DATE DUE

NO 2 02		
OC 5 02		
NO 26 02		
DE 16 02		
MR 2 2 10		

DEMCO 38-296

THE
PERSIAN GULF
CRISIS

THE
PERSIAN GULF
CRISIS

Steve A. Yetiv

Greenwood Press Guides to
Historic Events of the Twentieth Century
Randall M. Miller, Series Editor

Greenwood Press
Westport, Connecticut • London

Library of Congress Cataloging-in-Publication Data

Yetiv, Steven A.
  The Persian Gulf crisis / Steve A. Yetiv.
      p.   cm. — (Greenwood Press guides to historic
  events of the twentieth century, ISSN 1092–177X)
      Includes bibliographical references (p.   ) and index.
      ISBN 0–313–29943–9 (alk. paper)
      1. Persian Gulf War, 1991.   I. Series.
  DS79.72.Y48   1997
  956.7044′2—DC21   96–6554

British Library Cataloguing in Publication Data is available.

Library of Congress Catalog Card Number: 96–6554
ISBN: 0–313–29943–9
ISSN: 1092–177X

First published in 1997

Greenwood Press, 88 Post Road West, Westport, CT 06881
An imprint of Greenwood Publishing Group, Inc.

Printed in the United States of America

The paper used in this book complies with the
Permanent Paper Standard issued by the National
Information Standards Organization (Z39.48–1984).

10 9 8 7 6 5 4 3 2 1

Contents

A photographic essay follows page 92.

Series Foreword

As the twenty-first century approaches, it is time to take stock of the political, social, economic, intellectual, and cultural forces and factors that have made the twentieth century the most dramatic period of change in history. To that end, the Greenwood Press Guides to Historic Events of the Twentieth Century presents interpretive histories of the most significant events of the century. Each book in the series combines narrative history and analysis with primary documents and biographical sketches, with an eye to providing both a reference guide to the principal persons, ideas, and experiences defining each historic event, and a reliable, readable overview of that event. Each book further provides analyses and discussions, grounded in both primary and secondary sources, of the causes and consequences, in thought and action, that give meaning to the historic event under review. By assuming a historical perspective, drawing on the latest and best writing on each subject, and offering fresh insights, each book promises to explain how and why a particular event defined the twentieth century. No consensus about the meaning of the twentieth century emerges from the series, but, collectively, the books identify the most salient concerns of the century. In so doing, the series reminds us of the many ways those historic events continue to affect our lives.

Each book follows a similar format designed to encourage readers to consult it both as a reference and a history in its own right. Each volume opens with a chronology of the historic event, followed by a narrative overview, which also serves to introduce and examine briefly the main themes and issues related to that event. The next set of chapters is composed of topical essays, each analyzing closely an issue or problem of interpretation introduced in the opening chapter. A concluding chapter suggesting the long-term implications and meanings of the historic event brings the strands of the preceding chapters together while placing the event in the larger historical context. Each book also includes a section of short biographies of the principal persons related to the event, followed by a section introducing and reprinting key historical documents illustrative of and pertinent to the event. A glossary of selected terms adds to the utility of each book. An annotated bibliography—of significant books, films, and CD-ROMs—and an index conclude each volume.

The editors made no attempt to impose any theoretical model or historical perspective on the individual authors. Rather, in developing the series, an advisory board of noted historians and informed high school history teachers and public and school librarians identified the topics needful of exploration and the scholars eminently qualified to examine those events with intelligence and sensitivity. The common commitment throughout the series is to provide accurate, informative, and readable books, free of jargon and up to date in evidence and analysis.

Each book stands as a complete historical analysis and reference guide to a particular historic event. Each book also has many uses, from understanding contemporary perspectives on critical historical issues, to providing biographical treatments of key figures related to each event, to offering excerpts and complete texts of essential documents about the event, to suggesting and describing books and media materials for further study and presentation of the event, and more. The combination of historical narrative and individual topical chapters addressing significant issues and problems encourages students and teachers to approach each historic event from multiple perspectives and with a critical eye. The arrangement and content of each book thus invite students and teachers, through classroom discussions and position papers, to debate the character and significance of great historic events and to discover for themselves how and why history matters.

The series emphasizes the main currents that have shaped the modern world. Much of that focus necessarily looks at the West, especially Europe and the United States. The political, commercial, and cultural expansion of the West wrought largely, though not wholly, the most fundamental changes of the century. Taken together, however, books in the series reveal the interactions between Western and non-Western peoples and society, and also the tensions between modern and traditional cultures. They also point to the ways in which non-Western peoples have adapted Western ideas and technology and, in turn, influenced Western life and thought. Several books examine such increasingly powerful global forces as the rise of Islamic fundamentalism, the emergence of modern Japan, the communist revolution in China, and the collapse of communism in eastern Europe and the former Soviet Union. American interests and experiences receive special attention in the series, not only in deference to the primary readership of the books but also in recognition that the United States emerged as the dominant political, economic, social, and cultural force during the twentieth century. By looking at the century through the lens of American events and experiences, it is possible to see why the age has come to be known as "The American Century."

Assessing the history of the twentieth century is a formidable prospect. It has been a period of remarkable transformation. The world broadened and narrowed at the same time. Frontiers shifted from the interiors of Africa and Latin America to the moon and beyond; communication spread from mass circulation newspapers and magazines to radio, television, and now the Internet; skyscrapers reached upward and suburbs stretched outward; energy switched from steam, to electric, to atomic power. Many changes did not lead to a complete abandonment of established patterns and practices so much as a synthesis of old and new, as, for example, the increased use of (even reliance on) the telephone in the age of the computer. The automobile and the truck, the airplane, and telecommunications closed distances, and people in unprecedented numbers migrated from rural to urban, industrial, and ever more ethnically diverse areas. Tractors and chemical fertilizers made it possible for fewer people to grow more, but the environmental and demographic costs of an exploding global population threatened to outstrip natural resources and human innovation. Disparities in wealth increased, with developed nations prospering and underdeveloped nations starving. Amid the crumbling of former European colonial empires, Western technology, goods, and culture increasingly enveloped the globe, seeping into, and undermining, non-Western cultures—a process that contributed to a surge of religious fundamentalism and ethno-nationalism in the Middle East, Asia, and Africa. As people became more alike, they also became more aware of their differences. Ethnic and religious rivalries grew in intensity everywhere as the century closed.

The political changes during the twentieth century have been no less profound than the social, economic, and cultural ones. Many of the books in the series focus on political events, broadly defined, but no books are confined to politics alone. Political ideas and events have social effects, just as they spring from a complex interplay of non-political forces in culture, society, and economy. Thus, for example, the modern civil rights and women's rights movements were at once social and political events in cause and consequence.

Likewise, the Cold War created the geopolitical framework for dealing with competing ideologies and nations abroad and served as the touchstone for political and cultural identities at home. The books treating political events do so within their social, cultural, and economic contexts.

Several books in the series examine particular wars in depth. Wars are defining moments for people and eras. During the twentieth century war became more widespread and terrible than ever before, encouraging new efforts to end war through strategies and organizations of international cooperation and disarmament while also fueling new ideologies and instruments of mass persuasion that fostered distrust and festered old national rivalries. Two world wars during the century redrew the political map, slaughtered or uprooted two generations of people, and introduced and hastened the development of new technologies and weapons of mass destruction. The First World War spelled the end of the old European order and spurred communist revolution in Russia and fascism in Italy, Germany, and elsewhere. The Second World War killed fascism and inspired the final push for freedom from European colonial rule in Asia and Africa. It also led to the Cold War that suffocated much of the world for almost half a century. Large wars begat small ones, and brutal totalitarian regimes cropped up across the globe. After (and in some ways because of) the fall of communism in eastern Europe and the former Soviet Union, wars of competing cultures, national interests, and political systems persisted in the struggle to make a new world order. Continuing, too, has been the belief that military technology can achieve political ends, whether in the superior American firepower that failed to "win" in Vietnam or in the American "smart bombs" and other military wizardry that "won" in the Persian Gulf.

Another theme evident in the series is that throughout the century nationalism has continued to drive events. Whether in the Balkans in 1914 triggering World War I or in the Balkans in the 1990s threatening the post–Cold War peace—or in many other places—nationalist ambitions and forces would not die. The persistence of nationalism is yet another reminder of the many ways that the past becomes prologue.

We thus offer the series as a modern guide to and interpretation of the historic events of the twentieth century and as an invitation to consider how and why those events have defined not only the past and present but also charted the political, social, intellectual, cultural, and economic routes into the next century.

Randall M. Miller
Saint Joseph's University, Philadelphia

Acknowledgments

I would like to express my gratitude to Randall M. Miller, who initiated this series, and to the many people who consented to anonymous and on-the-record interviews. I am particularly grateful to General Colin Powell, Secretary of Defense Richard Cheney, Secretary of State James Baker III, General Brent Scowcroft, Ambassador Chas W. Freeman, Jr., Deputy Sandra Charles, Richard Haass, Admiral David Jeremiah, and Secretary Lawrence Eagleburger, and to various high-level Arab and European officials.

Finally, I thank Elaine Dawson for her superb computer support.

Abbreviations

CENTCOM	U.S. Central Command
DoD	Department of Defense
GCC	Gulf Cooperation Council
IAEA	International Atomic Energy Agency
NBC	Nuclear, biological, and chemical weapons
NSC	National Security Council
OPEC	Organization of Petroleum Exporting Countries
RRF	Ready Reserve Force
UAE	United Arab Emirates
UN	United Nations
UNIKOM	United Nations Iraq–Kuwait Observer Mission

Key Players in the Persian Gulf Crisis

The United States

James Baker, Secretary of State

George Bush, President

Richard Cheney, Secretary of Defense

Lawrence Eagleburger, Under Secretary of State

Chas W. Freeman, Jr., Ambassador to Saudi Arabia

April Glaspie, Ambassador to Iraq

Richard Haass, Special Assistant to the President for Near East and South Asian Affairs

General Colin Powell, Chairman, Joint Chiefs of Staff

General H. Norman Schwarzkopf, Commander in Chief, Central Command

General Brent Scowcroft, National Security Adviser

Dan Quayle, Vice President

Paul Wolfowitz, Under Secretary of Defense for Policy

Iraq

Abd al-Amir al-Anbari, Ambassador to the United Nations

Tariq Aziz, Foreign Minister and Deputy Prime Minister

Saddam Hussein, President

Hussein Kamel al-Majid, Minister of Defense

Ali-Hassan al-Majid, Minister of the Interior

Saudi Arabia

Crown Prince Abdullah Ibn-Abd-al-Aziz
Prince Bandar Ibn Sultan, Ambassador to the United States
King Fahd, Ibn-Abd-al-Aziz
Lt. General Khaled Ibn Sultan, Commander, Saudi Forces
Prince Sultan Ibn-Abd-al-Aziz, Defense Minister

The Broader Middle East

Sheikh Jaber al-Ahmad al-Sabah, Emir of Kuwait
Yasser Arafat, Chairman, Palestinian Liberation Organization
Hafez Assad, President of Syria
King Hussein, Jordanian Monarch
Hosni Mubarak, President of Egypt
Turgut Ozal, President of Turkey
Ali Akbar Hashemi Rafsanjani, President of Iran
Yitzhak Shamir, Prime Minister of Israel

United Nations

Javier Pérez de Cuéllar, Secretary-General

Europe

Helmut Kohl, Chancellor of Germany
John Major, Prime Minister of Great Britain (after November 1990)
François Mitterrand, President of France
Margaret Thatcher, Prime Minister of Great Britain (until November 1990)

The USSR

Alexander Bessmertnykh, Foreign Minister (from January 1991)
Mikhail Gorbachev, President
Yevgeny Primakov, Special Envoy to the Middle East
Eduard Shevardnadze, Foreign Minister (until January 1991)

Chronology of Events

1752

Sabah dynasty is established in the area of present-day Kuwait under Sheik Sabah bin Jabir al-Sabah.

Parts of modern-day Iraq were under the suzerainty of the Ottoman Empire from at least the mid-sixteenth century until the period 1914–1918, when the empire began to lose influence in World War I. Indeed, by November 1914, British troops had occupied Basra and undertook operations against Baghdad.

1920

April 25   Iraq is assigned to Britain as a mandate by the League of Nations.

1932

October 13   Iraq gains independence from Britain.

1961

June 19   Kuwait gains independence.

June 25   Iraq claims sovereignty over Kuwait; British deter Iraqi military action against Kuwait.

1969

Nixon Doctrine enunciated and sets up the U.S. "Twin Pillar" policy based on Iran and, to a much lesser extent, Saudi Arabia, as the U.S. regional pillars.

1973

March 20 Iraqi forces invade and briefly occupy the Kuwaiti border post at al-Samitah.

April 28 Iraq reasserts its claim to Warba and Bubiyan, two Kuwaiti islands that control Iraq's limited access to the Persian Gulf waters.

1979

January 16 The Shah of Iran, Mohammad Reza Pahlevi, flees Iran, and revolutionary leader Ayatollah Khomeini returns to Iran on February 1 to proclaim an Islamic republic.

July 17 Saddam Hussein officially becomes president of Iraq.

December 27 Soviets invade Afghanistan.

1980

January Three weeks after the Soviet invasion, the Carter Doctrine is enunciated, asserting that the United States will use force if necessary to protect the Persian Gulf.

September 22 Iraq invades Iran to touch off the eight-year war.

1988

August 20 Cease-fire is negotiated in the Iran-Iraq war.

1990

February 24 Saddam Hussein outlines a new offensive against the United States and Israel.

July 10 Kuwait agrees to abide by quotas in a meeting of oil ministers in Jeddah, but does not meet Saddam's demands.

July 15 A division of the elite Republican Guard moves from central Iraq toward the Kuwaiti border; by July 21, 35,000 Iraqi troops are on the Iraqi border near Kuwait.

July 17 Saddam threatens military action against Kuwait if it does not comply with his full set of demands.

July 25 Saddam tells Egyptian president Hosni Mubarak that Iraq will not invade Kuwait.

July 25 Saddam meets U.S. ambassador April Glaspie.

July 26 Kuwait reaffirms that it will lower production quotas and raise oil prices.

July 30   Eight Iraqi divisions, 100,000 of the best troops, and 350 tanks are poised on the Kuwait border.

August 2   140,000 Iraqi troops and 1,800 tanks invade Kuwait, spearheaded by two Republican Guard divisions.

August 2   UN Security Council votes 14–0 (with Yemen abstaining) to call for Iraq's withdrawal in Resolution 660.

August 6   UN Resolution 661 embargoes financial and economic resources to Iraq.

August 6   Saudi King Fahd requests the deployment of U.S. troops in line with Article 51 of the UN Charter.

August 8   Iraq annexes Kuwait; Bush addresses the nation, and Operation Desert Shield commences in full. By early November, U.S. forces number 240,000 military personnel and about 1,600 sophisticated combat aircraft.

August 9   UN Resolution 662 rejects Iraq's annexation of Kuwait as illegal.

August 10   In an Arab League meeting, 12 of 20 members vote to honor the UN embargo, support the deployment of U.S. troops, and agree to field an all-Arab military force to join the U.S.-led coalition.

August 12   Saddam Hussein presents a peace plan, rejected by Washington, linking Iraq's withdrawal from Kuwait to Syria's withdrawal from Lebanon and Israeli withdrawal from the occupied territories.

August 13   Iraq uses Westerners as hostages.

August 15   Saddam agrees to all Iranian demands to settle Iran-Iraq war.

August 16   United States begins naval blockade of Iraq.

August 25   UN Security Council votes 13–0 (with Yemen and Cuba abstaining) to allow allied ships to use force to uphold the embargo.

September 9   President George Bush and Soviet President Mikhail Gorbachev hold a summit in Helsinki, Finland, where they join to condemn Iraq's blatant aggression.

October 14   Soviets attempt unsuccessfully to negotiate a peaceful Iraqi withdrawal from Kuwait.

November 8   Bush announces plans to deploy up to 200,000 additional troops to insure what he refers to as "an adequate offensive option."

November 29   UN Security Council passes Resolution 678 authorizing the use of force.

November 30   Bush surprisingly invites Iraqi foreign minister Tariq Aziz to talks in Washington, and offers to send Secretary of State Baker to Baghdad, for talks to resolve the crisis. But diplomatic squabbles scuttle the plan.

December 6   Saddam announces release of all foreign hostages.

1991

January 9   U.S. Secretary of State James Baker and Iraqi foreign minister Tariq Aziz meet in Geneva to seek a peaceful end to the Gulf crisis, but the meeting proves futile.

January 12   The Senate gives the president the authority to wage war by a vote of 52 to 47. The House gives approval by a 250 to 183 vote.

January 15   At midnight, UN Security Council deadline for Iraq's withdrawal from Kuwait passes.

January 17   U.S.-led forces launch Operation Desert Storm.

January 18   Iraq attacks Israel with at least eight Scud missiles.

January 23   General Colin Powell announces that allied forces have achieved air superiority, after approximately 11,000 sorties.

January 25   Iraq dumps millions of gallons of Kuwaiti crude oil into the Persian Gulf.

January 26   Iraqi warplanes flee to Iran.

January 30   The first major ground battle is fought at Khafji in Saudi Arabia, after Iraqi troops attack. Saudi, Kuwaiti, and U.S. forces recapture Khafji on January 31.

February 6   King Hussein of Jordan abandons official neutrality and states that his country supports Iraq.

February 15   Iraq offers a plan for withdrawal from Kuwait with conditions attached that Bush finds absurd.

February 22   Bush and the allies give Iraq until 8 P.M. Gulf time on February 23 to initiate a withdrawal from Iraq or face a ground war.

February 24   Coalition launches the ground war.

February 26   Saddam announces the withdrawal of Iraqi forces from Kuwait.

February 27   Aziz accepts the twelve UN resolutions related to Iraq's invasion of Kuwait.

March 1   Civil unrest erupts in Iraq and threatens Saddam's regime.

March 3   At a meeting of allied and Iraqi commanders at Safwan, the groundwork for an official cease-fire is laid.

March 7   Anti-Saddam uprisings break out in fifteen Iraqi cities.

March 14   The emir returns to Kuwait after nearly eight months in exile.

March 31   Defeated Kurds flee into Turkey and Iran.

April 2   Iraq's army suppresses the month-long rebellion.

April 2   Security Council passes resolution 687, the "Mother of All Resolutions," which offers to end the Gulf War and lift most sanctions against Iraq if Baghdad abides by numerous punitive economic and military conditions.

April 6   Iraq accepts the UN cease-fire.

April 13   U.S. troops begin Kurdish relief in Iraq.

1994

October   80,000 Iraqi troops move toward the Kuwait border and cause international alarm and major U.S. military deployments.

1995

August 9   Lt. Gen. Hussein Kamel, head of Iraq's war machine, and Saddam Kamel Hassan Majeed, head of Saddam's secret services, defect to Jordan.

1996

September 1–9   Saddam invades northern Iraq to attack a Kurdish faction supported by Iran. The United States responds to the violation of UN Resolution 688 with two rounds of missile strikes on Iraqi military targets and by increasing the zone in southern Iraq beyond which Iraqi forces cannot move.

THE PERSIAN GULF
CRISIS EXPLAINED

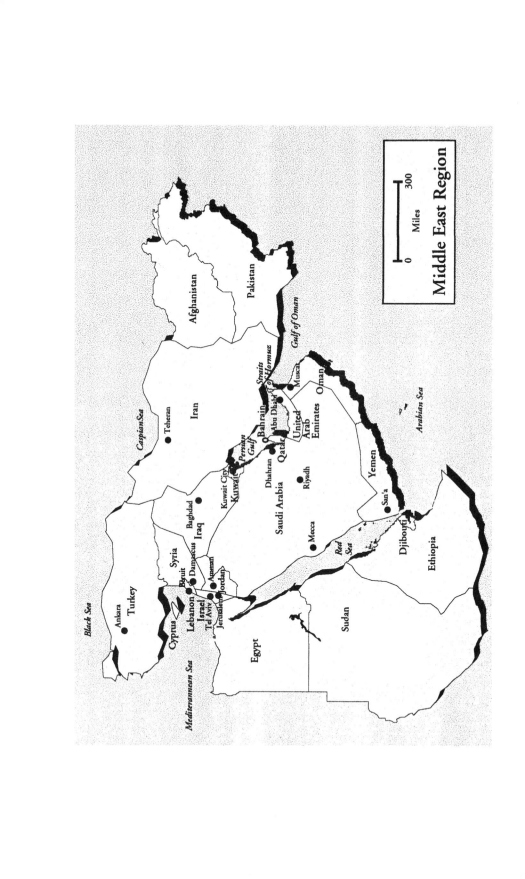

Middle East Region

1

Drama in the Desert: An Overview of the Crisis

On August 2, 1990, the world witnessed one of the most shocking spectacles of the twentieth century. One Arab country devoured another, annulled its very existence, and threatened to assert control over much of the world's oil resources. In past eras in which imperialism was more common, and where the world was less interdependent, such an event might have been unremarkable. Great powers crushed weaker ones without great fanfare. That was simply the way of the world. But not in modern times, not in a period where the end of the Cold War raised the prospect of a better world, not in a world dependent on Persian Gulf oil for economic growth, and not in a world where telecommunications and satellite television brought war into living rooms as if it were a rented video.

On that fateful day of August 2, Iraq did not just attack Kuwait, a tiny cosmopolitan state situated at the vortex of rivalry among Iran, Iraq, and Saudi Arabia. It attacked all nations that depended on oil at reasonable prices, that feared weapons of mass destruction in the hands of a brutal dictator who never met a weapon he did not use, and that sought to promote the romantic, hopeful concept of a new world order. As U.S. President George Bush stated, "Iraq's aggression is not just a challenge to the security of Kuwait and other Gulf nations but to the better world that we all have hoped to build in the wake of the Cold War. And, therefore, we and our allies cannot and will not shirk our responsibilities."[1] Thereafter, Bush, a World War II veteran and former director of the U.S. Central Intelligence Agency (CIA), dominated U.S. policy against Saddam Hussein, the fifty-three-year-old Iraqi dictator. In doing so, Bush mustered significant support from the world community and the American people. This chapter provides an overview of the crisis and puts the war in a broader political, military, and historical perspective.

THE INVASION IN HISTORICAL PERSPECTIVE

The Persian Gulf War was just one in a string of wars in and near the region. Earlier, in September 1980, Iraq, a country slightly larger in size than California, launched a major war against Iran. The bloody and lengthy Iran-Iraq war, which lasted until 1988, proved one of the deadliest of the century, with over a million casualties. In many ways, this war set the stage for Iraq's invasion of Kuwait in 1990.

Iran and Iraq, the two major powers in the Gulf region, had several reasons to fight, at least from their perspectives. They were split by long-standing territorial disagreements over control of the Shatt-al-Arab water-way (the confluence of the Tigris and Euphrates rivers, where ancient Mesopotamia flourished). And as had happened with so many other nations before them in the crucible of world history, a border issue would become a serious cause of war.

Personal hatred between Saddam and revolutionary leader Ayatollah Khomeini, who took control in Iran in early 1979, also created serious points of friction. Either of these leaders was more than a handful alone, but the two together made a volatile mix. In addition, Iran's theocratic rule, based on Islamic principles, as opposed to Iraq's more secular or nonreligious regime, and Iraq's Arab heritage versus Iran's Persian, non-Arab back-ground represented differences that made cooperation more difficult and war more likely.

Iraq, which is ruled by the Sunnis, but whose population is 67 percent Shiite, feared revolutionary Iran, whose leaders were from the more radical Shiite brand of Islam, which differs in its lineage and in some of its beliefs from its Sunni counterpart. Unlike Iran under the Shah, Khomeini's Shiite-led Iran sought to subvert Iraq's Shiite Muslims and to spread Iran's extreme brand of Islamic fundamentalism throughout the Gulf, thereby undermining Iraq's influence. Moreover, as the other major power in the Persian Gulf, Iran posed a threat to Iraq, particularly if it emerged intact from the revolutionary chaos generated by the overthrow of the Shah in 1979. In history, revolutionary states—for example, France, the Soviet Union, and China—have often found themselves at war with their neighbors shortly after their revolutions. So, Iraq had some reason to worry about its seemingly fanatical next-door neighbor.

By invading Iran, the egocentric Saddam also sought to advance his own grandiose plans for regional domination and to knock out Iran while it was still in the throes of revolution. Indeed, King Fahd of Saudi Arabia asserted that prior to Iraq's attack on Iran in 1980, Saddam told him that "it is more useful to hit them [the Iranians] now because they are weak. If we leave them until they become strong, they will overrun us."[2] From Saddam's perspective, the revolutionary chaos in Iran would allow Iraq to defeat Iran in a matter of months, if not sooner.

Saddam's peculiar combination of optimism and opportunism, however, met harsh reality on the bloody battlegrounds of the Persian Gulf. From Khomeini's perspective, Iraq's attack was sheer aggression, and Iran pledged to resist it literally to the last man. Iran would never surrender as long as Saddam Hussein, the "butcher of Baghdad" and the "heretic" who had lost his Islamic compass, ruled in Iraq. From the outset, the zealous, and in many cases, religiously inspired Iranian forces fought far harder than expected. In waves of human attacks, they died by the thousands, martyrs to Allah, sacrificed at the altar of piety and religion.

The war had ground to a stalemate by 1982 but dragged on until February 1986, when Iran won a major military victory at the Faw peninsula, and Khomeini, rejecting Saddam's overtures for a cease-fire, pledged zealously to fight on. A cease-fire came in August 1988, but the two states remained at war. Overall, the war accomplished nothing except much death and destruction. It would not be the last time that Saddam would underestimate the enemy.

WHY IRAQ INVADED KUWAIT

Iraq's stunning invasion of Kuwait, a nation the size of New Jersey, resulted from a complex set of factors, some immediate to the actual conflict, others flowing from the previous eight-year war in the region. The following factors were likely at play.

First, the Iran-Iraq war created a significant military imbalance in the region. Iraq emerged from the war a much stronger military power than its arch rival, Iran. Iraq's regular army quadrupled in size to 955,000 men, and the number of aircraft under its control increased by well over one-third. Meanwhile, the war significantly weakened Iran militarily. Coupled with the near cutoff of Western supplies of major equipment and spare parts, the war decreased Iran's air power by about 90 percent from 1980 to 1988. That Iraq did not have to contend with a powerful Iran on its border also made an invasion of Kuwait more plausible.

Second, after the Iran-Iraq war, Iraq's huge standing army could not be effectively reintegrated into the shaky Iraqi economy. Like Napoleon, Saddam probably understood that an idle, restless army could pose a much greater threat to his rule than one kept busy. Coups, after all, were often launched from within the military ranks. A military adventure, therefore, might have seemed more attractive to Saddam because it would at least have kept his army out of the barracks and his officers occupied.

Third, as suggested above, the Iran-Iraq war devastated Iraq's economy and left Baghdad heavily indebted to Kuwait and Saudi Arabia, both of which had loaned Saddam considerable amounts for the war against the feared, revolutionary Iran. Estimates suggest that Iraq began the Gulf War with $35 billion (U.S.) in reserve and ended it $80–100 billion (U.S.) in debt. Adding war reconstruction and debt repayment costs and basic yearly expenditures, it probably would have taken Iraq nearly two decades to recover from the Iran-Iraq war under optimal conditions. Thus, in theory, by invading Kuwait, Iraq would erase its war debt, control Kuwait's oil wealth, and increase world oil prices. In reality, Iraq did attempt to justify the invasion partly in economic terms. Iraq's foreign minister, Tariq Aziz, claimed shortly after the invasion that Baghdad had to "resort to this method" because its economic situation had deteriorated and it had no alternative.[3]

Fourth, Iraq and Kuwait had serious differences prior to Iraq's invasion of Kuwait. These disagreements constituted the immediate causes of the invasion. At the Arab League summit meeting in May 1990, Saddam attacked the Gulf states, particularly Kuwait, for ignoring oil production quotas, keeping oil prices down, refusing to forgive Iraq's debts from the Iran-Iraq war, and failing to extend reconstruction credits to Iraq after the destructive eight-year war. Because the Kuwaitis and Saudis were not forthcoming with economic support, and because Iraq's economy was devastated, Saddam sought to raise money for economic recovery by limiting Organization of Petroleum Exporting Countries (OPEC) production and thus increasing the price of Iraqi oil. By agreeing to production quotas, the many members of OPEC, which included the Gulf states, could control world oil prices. The less oil they pumped, the more expensive oil would be on the market. States that sought a shorter-term fix were more interested in pumping lots of oil, while those that had a longer-term view were less interested in doing so.

From February through late July 1990, Iraq issued various threats, backed at times by military maneuvers, that implied potential military action against Kuwait in retaliation for what Saddam termed economic war against Baghdad. Publicly, at least, the Kuwaitis were not bowed. Kuwait refused to forgive

Baghdad's war debts and to loan it more money for economic reconstruction. Moreover, Kuwait indirectly lowered oil prices by pumping too much oil, some from the Rumaila oil field, over which Iraq laid joint claim. Indeed, Iraq also accused Kuwait of angle drilling into this oil field. By starting oil wells on their side of the border, and angling their oil equipment under the border, the Kuwaitis could draw on oil from Iraqi sources.

While Saddam wanted higher oil prices to fund his postwar recovery, the Saudis and Kuwaitis initially opposed this approach based on their own national interests and oil-pricing strategies. Their actions were particularly annoying to Saddam, who reminded the other Arab states that Iraq had staved off the Iranian threat from 1980 to 1988 during the Iran-Iraq war and had positioned itself to carry the pan-Arab torch against Israel. Despite the fact that Iraq attacked Iran in 1980, Iraq repeatedly argued that it sacrificed treasure and blood to check Iran's fundamentalist Islamic threat to the entire Arab Gulf, to regain respect for all Arabs, and to advance the Arab cause. Thus, it deserved Arab allegiance and economic support, and Kuwait could not expect to get a free ride on Iraq's military back.

Even without these problems with Kuwait, Iraqis did not particularly like Kuwaitis. Indeed, many Arabs resented their wealth, their lavish country-club lifestyle, and the perceived outrageous displays of conspicuous consumption by some of the Kuwaiti elite. Never mind that Kuwaitis used some of their oil earnings to promote Arab causes—they were widely resented for being a family in charge of an oil well and a country.

Fifth, invading Kuwait had appeal among many Iraqis. This is because Kuwait was widely viewed in Iraq as part of historic Iraq. Since gaining its independence from Great Britain in 1932, Iraq had consistently challenged Kuwait's right to exist. In the 1930s, King Ghazi of Iraq openly demanded the incorporation of all of Kuwait into Iraq, a demand reiterated by Abd al-Karim Qassim, who overthrew the monarchy in July 1958. In 1961 Iraq actually invaded Kuwaiti border posts only to retreat under severe British political and military pressure. Again, in 1973, Iraqi forces occupied Kuwaiti territory along a narrow strip on the Iraq-Kuwait border on the pretense of protecting the Iraqi coastline against an alleged impending attack by Iran. These forces remained there for a decade against Kuwaiti wishes.

Prior to independence, Iraq was not a unified or independent state. Rather, it consisted of three disparate provinces—Mosul, Baghdad, and Basra. From Iraq's perspective, Kuwait was always part of Basra under the Ottoman Empire, which ruled the area now known as Iraq from the mid-sixteenth century to World War I. British agreements and maps bear this out. Kuwaitis viewed Iraqi claims to Kuwait, which have been made sporadically since 1932, as a smoke screen for Iraqi aggression. The al-Sabah royal family of Kuwait, after all, had established an autonomous sheikdom in Kuwait in 1756. Kuwaitis and many other observers considered Saddam's aggression as just one more power grab by a ruthless dictator looking for a quick monetary and power fix.

Sixth, by invading Kuwait, Iraq could gain control over the Persian Gulf islands of Warba and Bubiyan, and over Kuwait's huge natural harbor, along with approximately 120 miles of Gulf coastline. This was critical to Iraq, because its arch rival Iran enjoyed vast access to Gulf waters. By contrast, Iraq, a nation with 172,000 square miles and nearly 20 million people, was virtually landlocked, with only fifteen miles of coastline on the Gulf, some of which is inaccessible.

Seventh, a successful invasion of Kuwait offered Saddam perhaps the most prized goal of all: domination of the Persian Gulf and possibly the Arab world. Saddam, for his part, might not have been very knowledgeable about international relations, but he was aware of Iraq's glorious Babylonian past. Indeed, he fancied himself a modern-day Nebuchadnezzar, the Babylonian king who 3,800 years ago had fought against evil external forces and led the Babylonians to glory. Control of Kuwait, influence over Saudi oil, and more money for arms purchases and weapons of mass destruction would help Iraq surmount its economic problems and regain some of its ancient glory, as well as feed Saddam's inflated ego.

PRELUDE TO THE INVASION: ECONOMIC WARFARE

Whether Saddam developed a pretext for an already planned invasion is uncertain, but quite possible. At a minimum, Iraq was clearly making such an option feasible. On July 10, 1990, Kuwait, which had previously far exceeded its oil production quota, agreed to abide by quotas in a meeting of oil ministers in Jeddah, Saudi Arabia. But Iraq took the position that Kuwait remained condescending. While it is not clear to what extent Kuwait was uncooperative, it may be possible that it did not really understand, or care a great deal about, what would appease Saddam.

After the Jeddah meeting, Saddam upped the ante. By July 17, he threatened military action against Kuwait if it did not comply with his reiterated demands: to return $2.4 billion to compensate for oil "stolen" by Kuwait from Iraq's Rumaila oil field; to raise oil prices over $25 a barrel; to forgive completely Iraq's wartime debt; and, along with the Saudis, to lead an Arab financial assistance program for rebuilding Iraq. Furthermore,

Saddam rejected out of hand Kuwait's compromise positions, and appeared to want the Kuwaitis to fall short of meeting all of Iraq's demands.

From Kuwait's perspective, Saddam's demand for major Arab assistance to rebuild Iraq was a joke, because Iraq was one of the most resource-rich and advanced states in the Arab world. Moreover, the philosophy behind Kuwait's foreign assistance was to fund actual projects rather than to help countries deal with budget deficits. The Kuwaitis argued that Saddam should use his war debts as leverage with international lending institutions in order to obtain better terms than he otherwise could have received, and they believed that such an approach might appease Saddam.[4]

No matter what the Kuwaitis perceived, the stage was being set for the invasion. On July 15, a division of the elite Republican Guard, Saddam's best forces, moved from central Iraq toward the Kuwaiti border; by July 21, 35,000 Iraqi troops were on the Iraqi border near Kuwait. Meanwhile, Saddam was suggesting that his actions were meant only to frighten Kuwait into submission. Indeed, on July 24, Saddam told Egypt's president, Hosni Mubarak, whom the Arab League chose as a mediator between Iraq and Kuwait, that as "long as discussions last between Iraq and Kuwait, I won't use force. I won't intervene with force before I have exhausted all the possibilities for negotiation."[5] Mubarak, duped by Saddam's Machiavellian ploy, conveyed his message to the Kuwaitis and Americans, and dismissed the crisis as a "summer cloud" that fairer winds would soon blow away.[6] Mubarak would later express deep resentment and uncharacteristic anger at Saddam's lie and betrayal. In describing Saddam to U.S. Secretary of State James Baker, he called him "a crazy man" and asked: "How could he be so crazy? How can he delude himself this way? He doesn't listen to anybody."[7]

Better yet, Saddam was a master of deception. As late as August 1, Saddam told the Kuwaiti foreign minister that "he would gladly see him next week in Baghdad"[8]; and long prior to the invasion, Saddam told his son Uday, in front of the emir of Kuwait, "If anything happens to me, your uncle Jaber [referring to the emir] will take care of you."[9]

On July 26, while Kuwait had reaffirmed that it would lower production quotas and raise the benchmark price of oil to $21 per barrel, Saddam, in what appeared to be brinkmanship but turned out to be the real thing, was moving another 30,000 troops toward the border to add to the 35,000 already there. The stakes were rising. Saddam, untrusting of the Kuwaitis in any event, claimed to possess evidence that they intended to abide by the Jeddah agreement for only two months before changing their policy again.[10] Earlier, on July 11, Iraqi intelligence had reportedly intercepted transcripts of a telephone conversation between King Fahd and the emir of Kuwait, which Saddam interpreted as evidence of an Arab and American plot against Iraq.[11] By July 30, Iraq had eight divisions, 100,000 well-trained troops and 350 tanks, poised on the Kuwait border in formation for extensive operations. But not even the CIA was predicting an invasion. Earlier, on July 25, 1990, U.S. ambassador to Iraq April Glaspie had met with Saddam Hussein. The critical exchange in the meeting, for which Glaspie later was ridiculed in the press, is the following:

Saddam: The price at one stage dropped to $12 a barrel and a reduction of $6 billion to $7 billion in the modest Iraq budget is a disaster.

Glaspie: I think I understand this. I have lived here for years. I admire your extraordinary efforts to rebuild your country. I know you need funds. We understand that and our opinion is that you should have the opportunity to rebuild your country. *But we have no opinion on the Arab-Arab conflicts, like your border disagreement with Kuwait.*[12]

To what extent Saddam took Glaspie's words as a green light to invade Kuwait is not fully clear, and we might learn in the future that Glaspie was more clear about a strong U.S. response in classified diplomatic cables. Saddam may very well have interpreted her message as weakness or indifference in the face of his military posturing. That Saddam already doubted American resolve was clear. He told Glaspie that American society, unlike that of Iraq, "cannot accept 10,000 dead in one battle."[13] Later, Saddam and the Iraqi media returned time and again to the Vietnam issue, assailing American credibility. They would question whether a post-Vietnam country of spoiled Westerners, who had the good life in a land where there was no mandatory draft, could actually fight battle-hardened Iraqi troops.

The Glaspie meeting, and subsequent American actions, led Iraq's ambassador to Washington, Muhammad al-Mashat, to report in the days before the invasion that "few risks" existed of an American reaction in case of an attack on Kuwait.[14] While Saddam was sensitive to the possibility of American involvement, his actions showed that he discounted it.

WHY THE INVASION WAS SO SIGNIFICANT

On August 2, one week after the Glaspie meeting, 140,000 Iraqi troops and 1,800 tanks roared into Kuwait, spearheaded by two Republican Guard divisions: the Hammurabi (named after the famous Babylonian lawmaker) and the Medina. The Guard, conceived as Saddam's personal, loyal military force, was equipped with the best weapon systems, such as the Soviet T-72 tank. Unsurprisingly, Saddam spared these forces from the wrath of the

U.S.-led alliance by pulling them back to Baghdad during the end of the Gulf War (1991) and keeping some Guard divisions out of the fray altogether. They not only fought for Iraq, but, much more important, they protected Saddam himself. And for any dictator, self-preservation is the key goal.

The lightning-fast invasion was conducted professionally and successfully. Contrary to popular belief, the 16,000-strong Kuwaiti forces, while not fully mobilized, did put up some resistance. Kuwaitis were able to muster a small number of Kuwaiti A-4 aircraft, armored vehicles, Chieftain tanks, and elements of the navy to fight for about three days before running out of supplies. Iraq's blitzkrieg, however, proved far too much for Kuwait's small and untested military.

On August 2, 1990, Iraq installed in Kuwait a provisional government of nine hand-picked military officers whose origin is not altogether clear. This puppet regime replaced the ruling Kuwaiti al-Sabah family, which had fled to Saudi Arabia after the invasion, except for the emir's younger brother, Sheik Fahd, who was caught in the palace and killed. Although Saddam failed to seize the emir and other royal family members, Iraq tried quickly to make its takeover a fait accompli. President George Bush, however, would not tolerate this political maneuver. Asked how he could prevent the installation of the puppet government, Bush, his ire and resolve showing, responded with a terse, confident "Just wait. Watch and learn."[15] On August 8, Iraq annexed Kuwait as its nineteenth province as if this were a common practice in world politics, and by August 24, had ordered all countries to close their embassies in Kuwait. Most nations refused to comply with Iraq's demands or recognize its claim.

At the global level, Iraq's invasion was the first major crisis in the post–Cold War era of easing tensions between the superpowers, and a test of the New World Order. As Deputy Secretary of State Lawrence Eagleburger put it, if the United States did not take strong action, Iraq's aggression could set "all the wrong standards" for the post–Cold War world by suggesting to regional dictators that naked aggression pays and by hurting U.S. credibility at a critical juncture in history.[16]

Washington was fortunate that the invasion took place during a period of cooperation with the USSR. In the view of former Soviet leader Mikhail Gorbachev, which he made clear at a speech given at Hofstra University in April of 1997, had the invasion occurred "two or three years earlier, it could have been another Cuban missile crisis." At a minimum, Moscow would have been more inclined to protect its ally, Iraq

In the region, the invasion was the culmination of a tortuous decade, touched off by the Iranian revolution in 1979 and the Iran-Iraq war (1980–

1988). The invasion threatened U.S. interests, and drew Washington into the Gulf crisis militarily, for three key reasons. First, it suggested that if left unopposed, Iraq might use Kuwait as an example designed to intimidate other oil-rich Gulf states. Using this strategy, Iraq did not really need to invade and occupy Kuwait. It could just use its troop presence near Kuwait to threaten the region's oil-producing states, just as the Soviets had used their military position to bend Finland to their will—the famed Finlandization effect.

Second, and even more ominous, the invasion created the possibility that Iraq would also invade neighboring Saudi Arabia. Indeed, Bush was convinced that this was Saddam's plan, which added energy to his counteroffensive.[17] An invasion of Saudi Arabia would allow Saddam to gain direct or indirect control over major strategic facilities as well as more than half the world's oil resources, a frightening prospect, especially for countries such as Japan that relied heavily on Gulf oil. Moreover, it would allow Iraq to use its new possessions and monies to build nuclear weapons.

A number of factors raised the specter of an Iraqi invasion of Saudi Arabia. Iraq's 140,000 troops in Kuwait far exceeded the power necessary to dominate the area. Had Saddam only wanted to occupy and pillage Kuwait, why did he prepare for grander operations? Why did Iraqi units have the weapons, supply, and positioning for a forward thrust into the Saudi kingdom? Furthermore, U.S. satellite images revealed that at least six divisions of Iraqi forces were moving toward the Saudi-Kuwaiti border. On at least three occasions, beginning on August 3, Iraqi forces entered Saudi territory. Iraq explained the incursions as "mistakes," but, in reality, U.S. forces could have been overrun by the Iraqi military on its way to Riyadh in the first three weeks of the crisis. Such a prospect weighed heavily on the minds of U.S. officials.

Third, the Iraqi threat raised the prospect of significantly higher oil prices and a possible world recession. U.S. policymakers and the American public had not forgotten the devastating 1973 oil embargo that sent the U.S. economy into recession. The combination of a stagnant economy and high inflation in the 1970s, called "stagflation," was a significant factor in the defeats of two incumbent presidents—Gerald Ford in 1976 and Jimmy Carter in 1980. The Gulf crisis, as Secretary Baker would tell the president in private, had all the trappings of a situation that could bring down his presidency, if it went awry.[18] The stakes were getting higher.

On August 22, Bush, the former Texas oilman, suggested to the press for the first time that war was a real possibility. Asked if he was preparing Americans for the possibility of war and American deaths, he said yes after stating, "I think any time you move American forces and anytime you are up against what most of the world now considers to be an outrageous violator of international law that the best thing is to be prepared."[19] Wall Street went into a tailspin, Japan's stock market suffered its fourth worst loss in history, and oil prices jumped. This was ample proof that the entire world economy was linked to events in the oil-rich Gulf and that even minor statements about war in the region, much less actual events, could spook world financial markets.

The oil shock, however, was short-lived. On August 28, in order to provide for higher production and to ease stress on the world market, OPEC agreed to suspend quotas limiting oil production. Furthermore, over time, it became more clear that Iraq would not invade Saudi Arabia; Desert Shield, the name given to the U.S.-led operation intended to defend Saudi Arabia against any possible further Iraqi encroachment, was gaining momentum, the United States was asserting itself politically, and economic markets responded by settling down.

DESERT SHIELD: DRAWING A LINE IN THE SAND

Within forty-eight hours of the invasion, Prince Bandar bin Sultan, the pro-American Saudi ambassador to the United States, met with U.S. National Security Adviser Brent Scowcroft. Bandar, the son of the Saudi defense minister and the nephew of King Fahd, reminded Scowcroft about past Saudi questions regarding U.S. resolve during the time of the Iranian revolution, and expressed concern that America would lend a temporary hand against Saddam and then "pull it back," thus leaving Saddam on the Saudi border "twice as mad as he is now."[20] But, as discussed earlier in this chapter (and later, in Chapter 4, which deals with the decision-making process in more detail), the threat to U.S. interests was serious enough to warrant a major U.S. response. Since no other country in the world had the capability and stature to stop Iraq, the responsibility devolved to the United States.

By August 5, Bush stated publicly and unambiguously that he would accept nothing less than total Iraqi withdrawal from Kuwait. Moreover, U.S. officials had laid out for Bandar the U.S. strategy of starting out with 100,000 troops, a number that pleasantly surprised him.[21]

Meanwhile, Secretary of Defense Richard Cheney was in the air to Saudi Arabia on August 6 to gain permission for the entry of thousands of American troops in what would become Operation Desert Shield. U.S. officials initiated the trip in order to apprise Fahd of the threats that his country faced. Cheney was accompanied by the sometimes blustery General Norman Schwarzkopf, Deputy National Security Adviser Robert Gates, Under Secretary of Defense for Policy Paul Wolfowitz, and Chas Freeman, U.S. ambassador to Saudi Arabia, who served as a translator and a diplomatic aide.

At first, King Fahd briefly hesitated to give U.S. forces the right of entry into the kingdom, although the hesitation was not very serious. After Secretary Cheney and General Schwarzkopf made presentations for over two hours, King Fahd turned to Crown Prince Abdullah, Prince Sultan, and Prince Bandar, and engaged in a five-minute discussion that was not translated by the Saudis into English. Later, Freeman informed Cheney that the Saudis were debating not so much about whether to allow U.S. entry but in what form and how fast; they also discussed how steadfast Riyadh should be against Saddam.

The pro-U.S. faction, led by King Fahd and his brother Sultan, was willing to consider a major American role. The counter faction, led by Crown Prince Abdullah, the king's half brother, did not strongly oppose such a role, but did view a large American presence in the kingdom as potentially threatening to its traditional Islamic role and as introducing a destabilizing foreign presence. Even Saudi defense minister Prince Sultan, one of the leaders of the pro-American camp, no less, hinted earlier in the crisis that Iraq could be given some territory in Kuwait in exchange for withdrawal from Kuwait.[22]

Fahd, however, was convinced of and surprised by the Iraqi threat when he was shown CIA satellite photographs documenting that Iraqi divisions were sweeping southward toward the Saudi Arabian border, in striking distance of the Saudis' critical oil fields. Although U.S. officials expected Fahd to hesitate, he gave a fairly quick go-ahead nod once he realized that his kingdom was in danger. Fahd knew that he had to make a fast decision while Kuwait still existed. Abdullah, who wanted more discussion of the matter, responded that there still was a Kuwait, as if to downplay the urgency of the crisis. But according to an official present, Fahd retorted that this was not true because the Kuwaiti royal family is "living in our hotel rooms."[23]

In making a swift decision to allow U.S. forces into the kingdom, Fahd, for perhaps the first time in his life, bucked the Saudi tradition of consultation and consensus. Heretofore, Fahd had sought unanimity from other important royal family members and leaders in the kingdom before making critical decisions. But in the Gulf crisis, Fahd chose to act before gaining such consensus, despite modest pressures from Crown Prince Abdullah and others to do so.[24] Saddam, after all, had approached Fahd twice in the 1980s with a Machiavellian proposal to divide the small Arab Gulf states between Saudi Arabia and Iraq. Fahd knew what Saddam was capable of.[25]

The Saudis, however, did have three concerns about the huge U.S.-led deployment. First, they raised the issue of U.S. commitment and staying power. They did not want the United States to come into the kingdom, only to bolt at the first sign of trouble, thus leaving them at Saddam's mercy. The Iranian revolution and the U.S. inability to save the Shah of Iran, who had been one of Washington's closest allies in the Middle East, remained in the Saudi collective memory, as did the hasty U.S. departure from Beirut, Lebanon, in 1983 after a terrorist bomb killed 243 Marines there.

Second, while they wanted a strong U.S. showing against Saddam, they did not want Desert Shield to turn into a permanent presence. Thus, they asked for assurances that U.S. forces would depart as soon as the job against Iraq was finished. From Riyadh's perspective, the last thing King Fahd needed was to be accused of letting an infidel foreign presence onto sacred Saudi soil, and then of being unable to make the "infidels" leave.

Third, given the fact that the Saudis prided themselves on being the guardians of the two holiest sites of Islam at Mecca and Medina, they wanted to know that the Muslim way of life would be respected by allied forces. Schwarzkopf, who at age twelve had lived in Iran, understood what they meant and instructed his officers to be doubly concerned with respecting things Islamic. But this task of tolerance was not so simple.

At first, the Saudis refused to allow Bibles to enter the kingdom or to permit religious services for the 900 or so Jewish troops. Responding with some concern, Colin Powell asked Saudi Prince Bandar rhetorically, regarding the troops, "They can die defending your country, but they can't pray in it?" Although the question was as much in jest between two long-standing friends,[26] it did touch on an interesting issue. What rights did Americans have in a foreign land that they were protecting?

While Bandar certainly understood Powell's point, his concern was that the Saudi people, watching CNN, would wonder what was happening with all these foreign forces praying on their soil. Seeing the predicament, the two sides agreed that U.S. soldiers would wear crucifixes inside their clothing. Bibles would be flown directly to air bases for U.S. personnel, and Jewish soldiers would be helicoptered to U.S. naval ships for their services. Meanwhile, the Saudis would try to deal with the potential social consequences of the deployment.

After the details were hammered out, President Bush was ready to begin his effort to inform the American public of his approach to Saddam—the "butcher of Baghdad," as Bush sometimes called him.

On August 8, Bush outlined American goals in a national address:

- the unconditional withdrawal of all Iraqi forces from Kuwait;
- the restoration of Kuwait's legitimate government in place of the puppet regime put in place by Iraq;
- the protection of the security and stability of the region;
- the protection of the lives of Americans abroad.[27]

The United States also had some less clearly defined goals. Asked on August 11 if U.S. goals included overthrowing Saddam, Bush responded with trademark "eloquence" that he would "just leave it sit out there, and everybody can figure it out."[28] In other words, while removing Saddam was not an official goal, it could be interpreted to be an implicit and hoped for objective. Bush, balancing hardheaded statements on Saddam with hopeful visions of a future world, also asserted on September 11 that the United States had a "fifth objective," of producing a new world order that "one hundred generations have searched for"[29] in vain but have not achieved. This was heady stuff, given that the United States was moving toward one of its most serious confrontations since Vietnam.

For Bush, it was good that the Cold War was receding into the past and that communist regimes were falling like dominoes in the former Soviet bloc. The Soviets had long-standing relations with Iraq, were its top arms supplier, and were very reluctant to see it attacked by U.S.-led forces. With the end of the Cold War, however, Moscow was even more interested in good relations with the United States than with playing its Baghdad card. It needed Western technology and economic support to move its economy away from communism and toward capitalism, and it needed U.S. political support to integrate itself into the Western-dominated world economy. This consideration, and Saddam's blatant aggression against Kuwait, helped yield Washington the support it needed from the Soviet Union against Baghdad.

After King Fahd gave the nod, the 82nd Airborne Division and the first fighter squadrons were on their way. To illustrate American determination, Bush drew his famous "line in the sand" on August 8 (see Document 3). Upon his return from the presidential retreat at Camp David, Bush was handed notes by Richard Haass, special assistant to the president for Near East and South Asian affairs on the National Security Council (NSC). The notes indicated that Arab diplomacy was not working in getting Iraq out of Kuwait and that Saddam was consolidating his position. While it had become apparent in both formal and informal meetings between Bush and his advisers that Bush wanted Iraq forced out of Kuwait if necessary, the president had not yet made a forceful, dramatic comment to the press in that regard.[30] Turning to reporters near his helicopter, Bush stated in no uncertain terms that Iraq's aggression "would not stand." The president's "line in the sand" statement was of critical importance because it sent a strong message of American resolve, so strong that even some of his closest advisers, watching it on CNN, were taken by surprise. The president had suddenly moved from "not discussing intervention" to a "line in the sand." To Colin Powell, the respected chairman of the Joint Chiefs of Staff, that was a big step.[31]

Operation Desert Shield was in full motion one day after Bush's warning. It would become one of history's largest military deployments. Indeed, Washington assembled an alliance of twenty-eight member nations, which grew to thirty-seven by war's end and included more than half a million soldiers with a 10,000-soldier brigade from the Arab Gulf states, 7,000 Kuwaiti soldiers, and 15,000 reluctant Syrian troops who fought only on Kuwaiti soil.

On the European side, the British sent 43,000 troops and significant military equipment, while France sent 16,000 soldiers. The European countries depended on Gulf oil, had significant business interests in the region, and also wanted to protect their regional political influence. Thus, like the United States, which was outraged by the invasion, they sought to reverse Saddam's aggression. Japan, Kuwait, Saudi Arabia, and Germany helped foot the bill for the war, while the United States bore most of the burden in actual fighting. By November, U.S. forces numbered more than 240,000 military personnel and about 1,600 sophisticated combat aircraft; by January 1991, an incredible half of all U.S. combat forces worldwide had been deployed to the Persian Gulf theater.

Desert Shield, however, was not enough to give U.S.-led forces an offensive option against Iraqi forces in Kuwait. Bush's increasing impatience with Saddam and his interest in degrading Iraq's military capability inspired him to raise the heat, and in October 1990, he began to press for an offensive option to blast Iraqi forces out of Kuwait far sooner than his military officers had wanted.

On November 8, after consultation with King Fahd but not with the U.S. Congress, the administration announced plans to deploy up to 200,000 additional troops to insure an adequate offensive option, thus doubling U.S. troop levels in the region. The November decision, which drew serious criticism from a surprised and concerned Congress, ignited a national debate over the direction in which the crisis was headed, and was the opening salvo of the move away from Desert Shield to the offensive military attack against Iraq called Operation Desert Storm.

As a final step before Desert Storm, Bush sought to make one last, highly visible, effort at a negotiated settlement by advising Secretary of State Baker to meet with Iraqi foreign minister Aziz in Geneva. The tense meeting on January 9, 1991, proved entirely useless and helped convince the American people that war was inevitable. The divide between Aziz and Baker was wide enough to drive an armored division through.

THE DEBATE ON USING MILITARY FORCE

Before unleashing the military operation Desert Storm, President George Bush faced one last hurdle, imposed not by Saddam Hussein or by the complexities of war preparation, but rather by the vagaries of domestic politics. Seeking to strengthen his hand, the Republican president wanted the Democrat-controlled Congress to authorize the use of force against Iraq, thus lending Desert Storm more weight and public support. The central debate over whether to do so was heated, emotional, and historic, and gripped the nation for days beginning on January 10, 1990. Every member of Congress seemed to want to say something, to express a view, to take a stand, and they all had their chance in what was one of the most highly attended set of congressional sessions in American history.

Speaker of the House Thomas S. Foley described it as the most important debate that he had witnessed in over twenty years in Congress. Members of Congress who before had not spoken on the House and Senate floor felt compelled to express their views in a vote that could make or break them politically. The atmosphere was electric, the emotional statements genuine—this was serious business.

The debate in Congress hinged largely on whether the U.S.-led coalition should continue to use economic sanctions to pressure Iraq to withdraw, or resort to force. This national debate had begun earlier, in October, and carried through the January congressional hearings. (For representative positions on the issue, see Documents 6–8.)

Proponents of economic sanctions had earlier argued that it was too risky to march to war so soon, when UN economic sanctions might do the job of getting Iraq out of Kuwait. Indeed, in an interview in early October, Schwarzkopf, who was widely viewed as a "soldier's soldier," argued that there was evidence that sanctions were pinching, and rejected the war option as "crazy."[32] He did not want to put his young soldiers in harm's way without running the gamut of other options, and constantly expressed concern about casualties. Perhaps this was because of his Vietnam experience, or a result of his general approach to the basic soldier. Schwarzkopf was sometimes described as "a new breed of classless general, a guy to have a beer with."[33]

Perhaps the most stunning congressional testimony came in November from the two most recent chairmen of the Joint Chiefs of Staff, Admiral William Crowe, whose son Blake was a Marine captain in charge of 200 soldiers in the Gulf, and Air Force General David C. Jones. Both men suggested that Bush was moving too fast, argued that sanctions should be given a chance, and underscored the possible terrible consequences of war. In Crowe's words, war is "not tidy. And once you resort to it, it's a mess."[34] While not particularly profound, the statements of these two respected, hard-nosed military men made a national sensation and seemed to slow the momentum toward war.

Other observers who supported the continuation of sanctions raised doubts about sending U.S. soldiers to die for the nondemocratic royal family of Kuwait, which had provoked Saddam prior to his invasion. They just didn't think the Emir of Kuwait, or oil, was worth it.

Saddam seized on such misgivings to play up the possibility of a bloody ground war. On January 9, in characteristic fashion, he told members of Iraq's ruling Baath party, one of his instruments of power, "If the Americans are involved in a Gulf conflict, you will see how we will make them swim in their blood."[35] Bush viewed this as Saddam's way to exploit the Vietnam issue, which, in Bush's view, Saddam overestimated.[36]

Proponents of the use of force were given a big lift when a Kuwaiti woman, testifying at a hearing of the Congressional Human Rights Caucus, and identifying herself only as Nayirah, gave a tear-jerking, firsthand account of how Iraqi soldiers had taken babies out of incubators and absconded with the incubators. While it was one thing to the American people for armies to fight armies, killing babies for loot was too much. The public was clearly disgusted by this horrifying affair, and the president, as well as the media, made much of it. Before long, the story of baby-murdering, incubator-stealing Iraqi soldiers dominated the news. The only problem with the incident is that it may not have happened. Indeed, it was later discovered that the Kuwaiti woman who told the tale was the daughter of the Kuwaiti ambassador to the United States, and that the public affairs firm Hill and Knowlton Public Affairs Worldwide actually helped her prepare the testimony, which she had rehearsed before video cameras at the company's Washington offices.[37] Her story was never really corroborated by others, and its authenticity was cast into doubt, but the image of heartless Iraqis she helped create remained deeply etched in the public mind.

In the ongoing national debate and in the specific congressional debate from January 10 to 12, many proponents of the use of force doubted that the U.S.-led coalition could remain cohesive. They further doubted that

U.S.-led forces in the Gulf could remain alert and combat ready over a long period of time. The scuttlebutt from the region was that U.S. troops were tired of, as they would joke, "Kuwaiting" and wanted to get the job done and come home.

Furthermore, others argued that the United States needed to scale back Iraqi power. If Saddam withdrew from Kuwait with his army intact, he could still pose an enormous threat when U.S. forces left. Indeed, one of Bush's greatest fears, as well as that of most of his advisers, was that Saddam would engage in a partial withdrawal, remain in control of key sites in Kuwait such as the Rumaila oil field, split the coalition, and return at a later date to reconquer Kuwait.[38] This was such a serious concern that Bush instructed the Deputies Committee—the routine crisis management group that reported to the president and his chief advisers—to prepare contingency plans for a number of scenarios, including Iraq's full withdrawal from Kuwait. The analysis revealed that the amount of U.S. force that would have had to stay in the Gulf to deter Iraq would have been "enormous," and very costly.[39]

Finally, serious doubts arose about the effectiveness of economic sanctions against Iraq. William Webster, then director of the CIA, dismissed the impact of sanctions in congressional testimony in December. His judgment was, to some extent, on sound historical footing. Economic sanctions had only a mixed record of meeting critical political objectives. Iraq's dependence on oil exports and international unity against Saddam increased the possibility that sanctions could work in the Gulf crisis, but Iraq also had the political will and economic means to withstand them. Indeed, it achieved a bumper agricultural harvest in 1990, four times as large as its 1989 harvest, and was expected to have similar success in 1991. Moreover, Saddam's austerity measures also seemed to have worked in reducing consumption.

The prewar debate in Congress began in earnest on January 10. As a hedge against a war resolution, Sam Nunn and Majority Leader George Mitchell sponsored a draft resolution in the Senate that called for the use of force, but only to enforce the embargo, to defend Saudi Arabia, and to protect American forces. This fell far short of what the president sought. Congressional critics of Nunn and Mitchell accused them not only of playing politics and undermining the president, but also of sending Saddam a message of U.S. weakness. In the critics' view, Iraq was becoming more entrenched in Kuwait and showed little interest in withdrawing unconditionally. It had taken and manipulated human hostages, and was abusing and murdering Kuwaiti citizens.

On January 12, three days before the president's deadline for withdrawal from Kuwait, the final congressional votes were tallied. Would Congress support the notion that it was time for the U.S.-led coalition to support diplomacy "by other means"?

The House of Representatives voted 250 to 183 against the Nunn-Mitchell antiwar resolution and in favor of a resolution, sponsored by Representatives Stephen Solarz and Robert Mitchell, authorizing the president to use armed force, subject to UN Security Council Resolution 678 (see Document 8), so long as he exhausted all diplomatic means. The Senate also defeated the Nunn-Mitchell plan, by a 53 to 46 margin, and voted 52 to 47 in support of the president. Speaker Tom Foley summed up the serious mood in the House when he closed the emotional, perhaps unprecedented debate with a rare floor speech: "Let me offer a public prayer for this House, for all of us, for the Congress, for our president— and he is our president—and for the American people, in particular those young Americans who stand ready to make the supreme sacrifice. May God bless us and guide us and help us in the fateful days ahead."[40] The president, who earlier had criticized Congress for failing to send Iraq a clear signal of American unity against aggression, was now in position to deal Iraq a potential knockout blow.

THE ARAB WORLD'S RESPONSE

If Americans were struck by the brashness of the Iraqi dictator, so were many Arabs. At first, the Arab world's response was muted, largely because Arab states did not want to inflame Saddam further, and because the incredibly rich Kuwaitis were not widely loved by the poorer Arabs.

Even before the invasion, Saddam's Pan-Arab ideology was too extreme for moderate Arab states such as Egypt. His anti-American bent threatened Saudi Arabia and other Gulf states that cooperated with Washington, and his military bravado unnerved Gulf states as well as Syria and Egypt. While the perception existed that the war was principally between Iraq and the United States, in truth, many officials in the Arab world also wanted Saddam cut down to size. The American media underreported this aspect of the crisis, despite its importance in explaining why so many Arab states cooperated with the United States against a brother Arab state.

In the wake of Iraq's invasion, Arab leaders, shuttling back and forth between capitals, attempted to resolve the crisis. On August 2, the day of the Iraqi invasion of Kuwait, King Hussein of Jordan flew to Egypt to meet President Mubarak, and together they sought to produce a formula that would allow Saddam a dignified withdrawal. They also prevented the Arab League from condemning the invasion, an act which would have angered

Saddam, and pressured President Bush to hold back American action until an Arab solution had a chance to resolve the Gulf crisis.

They then sought to arrange for a small-scale Arab summit at Jeddah, Saudi Arabia, which Saddam could attend. Although Saddam accepted the invitation in theory, he rejected Mubarak's precondition that Iraq withdraw from Kuwait and restore the al-Sabah royal family prior to the meeting. For Saddam, the royal family was history, and he seemed to be in no mood to negotiate.

To induce Saddam's peaceful withdrawal from Kuwait, Mubarak, King Hussein, King Fahd of Saudi Arabia sought initially to reward Iraq, perhaps with a slice of Kuwaiti territory, but President Bush torpedoed this effort, partly due to the efforts of British prime minister Margaret Thatcher, the "iron lady" who was not known for her shyness. Prior to meeting her on August 2 in Aspen, Colorado, Bush was somewhat more open to peaceful dialogue. Questioned on the day of the invasion, after an NSC meeting on the crisis, Bush said that the United States was not contemplating intervention. According to General Scowcroft, this was widely misunderstood and chronicled in later books to mean that Bush was averse to using force, when in reality he meant that the NSC meeting was not a decision-making one.[41] Bush's statement may have also reflected some disagreement at the meeting about the best way to proceed against Iraq. Nonetheless, while Bush was inclined to use force prior to meeting Thatcher, she did impress upon him the importance of a firm stand against aggressors and the hazards of an Arab-brokered compromise, and did, as Bush would later recall, "reinforce" his convictions.[42]

The failure of the initial appeasement effort angered Jordan's King Hussein, who, in part because his predominantly Palestinian population was pro-Iraq, supported next-door Iraq. This failure moved the locus of Arab world attention to the Arab League. In supporting Saddam's invasion of Kuwait, King Hussein alienated the Gulf Arabs and his longtime friend, George Bush. According to Secretary Baker, Bush viewed the king's surprising and painful actions, actions that included calling U.S. policy against Iraq "criminal," as a "personal betrayal." Secretary Baker also found the king's use of the word "criminal" shocking.[43] The failed Arab effort also further convinced Bush that Saddam had to be dealt with more strongly.

While the United States was organizing the Desert Shield operation, the Arab League met in an emergency summit in Cairo. Twelve of the twenty members of the league voted that Iraq's invasion should be condemned and that individual Arab states could join Desert Shield. By November, Egyptian and Syrian forces in the U.S.-led alliance numbered almost 16,000 and 4,000 respectively.

For their part, Egypt and Syria were not very reluctant to join the U.S.-led coalition against Saddam. Egypt hoped to improve its relations with the United States and the oil-rich Gulf Arab states, have its American debt forgiven, and assume leadership in the Arab world—not a bad deal for an economically weakened nation that had been ostracized in the Arab world since signing the 1979 peace treaty with Israel. Syria, which had lost its Soviet patron, hoped to improve its image in the West, receive Saudi monetary support, and deal Iraq, its nemesis, a major blow.

In the Persian Gulf itself, the Saudi-led Gulf Cooperation Council (GCC), composed of Saudi Arabia, Kuwait, Oman, Qatar, Bahrain, and the United Arab Emirates (UAE), also reacted to the invasion. This military and political organization, formed in May 1981, condemned the invasion, called up its modest military forces, and served as a forum during the crisis for coordinating GCC military, economic, and social policy.

UN RESOLUTIONS AND COALITION-BUILDING

At the international level, Bush was busy, along with Secretary Baker and his State Department team, creating the anti-Iraq coalition and lobbying for UN resolutions against the Iraqis' actions. President Bush and Secretary Baker were critical in weaving together the U.S.-led international coalition. While Bush worked the phone indefatigably, Baker was on the road, twisting arms and making arguments on behalf of the U.S.-led coalition. As Baker points out, the overall political approach was a classic case of "coercive diplomacy" in which Washington led and said, "Do you want to be with us?" The United States made efforts at a multilateral approach so that European states, for instance, would not view the international effort as a "lone ranger operation," and so that the presence of Syria, for example, would provide political cover in the Arab world. But, in essence, as Secretary Baker later acknowledged, "this was not multilateralism. It was a U.S. operation that received financial support from states as powerful as Japan and Germany to those as small and unlikely as Malaysia."[44]

In early September, Secretary Baker went around the world in what would be known as the "Tin Cup Trip," an eleven-day journey to nine countries, including the wealthier states of Japan, Germany, and Saudi Arabia, to obtain financial support for the Gulf effort. While this effort underscored the limitations of U.S. power, in truth, the Europeans and Japan had a serious stake in the oil resources of the Gulf and in checking Iraq's nuclear program, which Saddam was developing with great effort and determination. From the U.S. perspective, they had a responsibility to finance part of Operations Desert Shield and Storm.

On the UN front, on the day of the Iraqi invasion the Security Council passed Resolution 660. (See Document 1.) With the exception of an abstention from Yemen, the council unanimously condemned the invasion and demanded that Iraq "withdraw immediately and unconditionally all of its forces to the position in which they were located on 1 August 1990." On August 6 the Security Council passed Resolution 661, which imposed economic sanctions on Iraq (except for humanitarian or medical purposes). (See Document 2.) President Bush, taking phone calls at all hours, worked feverishly to enforce the sanctions and to cultivate and maintain the U.S.-led alliance, using both carrot and stick.

The Turks, who shared a 200-mile border with Iraq, agreed on August 7, after some coaxing from Washington, to comply with UN sanctions and halt the flow of Iraqi oil through the 810-mile pipeline from Mosul to the Turkish port of Yumurtalik. Saudi Arabia followed suit and shut down its pipeline as well. These efforts were strategically important and let Saddam and the rest of the world know that states in the Middle East were willing to sacrifice and suffer, and to challenge Iraq's interests directly, in the effort to stop and reverse Iraq's aggression. This further emboldened other states to take an anti-Saddam stand and facilitated the U.S. effort to build and maintain the anti-Iraq coalition.

SELLING DESERT STORM

On the domestic front, the Bush administration used several different angles to communicate the importance of controlling Saddam. The public was initially skeptical about fighting a war to protect oil supplies or to restore the Kuwaiti monarchy. Major rallies against the war in Boston and San Francisco—bastions of liberal thinking—made famous the notion "No Blood for Oil." Other Americans did not fully understand what the United States intended to do in the faraway, exotic Persian Gulf.

The public, however, was concerned about Iraq's chemical and nuclear capacity, and the need to stop Saddam's aggression. Nuclear weapons were something that the public, having worried about the Soviet nuclear threat during the Cold War, could understand. A risk-taking, gun-toting, "irrational" dictator with nuclear capability posed a clear and present danger to peace.

The public also was anxious about American hostages seized in Iraq and Kuwait during and after the invasion who were being used by Saddam as human shields in Iraq, presumably to deter a U.S.-led attack on strategic sites.[45] In many ways, people could fixate much better on the issue of human shields than on strategic questions. This was made clear in one of Saddam's biggest blunders, which made headlines in the United States and was seized upon by the American people. In a classic television moment, Saddam, trying to show the world how much he really cared about the distraught hostages, put on a display of "affection" for them. In a demeaning and eerie spectacle, he had his advisers bring a young British boy to him, who was obviously terrified of the Iraqi dictator, despite his fine Armani-like double-breasted suit and pleasant smile. While running a fatherly hand through the boy's hair, Saddam asked whether he was getting enough food and being treated well. The boy flinched, scarcely uttered a word, and just stood there, petrified, for what appeared to be an eternity. Saddam's made-for-TV spectacle backfired. Viewers saw it as deception and chicanery, and sympathized even more with the frightened little boy and the plight of the hostages.

PRELUDE TO WAR: GOING THE EXTRA MILE

While war might have been avoided at critical junctures, Bush was unwilling to let Saddam save face by appeasing him; Saddam, for his part, was not willing to lose face by withdrawing unconditionally from Kuwait. Indeed, during King Hussein's talks with Saddam on September 5 in Baghdad, the Iraqi dictator called a staff officer to the room and asked him about the possibility of withdrawing from Kuwait. His reply: "Oh, God forbid, sir, please don't utter these words."[46]

By November 1990, it did not appear that Iraq was planning to withdraw from Kuwait, or even considering it seriously. President Bush was growing increasingly impatient with Saddam, and thus pushed for the UN to sanction the use of force against Iraq. This required that none of the five permanent members of the Security Council veto the American effort. France, the Soviet Union, and China were reluctant to support the American initiative initially. France and the USSR, in particular, had a long-standing political and military relationship with Iraq and wanted Iraq to repay them its debts from arms sales.

After some deliberation, however, these countries eventually signed on. The Soviets, as mentioned earlier, needed good relations with the United States in the post–Cold War era, and France did not want to appear too obstructionist, given Saddam's blatant aggression.

On November 29 the UN passed Resolution 678, authorizing nations to use force against Iraq. The next day, Bush, whose hand against Iraq was now strengthened, shocked many observers by announcing his readiness to go "an extra mile for peace." Bush's diplomacy, however, may very well have been mere show and tell. Indeed, National Security Adviser Brent Scowcroft told Saudi prince Bandar as early as December that Bush's offer to send James Baker to Baghdad and to invite Aziz to Washington for talks was window dressing and that he had already decided to be absolutely unyielding.[47] Nonetheless, the Bush announcement did catch many world leaders—who thought it might send Saddam a message of weakness—by surprise. However, after some diplomatic haggling, the two sides could not even agree on a date to meet. An elusive Saddam asserted that his schedule prevented him from meeting with Baker before January 12. Perhaps Saddam had already resigned himself to the prospect of war, or had boxed himself in with domestic rhetoric, or perhaps Bush's apparent turnaround had given him hope that Washington, after all, was cowardly. We may never know the exact truth.

Nonetheless, the United States and Iraq did resume their efforts at diplomacy. On January 3, Bush again proposed that Baker and Aziz meet in Geneva, with the proviso that Washington make no compromises and offer no rewards for aggression. The Baker-Aziz meeting of January 9, 1991, proved entirely fruitless. Rather than being compliant, Iraq argued that all allied forces must be replaced with a UN-directed, all-Arab force, that all political and economic sanctions against Iraq must end, and that Iraq's withdrawal must be met with similar action by Syria in Lebanon and Israel in the occupied territories. This was almost the opposite of American demands, and put some issues on the table that had absolutely nothing to do with Saddam's blatant aggression against Kuwait. Baker, who constantly sought to return the negotiations to the question of Iraqi withdrawal from Kuwait, handled each of Aziz's arguments with patience and did most of the talking for the American side, with sporadic interjections from his staff. While the U.S. team knew that only Saddam could give them assurances of Iraqi withdrawal, they thought Aziz might show at least a hint of flexibility. But Aziz proved quite stubborn. As one U.S. official in Geneva said, "We hoped he would at least blink!" But in reality Aziz tried to convince Baker that war would be bloody and that the U.S.-led alliance would fall apart.[48] In fact, Aziz did not put much stock in the Geneva meeting. He believed that Bush only sought to score public relations points and to obtain more congressional votes for going to war by showing that he had gone the last mile for peace.[49] And, indeed, the Geneva meeting did decrease public and congressional opposition to war.

Aziz even refused to take a letter, carried by Baker, from George Bush to Saddam. Among other things, the letter informed Saddam that dire consequences would follow if he refused to withdraw from Kuwait. After reading it for about ten minutes while flanked by Saddam's brother-in-law Barzan and Saddam's watchful personal interpreter, Aziz, a man very loyal to Saddam, acted shocked and insulted, and told Baker that the letter was "full of threats" and worded in a manner unfit for official discourse. In fact, the letter was not all that offensive, even for Arab discourse, which tended to be more polite than Americans might expect. (See Document 10.) Although phrased in strong terms, it also stated that if Saddam withdrew, "the Iraqi military establishment will escape destruction," that "Iraq will gain the opportunity to rejoin the international community," and that "the people of the United States have no quarrel with the people of Iraq."[50] In other words, Bush did hold out a carrot of sorts, to go along with his big stick.

Emerging from the meeting, a visibly agitated Baker, who had sought without great hope some kind of serious dialogue, summed up the conference to the international media by saying, "In over six hours of talks, I heard nothing today that suggested to me any Iraqi flexibility whatsoever on complying with the United Nations Security Council resolutions."[51] Later, Baker would write that his "heart knew . . . that America soon would be at war."[52] U.S. negotiators at Geneva believed that the Iraqi team doubted U.S. resolve and felt that the United States still carried the baggage of Vietnam, that the American public could not handle a major war, and that the U.S. Congress was not really aboard for the bumpy ride in the Gulf.[53]

NOTES

1. "The President's News Conference on the Persian Gulf Crisis," November 8, 1990, in George Bush, *Public Papers of the Presidents of the United States* (hereafter cited as *PPP*), vol. 2 (Washington, DC: United States Government Printing Office, 1990), 1581.

2. See text of interview with King Fahd, in *London AL-HAWADITH*, Foreign Broadcast Information Service (FBIS): Near East and South Asia (NESA), February 14, 1992, 21.

3. *Cairo MENA*, in FBIS: NESA, August 13, 1990, 5.

4. Author's interview with high-level Arab official, off the record, Washington, DC, June 27, 1996.

5. Lawrence Freedman and Efraim Karsh, *The Gulf Conflict 1990–1991: Diplomacy and War in the New World Order* (Princeton: Princeton University Press, 1993), 50.

6. John K. Cooley, *Payback: America's Long War in the Middle East* (London: Brassey's, 1991), 186.

7. Quoted in James A. Baker III, *The Politics of Diplomacy: Revolution, War and Peace, 1989–1992* (New York: G. P. Putnam's Sons, 1995), 290.

8. Author's interview with high-level Arab official, Washington, DC, 6/27/96.

9. Ibid.

10. Freedman and Karsh, *Gulf Conflict*, 47.

11. The text of the conversation appears in Dilip Hiro, *Desert Shield to Desert Storm* (London: Routledge, 1992), 85–86.

12. Emphasis added. For the text of the transcript of the Glaspie meeting, see "Excerpts from Iraqi Document on Meeting with U.S. Envoy," *New York Times*, September 23, 1990, A19.

13. For details of the Glaspie meeting and its potential implications, see Michael A. Palmer, *Guardians of the Gulf: A History of America's Expanding Role in the Persian Gulf, 1833–1992* (New York: The Free Press, 1992), 158–60.

14. Quoted in Freedman and Karsh, *Gulf Conflict*, 59.

15. "Remarks and an Exchange with Reporters on the Iraqi Invasion of Kuwait," August 5, 1990, in Bush, *PPP*, vol. 2, 1101.

16. Author's interview with Lawrence Eagleburger, Under Secretary of State, Washington, DC, July 23, 1996.

17. George Bush, interview with Sir David Frost, PBS, January 16, 1996.

18. Author's interview with Secretary of State James Baker III, Washington, DC, 4 June 1996.

19. "The President's News Conference on the Persian Gulf Crisis," August 22, 1990, in Bush, *PPP*, vol. 2, 1160.

20. For an extended analysis of U.S.-Saudi interaction immediately after the invasion, see Bob Woodward, *The Commanders* (New York: Simon and Schuster, 1991), 218–60; Colin Powell, *My American Journey* (New York: Random House, 1995), 465–66.

21. Author's interview with General Colin Powell, Chairman, Joint Chiefs of Staff, Alexandra, VA, May 30, 1996.

22. *Belgrade TANJUG*, in FBIS: NESA, October 24, 1990, 7.

23. Author's interview with Chas W. Freeman, Jr., U.S. ambassador to Saudi Arabia, Washington, DC, June 26, 1996.

24. Ibid.

25. Ibid.

26. Author's interview with Colin Powell, 5/30/96.

27. "Address to the Nation Announcing the Deployment of United States Armed Forces to Saudi Arabia," August 8, 1990, in Bush, *PPP*, vol. 2, 1107.

28. "Remarks and an Exchange with Reporters on the Persian Gulf Crisis," August 11, 1990, in Bush, *PPP*, vol. 2, 1126.

29. "Gulf Crisis an Opportunity for a 'New World Order' " (Presidential Address to Congress), *Congressional Quarterly* (hereafter cited as CQ), September 15, 1990, 2953.

30. Author's interview with Richard Haass, Special Assistant to the President for Near East and South Asian Affairs, phone interview, June 13, 1996.

31. Powell, *My American Journey*, 456–57.

32. Quoted in Freedman and Karsh, *Gulf Conflict*, 204.

33. Roger Cohen and Claudio Gatti, *In the Eye of the Storm: The Life of General H. Norman Schwarzkopf* (New York: Farrar, Straus and Giroux, 1991), 8.

34. Admiral William Crowe, "Testimony Before the Senate Armed Services Committee," November 28, 1990.

35. Extracted in *CQ*, January 12, 1991, 71.

36. George Bush, interview with Bernard Shaw, CNN, March 2, 1996.

37. Jarol B. Manheim, "Strategic Public Diplomacy," in W. Lance Bennett and David L. Paletz, eds., *Taken by Storm: The Media, Public Opinion, and U.S. Foreign Policy in the Gulf War* (Chicago: University of Chicago Press, 1994), 138–40.

38. George Bush, interview with David Frost, 1/16/96.

39. Author's interview with Richard Haass, who helped prepare the analysis, 6/13/96.

40. Quoted in John E. Yang, "Somber Decision," *Washington Post*, January 13, 1991, A1, 24.

41. Author's interview with General Brent Scowcroft, National Security Adviser, Washington, DC, June 26, 1996.

42. George Bush, interview with Bernard Shaw, CNN, 3/2/96.

43. Author's interview with James Baker, 6/4/96.

44. Ibid.

45. John Mueller, *Policy and Opinion in the Gulf War* (Chicago: University of Chicago Press, 1994), 42.

46. Quoted in Freedman and Karsh, *Gulf Conflict*, 162.

47. Jean Edward Smith, *George Bush's War* (New York: Henry Holt, 1992), 222.

48. Author's interview with Sandra Charles, Deputy National Security Adviser, Washington, DC, June 5, 1996.

49. *Frontline* interview with Tariq Aziz, rebroadcast 1/27/97.

50. Text of "Bush Letter to President Hussein," January 9, 1991, in Bush, *PPP*, vol. 2, 36–37.

51. Remarks of Secretary of State James Baker, January 9, 1991, after his January 9 meeting with Iraqi foreign minister Tariq Aziz.

52. Baker, *Politics of Diplomacy*, 346.

53. Author's interview with Sandra Charles, 6/5/96.

2

War Erupts in a Storm: The Continuation of Diplomacy by Air and on the Ground

We make war that we may live in peace.

—Aristotle

In one of the more famous lines of statecraft, Carl von Clausewitz, the nineteenth-century Prussian strategist, asserted that war was simply the continuation of diplomacy by other means. By this, he meant that states used force as an extension of politics in order to obtain what they failed to obtain through diplomacy. War, then, was not really a substitute for diplomacy. Rather, as in the case of the Persian Gulf War, channels of communication to the adversary were kept open so as to achieve critical goals peaceably if at all possible, while military force was applied at the same time. Indeed, the U.S.-led coalition initially tried diplomacy to deal with Iraq's aggression, then economic sanctions and more diplomacy, and finally war, while at the same time seeking Saddam's withdrawal from Kuwait.

This chapter examines the air and ground phases of the Gulf War as the continuation of diplomacy, and the U.S. decision not to march on Baghdad to depose Saddam Hussein. In the process, it raises a number of questions. Can air power alone defeat an enemy, as an extension of diplomacy? Should U.S.-led forces have marched on Baghdad? Did Washington achieve its political goals?

SMART BOMBS AND THE PUBLIC IMAGINATION

On Wednesday, January 16, 1991, the world witnessed an unforgettable sight. On a night purposefully chosen because it was moonless, the sky over Baghdad erupted in a flash of light reminiscent of an endless, far-reaching fireworks display. This, however, was no holiday spectacle. Desert Storm had begun; diplomacy by other means was at hand.

In an intense bombardment, even by history's toughest standards, the allies flew one sortie every single minute against Saddam's virtually hapless military, hoping to degrade and weaken it, knock out Iraq's strategic facilities, isolate its front-line troops from resupply, destroy its troop formations and front-line defensive fortifications, and possibly kill Saddam in the process.

During the air war, the U.S. Air Force expended more than half of its total inventory of nonnuclear missiles. Of all high-explosive bombs used during the war, a shocking 98 percent of the 82,000 tons dropped were American.

Desert Storm was a high-tech extravaganza, broadcast to viewers worldwide, with a significant impact on the public imagination. The "surgical" strikes captured on television gave a surreal, antiseptic quality to the war. The last time Americans viewed war, U.S. soldiers were being blown up in Vietnam and civilians were being burned with napalm or killed in fire fights. This time around, media coverage created the impression that no one was really dying on either side of the battle line and that all bombs were going directly down the air shafts of buildings. Was this dangerous in its own way? Did it distort the real horror of war? Such questions were inevitably asked and would remain salient long after the war.

COMPLETE SURPRISE

In the process of using force to obtain what diplomacy had failed to achieve, the U.S.-led coalition sought to devastate Iraq's military. The air attack achieved complete tactical surprise. This was due, in part, to the Iraqis' decision, earlier in the crisis, to turn off their radars so as to prevent allied aircraft from recording and jamming their radar transmissions. The attack was planned so that the aircraft could strike in the dead of night and return in near-total darkness, thus adding to the surprise and minimizing civilian casualties. On the night of the attack, the Iraqis were blinded to the reality befalling them, to the fact that, as General Colin Powell put it, F-117A Stealth fighters were slipping "through the Iraqi air defenses like ghosts."[1]

New technology gave U.S. pilots a huge edge. The ghostly nature of the U.S. Stealth aircraft resulted from a combination of technology and modern-age design that deflected radar and minimized the ability of heat-guided weapons to home in on its engine exhaust. For its part, the Tomahawk cruise missile flew at a low altitude of 500 feet at over 500 miles per hour, thus making it hard to detect. Shot from a ship or submarine, the Tomahawk uses a Terrain Contour Matching system that scans the landscape and matches the data to a preconfigured computer map, thus allowing redirection in flight toward its target.

The major air attack was preceded by special forces in Apache helicopters that destroyed Iraqi border radars, designed to protect two main air defense radars from a low-altitude attack. The Air Force F-4G Wild Weasel aircraft and the Navy F/A-18 Hornets carrying high-speed antiradiation missiles (HARMs) also began to take out the major portion of Iraq's active radar-guided surface-to-air missiles.

The first allied air strike included 400 aircraft in a carefully organized operation. The main attack came from the triangular, sleek F-117A Stealth aircraft, which was the only aircraft to attack in downtown Baghdad, and terrain-reading Tomahawk cruise missiles that struck at three main air defense centers and key military and political buildings in Baghdad, six minutes after the Stealth aircraft attacked. At just before 3 A.M.., Stealth fighters flew over Baghdad and destroyed the headquarters of the Iraqi air force. Saddam's Presidential Palace along the Tigris River was targeted by at least eight computer-guided Tomahawk missiles, which flew 700 miles to hit their target directly, as well as by U.S. air power.

It was not exactly clear how the campaign would go. U.S. F-16 pilots were very anxious prior to the attack because they expected to lose many planes to Iraqi antiaircraft missiles. Moreover, some of the weapons to be used had not been tested under desert conditions, and in the fog of war just about anything could happen. Already, during the Desert Shield phase of bringing an American military presence to the region, planes and other highly technical, sensitive equipment had performed somewhat erratically in the sand and heat of the desert.

Lieutenant General Charles Horner, who guided the planning and execution of the air war, received some quick assurances that the Stealth aircraft were finding their targets just fine. In what might have been viewed as ironic by Horner, CNN's Bernard Shaw, who some in the military considered a bit too far to the left in his politics, went off the air when a precision bomb knocked out Baghdad's telephone exchange grid.[2] Clearly, the U.S. attack was basically on target; Iraq's communication grid was taking direct hits as planned. Shaw and his CNN colleagues, Peter Arnett and John Holliman, continued to offer the world a peek into the ongoing drama from the ninth floor of Baghdad's Rasheed Hotel, while television watchers wondered if the reporters also might get hit in what appeared to be a total, deadly barrage of the entire city, but what in reality was an attack confined to particular areas and buildings. Thereafter, CNN, the only major news network that kept its people in Baghdad on the night of the attack, would become a bona fide worldwide news phenomenon.

One look at Baghdad from the sky told the tale. By and large, unlike the cities of World War II, Baghdad did not look bombed out; rather, buildings that were not targeted were left standing next to those hit. Overall, approximately 155 cruise missiles were used and 300 F-117 sorties were flown against forty-five specific targets in Baghdad. By war's end, the allied coalition flew about 100,000 sorties-the most severe, concentrated air attack in strategic history.

The first phase of Desert Storm, which was intended to achieve air supremacy, was a great success. As Schwarzkopf asserted excitedly on the night of the attack, when Powell asked apprehensively about losses, "it's incredible," because only two aircraft went down.[3] In the entire air campaign, the allies lost only thirty-six planes, of which twenty-seven were American.

U.S. technology was good enough that Iraq's planes could be identified and targeted from a long distance. After a while, Iraqi pilots were too intimidated to go airborne. U.S. F-16 pilots could hear them communicating engine problems, malfunctions—almost any excuse not to have to face devastating U.S. technology.[4] Had Iraqi's air force even modestly challenged the U.S. attack, it would have thrown U.S. aircraft off their trajectories and made it much harder for them to drop their bombs.

After gaining air supremacy, allied air forces used smart bombs, highly precise weapons, to target Iraqi aircraft bunkers, specifically hardened to take direct attacks. These attacks were accurate enough that Saddam, in what appeared to be a desperate move, sent 122 aircraft to his archenemy, Iran, as early as January 28. At first, it appeared that the two sides had agreed that the planes would be returned in exchange for some Iraqi concession. But Iran had other plans. This incident further convinced Bush that Saddam was psychologically unstable. Indeed, when asked what surprised him most during the entire Gulf War, Bush referred to this "man sending his air force to Iran. What the hell is going on here? Why is he sending his air force to his enemy Iran?"[5]

Meanwhile, back in Iraq, Saddam was parading captured American, British, Italian, and Kuwaiti pilots on television on January 20, forcing them to read carefully scripted statements condemning the allied attack. In yet another media fiasco for Saddam, these battered men were forced to go on television, repeating, like zombies, verbatim statements that were clearly coerced and would have been viewed as totally absurd under any other circumstances. Like Saddam's television fiasco with the hostages, the exploitation of the airmen backfired.

In response to the dramatic success of the air attack, Saddam moved quickly to try to draw Israel's fire. On January 18, two days after the war began, the first al-Hussein Scud missiles were fired at Israel and Saudi Arabia. Initially, it appeared that Saddam might have used chemical or nerve weapons. Indeed, in one gripping newscast, Frank Reynolds of ABC News, shackled with a gas mask and visibly agitated, went off the air after reporting that Scud warheads had hit nearby. Although he came back on the air in a matter of seconds, the fear was that a nerve gas bomb might have hit close to Reynolds's base of operations. This brought home to viewers the real seriousness of the war in a manner that few other events could. Here, after all, was a human being that Americans knew, who was openly frightened and potentially imperiled. It made for sobering drama.

Rumors of Iraqi nerve gas and chemical attacks continued for several hours. Given the Holocaust experience of the Jewish people, serious use of nerve or chemical agents by Iraq could have triggered an Israeli nuclear response, and, indeed, Israel did go on nuclear alert. For those few fateful hours, the world sat riveted to the television, wondering if the war would expand in scope and intensity. However, beyond terrorizing civilians, the inaccurate, conventional Scud missiles caused few fatalities, with the exception of one lucky hit on U.S. personnel barracks in Dhahran, Saudi Arabia, where twenty-eight soldiers were killed.

Saddam's key goal in attacking Israel was to draw return fire, thus pulling Israel into the war. From Saddam's perspective, this would have splintered the U.S.-led coalition, because Arab states would not have wanted to be perceived as fighting with Israel against Iraq. The United States, however, successfully persuaded the Israelis not to attack. Bush and other U.S. leaders convinced them that an Israeli attack could severely disrupt the anti-Saddam coalition, offered Israel the use of Patriot antimissile batteries against Scud attacks, refused to give Israel the aircraft codes necessary to identify friend and foe in the skies, and promised to do all that it could to find and destroy Iraq's Scud launchers. This combination of approaches kept Israel at bay, against its basic instincts.

Allied aircraft were diverted to become Scud busters. "Stormin' Norman" Schwarzkopf described the hunt as "searching for a needle in a haystack" and viewed it as an unfortunate diversion from attacks on more important targets. He would have preferred concentrating on military targets in Iraq, but was overruled by Secretary Cheney, who believed it was critical to keep Israel out of the war.[6]

THE AIR-POWER DEBATE

America's smart bombs were fairly accurate, although, as a General Accounting Office (GAO) report would show in 1996, not nearly so accurate as initially believed.[7] The accuracy achieved was made possible by an array of technologies such as global positioning satellites (GPS) and ring laser gyro inertial navigation systems, which allowed pilots to lock in on targets even in bad weather. Once over their targets, U.S. aircraft used another array of navigational and precision-bombing technologies to assure greater accuracy, although the effectiveness of infrared, electro-optical, and laser systems was degraded seriously by clouds, rain, fog, smoke, and even high humidity.

Of all the bombs dropped by U.S. forces, approximately 178,000 were basic unguided bombs ("dumb" bombs), and only 17,109 were smart ones. The dumb bombs such as those dropped from the ancient B-52s had a terrorizing impact on Iraqi soldiers and helped break their morale prior to the ground war, while the smart bombs hit Iraqi assets.

The U.S. Air Force deployed 46 percent of its total combat force to Saudi Arabia. The coalition had approximately 2,500 aircraft at the time of the January 16 attack, and the devastating air attack raised serious questions about whether a ground war would even be needed. Iraq's air force, the sixth largest in the world, had been completely suppressed within one week, and allied aircraft were hitting Iraqi targets with virtual impunity. Iraq's thick air defense system—composed of as many as 16,000 surface-to-air missiles and 10,000 antiaircraft artillery pieces as well as complicated radar systems—also proved relatively ineffective.

For perhaps the first time in strategic history, air power alone seemed to cause enough damage to the adversary to make capitulation quite possible. The national debate on air power had begun even before Desert Storm was initiated. Indeed, a headline in the *Washington Post* on September 16, 1990, would prove quite controversial: "U.S. to Rely on Air Strikes if War Erupts." Powell viewed it as "the worst possible message at this time" because he thought the president was already "being oversold on air power," on its ability to make the Iraqi army fold.[8] Powell, who seriously doubted that air power alone could win any war, advised the president against such assumptions. The source of the *Washington Post* story, General Michael Dugan, the

Air Force chief of staff, was fired for the gaffe, and for some time talk of air power being decisive was suppressed.

Ironically, Defense Secretary Cheney, who had a major role in firing Dugan, would later recall that "special credit" should go to the air war, which was decisive in determining the outcome.[9] The notion of dominant air power, however, would arise again once the air war began and proved so effective, and would later recur in the post–Gulf War period. Indeed, Powell would later note that President Bill Clinton asked him about influencing the Bosnian situation among the Serbs, Croats, and Muslims of the former Yugoslavia by using air power. To Powell, this was the "air power" notion, made famous in the Gulf, once again surfacing; according to Powell's memoirs, he disabused Clinton of this notion.[10] But there is no doubt that, to the chagrin of the U.S. Army and Navy, the use of effective and decisive air power in wars and crises would be much more seriously considered as a result of the Gulf War. Whether the war set a precedent for air power as a dominant strategic tool is a question that is still being debated. But in all likelihood the answer to the question will depend on the case at hand—on the target, geography, balance of forces, and objectives of any future conflict.

A LAST ULTIMATUM

At the outset, questions arose about whether to launch a ground war at all. Soviet leader Mikhail Gorbachev appeared particularly eager, after seeing the drubbing Iraq was receiving from the air, to have a cease-fire negotiated, followed by Iraqi withdrawal from Kuwait. From Baghdad, Iraqi statements suggested that Saddam expected Moscow to deliver Iraq from an American ground attack. From Gorbachev's perspective, the Soviets were trying to throw "a life raft to Iraq,"[11] but only Saddam could save himself.

Under Gorbachev's pressure, Bush agreed to let Baker meet with Moscow's new foreign minister, Alexander Bessmertnykh. This was diplomacy as the continuation of war rather than war as the continuation of diplomacy. But in a sense, Washington was also stepping back to see if diplomacy might accomplish the objective of getting Iraq out of Kuwait.

To the surprise of Bush and many other actors, the two emerged from a meeting and made a statement offering Saddam a cease-fire in exchange for withdrawing from Kuwait, and also promised to promote Arab-Israeli peace. While Baker later argued that the statement represented no change in policy on unconditional Iraqi withdrawal,[12] it was applauded by the French, who sought some compromise with Saddam, and embarrassed

Bush. The White House, thereafter, carefully scaled the statement back and then denied it altogether. Bush wanted to avoid even the appearance of offering Saddam any compensation for aggression.

This incident reflected the difference in opinion between the Soviets and Americans. Moscow had long-standing relations with Iraq extending at least as far back as the 1972 Soviet-Iraqi Treaty of Friendship and Cooperation. Soviet and Iraqi military and political officials had an established rapport at many levels of interaction, and Gorbachev must have been under pressure to offer Saddam a face-saving escape from Kuwait.

Bush, by contrast, found the face-saving formula an unacceptable reward for aggression. While both leaders agreed that Saddam had to leave Kuwait, and although the cooperation that they were exhibiting was unprecedented in the post–World War II period, they differed on how to get Iraq out of Kuwait.

By February 15, Iraq was so shell-shocked, and Saddam so out of tricks, that for the first time the Iraqi president grudgingly referred to the possibility of leaving Kuwait, and the Soviets pushed their peace plan. Politburo member Yevgeny Primakov, a well-known face in elite circles in Baghdad and the Soviet foreign ministry's leading Arabist, met with his friend Saddam in Baghdad and argued that the Americans were preparing for a crushing ground war and that Iraq should withdraw. Saddam, while open to discussion, wanted assurances that retreating Iraqi forces would not be attacked and that sanctions would be lifted. Bush, however, was not in a negotiating mood. He stated emphatically on February 19, when asked about the Soviet peace initiative, that there "are no negotiations. The goals have been set out. There will be no concessions—not going to give."[13] The only guarantee Bush would give was that retreating Iraqi forces would not be shot in the back.

In any event, Saddam clearly did not meet Bush's demands. After reading Iraq's statement, which aimed at less than unconditional withdrawal, the White House asserted that it contained conditions in violation of UN Security Council resolutions, which called for complete and unconditional withdrawal.[14] If diplomacy was not likely to meet all of Bush's conditions, he would clearly return to war.

While negotiations on terms for Iraq's withdrawal were proceeding unsuccessfully, Iraqi forces began to set over 600 Kuwaiti oil wells afire on February 22, in one of the more dramatic incidents of environmental terrorism in this century. The fires would burn for months, transforming the regional landscape with a hellish blackness that descended like a veil of darkness. Despite this environmental terrorism, the coalition gave Saddam one last chance to withdraw by February 23. As Bush put it, "The coalition will give Saddam Hussein until noon Saturday to do what he must do: begin his immediate and unconditional withdrawal from Kuwait. We must hear publicly and authoritatively his acceptance of these terms."[15] Saddam, perhaps fearing capitulation to such an ultimatum or resigned to the prospect of war, rejected this offer. And so the stage was set for the land war.

100 DAYS: THE GROUND WAR

The failure of yet another round of diplomacy put Iraq and the United States into the ground phase of the war. Saddam may very well have waited for the damaging air war to end and the ground war to begin. Indeed, while his air force was ineffective, his ground forces had experience from the Iran-Iraq war, and could possibly inflict allied casualties.

Saddam was so eager, or desperate, that he had earlier ordered an Iraqi attack on a small, abandoned, and lightly defended Saudi border town called al-Khafji. On January 30, Iraq began its incremental attack, with about 4,000 men and eighty tanks. Saudi and Qatari military units launched a counterattack on January 31 to recapture the town, in which a twelve-man U.S. reconnaissance unit was trapped. Although Iraqi troops were roundly defeated in the battle that ensued, Saddam tried to portray al-Khafji as a psychological victory. After all, Iraqi troops did occupy and control al-Khafji until they were either ejected or captured by Saudi troops supported by U.S. Marines. In the process, twelve U.S. Marines were killed, an outcome that Saddam must have relished. In reality, al-Khafji was at best a fleeting minute of glory for Saddam, and a failed attack that really betrayed how ineffective Iraq's ground forces were. It merely reinforced Schwarzkopf's view that Iraq would go down hard.

The U.S.-led ground war plan had three major parts. In the first part, Iraqi soldiers were subjected to severe bombardment by multiple-rocket launchers, naval guns, helicopter gunships, and, most important, punishing B-52s. This disoriented, demoralized, and undermined Iraqi divisions.

On February 24, the second phase of the plan was implemented. Allied forces faked an amphibious assault off the Kuwaiti coast with 18,000 U.S. Marines, in order to tie down some Iraqi divisions and to allow for a surprise attack to the west. This objective was achieved with surprising success. Iraqi generals clearly believed that there would be a Marine landing from the Gulf, north of Kuwait City into Kuwait, aimed at cutting the Iraqi army in half. To deter or address such an attack, Iraq built extensive defenses, including mines, sand dunes, and antiaircraft guns, and placed two infantry divisions, backed by additional mechanized and armored divisions, there.

Indeed, the bulk of Iraq's 500,000 troops, except for the Republican Guard, were dug in either along the coastline, expecting an amphibious assault, or on the Kuwait-Saudi border.

Approximately 300 miles west of the Iraq-Kuwait border, under the cover of the allied air attack, U.S.-led forces engaged in a major flanking maneuver, involving highly complex logistics. All in all, 65,000 vehicles were involved in the attack, moving twenty-four hours a day, each with a particular destination and objective. The U.S. XVIII and VII Corps, with 240,000 troops, 95,000 trucks, and 12,000 tanks and other armored personnel vehicles, including supply trucks, moved westward undetected. Iraq's surveillance capabilities had been severely degraded by the air war, and Saddam was lucky to know where his own forces were, much less the allied armies. The primary objective of the XVIII and VII Corps was to destroy Saddam's elite Republican Guard and to entrap key Iraqi divisions for elimination.

On February 24, the U.S.-led forces initiated part three of the attack. U.S. Marines and Saudi troops attacked across the Kuwait-Saudi border in the direction of Kuwait City. Both attacks were highly successful and met surprisingly little opposition from Iraqi forces, who often did not know where the attack was coming from and were usually facing in the wrong direction when it did come. The allied forces quickly breached the vaunted "Saddam line," composed of antitank ditches, minefields, and deep trenches filled with ignitable oil. Rather than facing fierce fighting, the allies were met with the surrender of thousands of Iraqi troops. While U.S. forces might have expected hardened, dangerous Iraqi soldiers willing to die rather than surrender to the "imperialist Americans," what they found in many cases were confused, starving, broken men, unsure and fearful of their fate. So much for Saddam's million-man machine.

While Iraq did fight hard in several tank battles to the west, by and large the Iraqi army proved no match for the better trained, equipped, and rested U.S.-led forces. Saddam's model was the unimaginative, unmaneuverable Soviet defensive posture. This was particularly unfortunate for his military, because U.S. forces had trained throughout the Cold War to defeat precisely such a posture. Almost any other strategy could have thrown at least a small monkey wrench into U.S.-led military operations. In less than two days, the allies broke the enemy's military position, leaving Iraqi forces at the mercy of the coalition.

On February 25, when it had become clear that Iraqi forces were routed, Baghdad boldly announced the withdrawal of Iraqi troops from Kuwait. With characteristic bravado, Saddam proclaimed that the forces had "proven their ability" to fight and were heroes, but this must have fallen on deaf ears.

After all, except for the Republican Guard, this was a broken army that had suffered possibly tens of thousands of deaths and many more casualties.

While Saddam became increasingly compliant, he also remained reluctant to accept all of the UN resolutions. The next day, Foreign Minister Aziz announced Iraq's willingness to rescind its official annexation of Kuwait, release all prisoners of war, and pay war reparations in exchange for a cease-fire. On February 27, Iraq finally announced that it would comply with all twelve UN resolutions.

Meanwhile, on the evening of February 25, rather than surrendering, Iraqi troops attempted to escape in the dark from Kuwait with their equipment and stolen booty. The ploy failed. The allies discovered a large convoy of over 1,000 vehicles moving toward Basra on Highway 6 and attacked it with a dozen F-15s and F-16s. American pilots described the attack as a "turkey shoot." Their technological wizardry allowed for pinpoint attacks on military vehicles from far away. As one pilot put it: "I could see Iraqi trucks from a long distance. I then locked on target and fired away knowing that the hapless Iraqi on the other end never had a chance."[16] Within hours, Highway 6 had become the "highway of death," filled with bombed-out vehicles hopelessly stuck in a traffic jam of hellish doom.

The carnage, however, did not make for good copy and raised moral questions about destroying an army that was already defeated. President Bush had the option of continuing the attack against Iraqi forces and attempting to weaken further Iraq's Republican Guard, or calling the cease-fire. The president agreed to a cease-fire approximately 100 hours after the ground war had begun.

To be sure, U.S.-led forces had wreaked great damage on Iraq's military. By the war's end, the world's sixth largest air force had been severely damaged, and Iraq's army was halved in size. Iraq lost an estimated 2,633 tanks out of 5,800, 2,196 artillery pieces out of 3,850, and 324 fixed-wing combat aircraft out of an estimated 650–700. Its navy, which was not particularly strong, but nonetheless dangerous, was destroyed.

In the nuclear area, U.S. air attacks devastated Saddam's strategic facilities, and postwar UN inspections revealed that Iraq had been closer to developing nuclear weapons than had been expected. Inspectors found a multibillion-dollar nuclear program that could have produced its first nuclear weapon not in ten years, as some U.S. intelligence agencies had thought, but in one to two years had Iraq not invaded Kuwait.

Although Iraq initially defied the UN resolution requiring full disclosure of nuclear materials, over time the UN Special Commission and the International Atomic Energy Agency made substantial progress toward eliminating Iraq's programs of mass destruction. All major parts of Iraq's nuclear program were destroyed or seriously damaged either by Desert Storm or by UN inspection teams. This included Iraq's nuclear reactor and major nuclear labs, and the various high-tech machines that were used for producing weapons-grade materials. Its uranium mine was also located and its processes for turning uranium ore into oxide controlled.

Nonetheless, while the war cut Saddam down to size, Bush would be severely criticized for not supporting uprisings against Saddam immediately after the war. The southern Iraqi city of Basra was the first to erupt. The rebellion spread to other key areas of Iraq's primarily Shiite south, including the holy cities of Najaf and Karbala. In the north, the Kurds, long brutalized by Saddam and in search of their own state, also took to the streets. Within days, Saddam faced a major insurrection in the south and in Kurdistan. His military forces viciously suppressed the rebellion and produced a human tragedy of major proportions, including the brutalization and murder of civilians.

By March 1991, 1.5 million Iraqi Kurds fled to the Turkish border and Iran. Although the United States did not want to support the rebels directly for fear of being dragged into the Iraqi quagmire, it did establish safety and no-fly zones to protect Kurdish refugees. Iraqi citizens, suffering under UN-mandated economic sanctions and Saddam's refusal to sell oil for medicine and food, met unfortunate death by the thousands.

Bush and his military brass were also criticized for not having destroyed, when they had the chance, Iraq's Republican Guard divisions, a military force that would prove instrumental in violently suppressing the postwar northern Kurdish and southern Shiite rebellions against the Iraqi dictator. This was certainly the view of the Kurds. Indeed, in a meeting with a delegation of Kurdish refugees, amid the "heartbreaking beauty," as Secretary James Baker put it, of the snow-capped mountains of northwestern Iraq, Baker was given a letter by them which had two sentences that struck him in particular: "All Iraqis were waiting for freedom and [a] democratic regime in Iraq. But the mistakes and wrong decisions that allowed the Iraqi regime to use tanks and helicopters caused this tragedy."17 In defending his decision, Bush would later say that we "don't measure the extent of victory by killing 25,000 more Iraqis. We won the war by then."18 As discussed in Chapter 7, the war already had taken its toll on the Iraqis (and also produced some casualties and postwar medical problems on the American side).

While the U.S.-led coalition did impose some severe cease-fire terms on Iraq, including economic sanctions and the dismantling and permanent monitoring of its potential nuclear program (see Chapter 7, and Document

13), other critics would go even further and say that the United States should
have found Saddam and eliminated him. This raised the not unpopular idea
of whether U.S.-led forces should have marched on Baghdad and produced
a clear, decisive end to the Iraqi regime. For such critics, as for the Kurds
and Shiite Muslims opposed to Saddam, the Gulf War would not be over
with Saddam still entrenched in power in Baghdad.

TO BAGHDAD OR NOT?

Although Bush derided Saddam as another Hitler, he sought a different
solution for Saddam and Iraq than the one imposed on Germany in 1945.
He wanted to evict Iraq from Kuwait, destroy Saddam's war-making potential, and probably kill Saddam in the process if possible. No one wanted the
brutal dictator to survive, only to fight another day. Bush, however, did not
want to remake Iraq in America's image. While he was criticized in some
elite quarters for not marching on Baghdad and taking Saddam, this would
have involved several risks. Thus, it did not become a plausible option.

First, the UN mandate governing Operations Desert Shield and Storm
did not allow for a march into Baghdad, and America's Arab allies, some
of whom would not even fight Iraq, would have opposed such action.
Therefore, the United States would have been acting without the great
international support that it enjoyed thus far during the war, and may have
appeared more like a bully than an enforcer of peace. Multilateral political
action, which a majority of Americans supported, was important during the
war. It continues to be the principal way to avoid the appearance of Yankee
imperialism in the Arab world.

Second, nations historically fight much harder to protect their homeland
than to hold onto foreign booty. Saddam's Republican Guards, which he
pulled back to the Baghdad area for safekeeping, no doubt would have
resisted U.S. forces vigorously around and in Baghdad, thus imposing
serious casualties. Although Saddam was reluctant to use the Guards to keep
Kuwait, the same was not true of Baghdad, Iraq's capital and the heart of
what many consider to be Arab history.

Third, finding Saddam, which coalition bombs failed to do during the
war, would have been difficult. Iraq is a big country, and Saddam, who has
at least two doubles, knows where to hide. Fourth, even if the United States
could have accomplished its mission, what next? Iraqis might dislike
Saddam, but they hate U.S. forces even more. As Bush would later recall,
there wasn't even a legal basis for "getting" Saddam.[19] And the United
States would have a hard time finding an alternative Iraqi group to lead a

post-Saddam Iraq. Iraqi opposition to Saddam after the war and today consists of five separate groups: communists, Kurds, Islamists, Arab nationalists, and so-called democratic forces. They all agree on four things: (1) Saddam should be ousted, (2) Iraq should remain whole, (3) democratic elections should be held, and (4) the Kurds should get some autonomy. Beyond that, their views diverge significantly, and they lack unity, experience, legitimacy, and the connections necessary for governance. They would likely fight any members of the current elite for power, creating a power vacuum after Saddam.

Fourth, if regional security is served when neither Iran nor Iraq has the ability or inclination to dominate the region, then marching on Baghdad could probably have knocked Iraq out of this balancing role, at least in the short term. This would have put even greater pressure on the United States to check Iran—a difficult and unsavory job.

WAR TERMINATION AND CLAUSEWITZ

Clausewitz put great emphasis on how military force should be used as an instrument to achieve political goals. And while President Bush was effective during the crisis in meeting political goals, more attention could have been devoted to the issue of how to translate a brilliant military victory into political humiliation for the Iraqi dictator. Indeed, the United States could have attacked Iraq's Republican Guards for another twenty-four hours, which is something that many U.S. commanders on the ground, including Schwarzkopf, wanted. U.S.-led ground forces were in a position to deal three Iraqi divisions severe blows prior to the decision to end the war at one hundred hours. It is possible that such attacks would have further crippled Saddam without leaving Iraq unable to play a future balancing role against Iran.

Moreover, Washington could have pushed for stronger terms for Iraq's capitulation at the cease-fire talks at Safwan. But the administration, as Richard Haass would later assert, may not have been thinking "hard enough about humiliating the political leadership."[20] From Scowcroft's perspective, the administration should have insisted on Saddam's presence at Safwan. "That was our mistake, because that allowed him to blame his generals for the defeat, and not he himself."[21]

While Chas Freeman, U.S. ambassador to Saudi Arabia, pressed the Bush administration for a war-termination strategy, no real action was taken because, in Freeman's view, the administration was concerned that the coalition would break down if such a strategy were formulated and leaked. Schwarzkopf, for his part, was very "agitated" when he received little direction from Washington regarding the talks at Safwan; Iraqi generals must have "walked out of Safwan with smiles on their faces, wondering why the U.S. position was so apolitical." Schwarzkopf wanted instructions from Washington on how to negotiate at Safwan, and in the absence of such direction was forced to treat the talks in military rather than political terms.[22]

Schwarzkopf did not even insist on preventing the Iraqis from flying attack helicopters, a decision that General Scowcroft wanted reversed. The Iraqis subsequently used helicopters to put down the postwar uprisings against the regime. Schwarzkopf was more concerned with terminating the war cleanly than with crippling Saddam politically. Yet, the U.S.-led coalition, with dominant military force and a clearly defeated adversary, was in a position to impose more severe cease-fire terms.

An overriding concern among high-level U.S. policymakers, however, was to avoid getting "stuck in the Gulf." This concern "seriously affected the war-termination approach" because, as one policymaker close to events later put it, "After achieving our critical objectives, Bush did not want to stick around and lose Arab support and get into the types of troubles that U.S. forces faced in the terror bombings in Saudi Arabia in 1996."[23] Moreover, Bush believed that Iraqi forces were more devastated than was really the case, and was concerned about exceeding the coalition's mandate. His advisers were also concerned that additional U.S. attacks, after the surrender of thousands of Iraqi soldiers, would look like a massacre, and in Powell's words would be "un-American" and "unchivalrous."[24]

Whether or not it was possible to humiliate Saddam politically, thus weakening his domestic position, without further insinuating U.S. forces in harm's way is an issue that deserves more serious consideration, particularly as new information comes to light. Current information suggests that more could have and should have been done in the form of weakening Iraq's Republican Guards and in imposing more humiliating cease-fire terms. But, then again, hindsight is always 20/20.

CONCLUSION

The U.S.-led coalition used many forms of diplomacy, various types of sanctions, and, only as a last resort, force to achieve the objective of reversing Iraq's invasion of Kuwait. In this sense, the Gulf War was a classic case of war as simply the continuation of diplomacy by other means. To what extent the war actually achieved long-term political objectives, in addition to its military goals, will remain a matter of great debate as history continues to unfurl in the region, into the twenty-first century.

NOTES

1. Colin Powell, *My American Journey* (New York: Random House, 1995), 508.

2. Roger Cohen and Claudio Gatti, *In the Eye of the Storm: The Life of General H. Norman Schwarzkopf* (New York: Farrar, Straus and Giroux, 1991), 262.

3. Powell, *My American Journey*, 508.

4. Author's interview with Keith Rosenkranz, Desert Storm F-16 pilot, Boston, MA, March 3, 1996.

5. George Bush, interview with Bernard Shaw, CNN, March 2, 1996.

6. *Frontline* interview with Richard Cheney, rebroadcast January 17, 1997.

7. *Operation Desert Storm*, Report to Congressional Requesters (Washington, DC: GAO, July 1996).

8. Powell, *My American Journey*, 476–77.

9. Richard Cheney, interview with Bernard Shaw, CNN, March 2, 1996.

10. Powell, *My American Journey*, 562.

11. *Frontline* interview with Mikhail Gorbachev, broadcast January 9 and 10, 1996.

12. James A. Baker III, *The Politics of Diplomacy: Revolution, War and Peace, 1989–1992* (New York: G. P. Putnam's Sons, 1995), 393–95.

13. "Exchange with Reporters on the Soviet Peace Plan Proposal for the Persian Gulf Conflict," February 19, 1991, in George Bush, *Public Papers of the Presidents of the United States* (hereafter cited as *PPP*), vol. 2 (Washington, DC: United States Government Printing Office, 1990), 153.

14. "Statement by Press Secretary Fitzwater on the Iraqi Offer to Withdraw from Kuwait," February 15, 1991, in Bush, *PPP*, vol. 1, 144.

15. "Remarks on the Persian Gulf Conflict," February 22, 1991, in Bush, *PPP*, vol. 1, 166.

16. Author's interview with Keith Rosenkranz, 3/3/96.

17. Quoted in Baker, *Politics of Diplomacy*, 431.

18. George Bush, interview with Bernard Shaw, 3/2/96.

19. Ibid.

20. *Frontline* interview with Richard Haass, Special Assistant to the President for Near East and South Asia, January 9 and 10, 1996.

21. *Frontline* interview with Brent Scowcroft, National Security Adviser, January 9 and 10, 1996.

22. Author's interview with Ambassador Chas W. Freeman, Jr., Washington, DC, June 26, 1996.

23. Author's interview with Lawrence Eagleburger, Under Secretary of State, phone interview, July 23, 1996.

24. *Frontline* interview with Robert Gates, Deputy National Security Adviser, January 9 and 10, 1996.

3

From Truman to Desert Storm: The Rising Eagle in the Persian Gulf

After Iraq invaded Kuwait, one of the biggest questions worldwide was how the United States would respond. Would Washington send major forces to the Gulf? Could the Saudis trust U.S. determination? Would the United States be able to stop Saddam? At stake were even more fundamental questions about the U.S. role in world politics. Was the United States in decline, as one major school of thought argued? Had its heyday as a great power passed? Would other states such as Japan and Germany rise in influence in world politics? The Gulf crisis was a test of sorts of the U.S. role in world politics, and it passed the test quite well. While in retrospect it may seem eminently sensible that the U.S.-led coalition did so well in the Gulf, in truth Operations Desert Shield and Storm were complicated, and history could have taken another turn had Washington not been so well prepared and disposed to challenge Iraq.

The United States had been unknowingly preparing for the Gulf War for decades, and in particular from 1979 to 1990. Indeed, the rise of American power and presence in the Persian Gulf over the past four decades, and particularly in the 1980s, represents one of the distinguishing features of the regional and international politics of the area.[1] Without understanding this vital piece in the complex puzzle of regional politics, it is impossible to understand the U.S.-led military victory in the Persian Gulf War. This chapter explores this piece of the puzzle, and in so doing, helps explain how the United States, over time, prepared itself for the Gulf War, a war that elevated United States prestige in world politics and cast serious doubt on the notion that the United States was in decline.

TRUMAN AND KING SAUD

In the nineteenth century, before the discovery of oil there, the Persian Gulf was important for strategic purposes in terms of Britain's great rivalry with Russia in Asia. By the 1920s, this picture began to change with the discovery of oil. The acceleration of oil exploration in the mid- to late 1930s and the onset of World War II thrust the Persian Gulf into U.S. strategic considerations. Indeed, in that war not only was the region's oil an issue of rivalry among the great powers, but so was its critical position astride three continents. Control of the Persian Gulf facilitated military efforts to contain Nazi Germany in Africa, the Middle East, and Asia.

The region grew increasingly vital over the next forty-five years, particularly during the Cold War. The Soviet Union hardly disguised its desire to shape events in the Persian Gulf, while the United States struggled to reduce Soviet regional influence and to shore up its own security position.

At least as early as 1935, the United States began to appreciate the vital role of Saudi oil as an economic source, and as a potential political weapon for any actor that could influence or control it. This recognition pushed President Harry S. Truman, on September 28, 1945, to approve the completion of the air base at Dhahran, Saudi Arabia, which when expanded would later play an important role in Operations Desert Shield and Desert Storm. While the United States had made informal commitments to Saudi security in the early 1940s, we now know that it was formally committed to Saudi security at least as early as 1947, when Truman and King Ibn Saud made a pact. As described in a State Department cable, the United States pledged that if Saudi Arabia were attacked by another power, or under threat of attack, Washington would take "energetic measures under the auspices of the United Nations to confront such aggression."[2]

Although the United States did make certain commitments to the Saudis from 1945 to 1971, it remained unable to protect the region either by proxy or by means of its own power. It had neither the will, the regional stature, nor the military forces to accomplish this goal. Rather, Great Britain was largely responsible for regional security, with the United States playing a distant secondary role. While the United States continued to compete with Great Britain for economic and political influence in the region, it took a back seat in the security arena.

POWER AND PROXY

In 1968 the British announced that they would withdraw "East of Suez." By 1971 they had accomplished this task, thus leaving principal responsibility for regional security to the United States. Washington did not assume this responsibility directly. Rather, Iran and, to a much lesser extent, Saudi Arabia formed the pillars of the Nixon administration's "Twin Pillar" policy, which was designed to protect the American-favored status quo. Under the Twin Pillar policy, the United States could rely primarily on Iran to safeguard regional security in exchange for American arms and technical support. This policy appealed to American policymakers because it obviated the need for Washington, in the post-Vietnam period, to intervene directly in the region. As is well known, the last thing the American public wanted in the 1970s was yet another set of U.S. commitments in a region far away that Americans neither cared about nor understood. Little did the United States know that its reliance on regional actors would leave it highly vulnerable in 1979 when the Shah of Iran was overthrown, American hostages were seized by Iranian Islamic militants, and the Soviets invaded Afghanistan.

In the 1970s, the United States counted on Iran to help protect U.S. regional interests, but U.S.-Iranian relations faced some significant problems. At times, the ego-driven Shah of Iran appeared more willing to take American arms than advice, and seemed to be making critical domestic and foreign policy decisions in a vacuum. While Washington expected Iran to support higher oil production and lower oil prices, it was surprised to find that the Shah led an effort in the 1970s for higher oil prices.

In addition, considerable concern existed in the U.S. Congress regarding the pace, scope, and implications of Iran's massive, U.S.-supported military buildup. The Shah bought arms right and left, in a manner that did not always jibe with military sense. The possibility that all these arms and technical information could fall into revolutionary hands was feared in some congressional quarters, but it did not weigh very much on the minds of U.S. policymakers, who did not anticipate the fall of the Shah.

The Shah's dismal human rights record also raised questions about the morality of supporting his regime. His disregard for basic American values as reflected in the repressive, far-reaching, and shady nature of his secret police, SAVAK, was viewed as troublesome in some quarters. The Iranian people, who associated the CIA with the hated SAVAK, would later retaliate against the United States and American citizens in part because of such perceived, seedy connections.

Although America's support of the Shah was problematic, it also offered Washington numerous strategic benefits. Between 1974 and 1979, the Shah established acceptable relations with all Gulf states, and was, by and large, a mediating influence. The Arab Gulf states were uneasy with the Shah's imperialist designs, found his arrogance annoying, and even feared that he might one day turn Iranian power on them. But they also perceived Iran under the Shah as a moderating force. Iran helped stabilize the region and overall had a positive impact on world oil prices as well. The Shah was a difficult ally for the United States, but he also played a security role in the region that the United States preferred not to assign itself.

Enter Ayatollah Khomeini, the Islamic cleric who would spearhead the Iranian revolution and replace the ousted Shah in early 1979.

AMERICAN DEBACLE AND ACTIVISM

When the Shah of Iran fell in 1979, the United States, having relied on Iran and, to a lesser extent, Saudi Arabia to defend its goals, lacked its own military capability for Gulf contingencies. Meanwhile, revolutionary Iran appeared bent on dominating the region, overthrowing the "corrupt" regimes in Saudi Arabia, Kuwait, and other Arab Gulf states, and kicking the United States out of the region.

The surge of anti-American feeling that the Shiite Muslim revolution unleashed in Iran surprised and confounded Americans, who did not understand that Iranians associated the United States with the repressive, hated Shah. The humiliation of watching the Iranian "revolutionary guard" storm the American embassy in Tehran, seize fifty-two hostages, and hold them for 444 days especially pointed up American weakness. U.S. defense officials had to inform President Jimmy Carter in late 1979 that the United States was virtually powerless to release the American hostages held in Iran. The United States simply did not have the political contacts, rapid deployment capability, and regional infrastructure to accomplish this task. This weakness would have been bad enough were it not for the wars to come.

Indeed, the occurrence within a similar time frame and geographical area of the 1978–1979 Iranian revolution, the 1979 Afghanistan intervention by the Soviet Union, and the Iran-Iraq war (1980–1988) raised the specter of American regional decline. Analysts feared an increase in Soviet influence or an outright military invasion of the region by the USSR, the spread of Islamic fundamentalism, the domination of the region by Iran or Iraq, an alignment of anti-American radical forces around such aggressive states as Syria, Libya, and Iraq, and the weakening or collapse of the generally pro-American Saudi regime. If there was a time when talk of U.S. global decline made sense, this was it. America's adversaries appeared to be on the move, its allies were weakened, and Washington seemed unable to change the tide.

The Iranian revolution seriously weakened the U.S. position. It undermined relations between Iran and most Arab Gulf states, disrupted the regional balance of power such that Iraq gained the upper hand over Iran, and threatened Saudi stability. It also sounded the death knell for the twin pillar policy of U.S. reliance on Iran and Saudi Arabia for protecting U.S. interests, by transforming U.S.-Iranian relations from cooperation to confrontation. This placed the burden for Gulf security directly on America's shoulders for the first time. Not only could the United States no longer rely on Iran to support its regional goals, but it now had to deal with Iran's efforts to undermine them. In a few months, U.S. regional security went from fairly stable to volatile, and U.S. credibility was also hurt worldwide.

Unfortunately, the United States found itself in a poor position to protect its interests in the region. Saudi Arabia was the Arab state in the Persian Gulf region most likely to cooperate with Washington, but the Saudis could not be counted on for political and military support. Saudi regional influence had decreased, and the Saudis had trouble protecting their own interests.

Riyadh was also reluctant to associate closely with Washington because of the negative reaction in the Arab world to the 1979 peace treaty between Israel and Egypt. Adding to the Saudis' caution were rising anti-American fervor generated by the Iranian revolution and fear of the growing influence of hard-line anti-American Arab states such as Iraq, Libya, and Syria. This was a problem because U.S. interests in the region depended very much on stable U.S.-Saudi relations. The perception of Soviet political and military gains in Angola, Ethiopia, South Yemen, and Afghanistan, coupled with America's loss of Iran as an ally, further damaged Washington's reputation. Moscow looked like it was on the move, while the United States looked increasingly inept.

To worsen matters, America lacked the military capability to cope with major regional threats. The U.S. rapid deployment force, which later would play a critical role during the 1990–1991 Persian Gulf crisis, had not been developed, and the regional military facilities which later hosted the forces of Operations Desert Shield and Storm had not been built to any significant extent. Nor were any regional actors capable of providing logistical or political support for American military efforts.

Against this backdrop, the December 1979 Soviet invasion of Afghanistan appeared particularly ominous. At the time, there was ample opportunity for states in and outside the region to improve their position at America's expense. This is particularly true because U.S. credibility was in question across the region after the Iranian revolution, and as a consequence of the Iranian hostage crisis. Day after day pictures of blindfolded hostages were shown worldwide; day after day President Carter was shown struggling painfully with the crisis, a crisis that consumed him, aged him, and hurt his political career. The impact of the hostage crisis, and of the failed, aborted American attempt to rescue the hostages, could not be underestimated. It was one of those rare events that, because of its agonizing duration and media coverage, could highlight and lay bare all those things that made America weak rather than strong.

In response to the Iranian revolution and the Afghanistan intervention, the United States was forced, for the first time, to develop substantial military capability and regional support to protect its own interests. The Persian Gulf emerged for the first time in U.S. history as a region on a par in importance with other major regions of the world. At the highest levels of government, it was recognized that the U.S. defense and foreign establishment would have to pump significant resources into this region, which until 1978–1979 had been of great concern only to Middle East experts, and on occasion to the public, which counted on a ready supply of low-cost gasoline at the pump.

In 1983 the federal government funded and developed the Rapid Deployment Force (RDF), renamed U.S. Central Command (CENTCOM), which later formed the heart of American-led forces under the direction of General H. Norman Schwarzkopf. In addition, the U.S.-operated naval and air bases at Diego Garcia in the Indian Ocean were upgraded, the scale and pace of U.S. periodic naval force deployments increased, and the United States gained access to key regional military facilities. Washington's ability to project force improved considerably between 1980 and 1990.[3] The Iranian revolution and the nearby Soviet invasion of Afghanistan awakened the American public at least temporarily to the vital importance of the Persian Gulf and put the entire region on the map of the American consciousness, if only briefly.

The American public, however, still was oblivious to the rise of a dictator who one decade later would become a household name. Indeed, Saddam's rise to power in July 1979 was covered by only a total of seven television news items amounting to less than three minutes of air time.[4] No cameras covered his bloody purges of possibly hundreds of Baath party officials after he took power; no Diane Sawyers were there to gauge Saddam's every view; CNN was yet to be born as a dominant global television news force. The Persian Gulf had become a high-level policy concern, but it still attracted only fleeting attention from the public as a national security issue.

The 1973 Arab oil embargo taught Americans the importance of Gulf oil, but it did not create the specter of American military involvement in the region. Some plans did exist for invading the Gulf oil fields during the embargo, but they were not very serious. The Iranian revolution and Afghanistan intervention, however, did increase the prospect of U.S. intervention in the region, and it is for this reason that these two events inaugurated a new period in American regional involvement. It was one thing to need the region for oil, which one pumped at a gas station, and quite another to think that American men and women would actually have to go there to fight wars. One need was concrete, the other abstract.

Concerned with global and regional threats to Gulf security, Washington was determined not only to improve its capability to deter outside pressure on the Gulf, but also to deal with growing internal pressures. In that spirit, President Ronald Reagan stated in October 1981 that there was "no way" the United States could "stand by" and see Saudi Arabia threatened to the point that the flow of oil could be shut down.[5] This statement and others of a similar kind later became associated with the Reagan Doctrine, which was widely perceived as a U.S. commitment to protect Saudi Arabia against not only external threats but also internal ones. The United States had made a tacit agreement to protect the Saudis in the 1940s; now Reagan jacked it up at least one notch.

The improvements in U.S. force projection capability during the 1980s were significant. In 1980 movement of minimal U.S. forces to the Gulf would have taken many weeks.[6] In contrast, by 1983 America could have had the first ground forces to the Gulf in a few days. U.S. airlift, sealift, and prepositioning capabilities continued to improve substantially throughout the decade.[7] From 1980 to 1987, American airlift capabilities increased from 26.9 to 39.6 million ton-miles per day. The United States also enhanced the Military Sealift Command active fleet from forty-four to fifty-seven ships, and the Ready Reserve Force (RRF) from twenty-seven to eighty-two ships.[8] Overall, the Department of Defense (DoD) spent over $7 billion to improve sealift capabilities in the 1980s. Key improvements included a prepositioned force of twenty-five ships, some of which provided the first supplies during the Persian Gulf crisis; eight fast sealift ships especially suited to transport heavy Army unit equipment; and an additional increase in the Ready Reserve Force to ninety-six ships.[9]

While all these military efforts were going on, the American public still was not all that familiar with the Gulf. Yes, they remembered the Iranian hostage crisis; they also could recall that the Soviets invaded Afghanistan, and they knew about Oliver North's Iranian arms-for-hostages imbroglio and about a nasty war between Iran and Iraq. But the Persian Gulf still remained largely an abstraction, and it was not clear to most Americans exactly how the United States was involved there. Indeed, prior to the May 1987 Iraqi Exocet missile attack on the USS *Stark*, a Navy frigate that was on patrol in the Gulf, 32 percent of the U.S. public described itself as paying "no attention" or "not too much attention" to events in the Gulf. The *Stark* attack, which killed thirty-seven American sailors, briefly raised this level much higher, but attention soon returned to lower levels.[10]

On the military front, the United States continued to make good progress. By 1988 it had reached 89 percent of the DoD sealift goal, although its capability in this area declined in the post–cease-fire period following the Iran-Iraq war.[11] In addition, the Maritime Prepositioning Ships program that had been put into effect in 1980 became a distinct capability, enabling forces to reach critical contingency areas within seven days. This would prove critical in the first weeks of Operation Desert Shield, when it seemed that Iraq's forces might invade Saudi Arabia before the U.S. armed forces could get there, or might wipe out U.S. forces before reinforcements made it to the Gulf.

Moreover, the Iran-Iraq war contributed to Saudi interest in funding and building an estimated $200 billion military infrastructure for the entry of massive American forces. The improvements in the Saudi military infrastructure made Desert Shield and Storm possible. In 1980 there had only been two major nonoil docks in Saudi Arabia, each capable of unloading only one ship at a time. By 1990 dozens of ships could be unloaded simultaneously at nine major ports. Saudi airfields became significantly more sophisticated and doubled in number. The Saudis also integrated their ground-based radar missile systems, fighter bases, fighters, and command-communication posts into a single network. Military roads, emergency fuel storage facilities, air-conditioned bunkers, nuclear-proof command posts— all became part of the elaborate military infrastructure that Americans saw on television during the war. It was the base of operation for most of the allied forces.

General Schwarzkopf, commander of allied forces during Desert Shield and Storm, stated that had this infrastructure not existed, U.S. CENTCOM would not have recommended sending in such a substantial American force. And had war been launched in the absence of such a complex supporting infrastructure, the outcome would have been different. At a minimum, the victory would not have been as quick and decisive.[12] That is almost certainly true. So much of the efficiency and success of the attack was related to this tremendous infrastructure, which was in large part a product of the late 1970s and the 1980s.

INTERVENTION AND RISING INFLUENCE

Just as Iraq's invasion of Kuwait was the result in part of numerous events that occurred long before, the U.S.-led success against Saddam was also the product of long-term developments and policies. In Desert Storm, the United States for the first time actually utilized in a full-scale manner the major capabilities it had been developing for forty years, particularly those capabilities developed during the 1980s. The massive movement of tanks, troops, ships, and equipment across long distances would have been impossible without the great improvements in rapid deployment in the 1980s.

Desert Shield and Storm were multilateral military operations, conducted under the umbrella of the United Nations. In reality, the United States directed the political and military policies of these operations, with only secondary involvement by other nations. Before the Gulf War, it was fashionable to talk about American decline and to discuss the rising power of Germany and Japan. After the war, such talk subsided. Germany and Japan, which made no strong stand against Iraq, looked weak during the crisis, while the United States appeared confident, capable, and even dominant. Were it not for the United States, and in particular President George Bush, it is highly doubtful that Saddam would have faced such serious opposition.

On the domestic front, the Gulf War etched the Persian Gulf into the American mind with a firebrand in a way the Ayatollah in Iran or the Soviets in nearby Afghanistan never could. The media covered the war relentlessly, almost to the point of redundancy. Between August 2, when Iraq invaded Kuwait, and November 8, 1990, the *New York Times* and *Washington Post* published a combined total of 4,214 stories, editorials, and columns on the crisis. These numbers increased dramatically during the war.[13]

The media saturation, the involvement of America's men and women in a spectacular military success, the great debates that raged in Washington and on street corners around the country, when added to the high drama of it all, finally elevated the Persian Gulf region to special status in the American ethos. The age of the Gulf had arrived.

CONCLUSION

The United States could not have launched Desert Shield and Desert Storm had it not been for the substantial changes that took place during the 1980s in American military capability and regional politics. In 1979 Saudi Arabia seemed highly unstable; Iraq was a dominant regional power; Iran, previously America's key regional ally, had become an enemy; U.S. military capability for Persian Gulf contingencies was so questionable that a large-scale operation such as Desert Shield was unthinkable; the Saudi military infrastructure that supported American-led forces against Iraq was largely absent; and the American public was not in a mood to support military operations in a region that it could scarcely find on a map.

One decade later, King Fahd, whose father had always told him to cultivate relations with the United States,[14] was inviting U.S. armies onto sacred Saudi soil, and the United States, leading an international coalition of strange bedfellows, would be in a position to spearhead one of the most intense aerial bombardments in world history and to evict a well-armed, million-man army from Kuwait with relative ease.

The change in American power and position in the Persian Gulf prior to the war was nothing less than remarkable. Desert Shield and Desert Storm continued this trend by establishing the United States as the clear power broker of security in the Persian Gulf and by significantly elevating its prestige in global politics.

NOTES

1. For extensive evidence, see Steve A. Yetiv, *America and the Persian Gulf: The Third Party Dimension in World Politics* (Westport, CT: Praeger, 1995).

2. Walter Pincus, "Secret Presidential Pledges over Years Erected U.S. Shield for Saudis," *Washington Post*, February 9, 1992, A20.

3 For details, see Witness Statement by General H. Norman Schwarzkopf, Commander in Chief of the U.S. Central Command, before the Senate Armed Services Committee, February 8, 1990 (hereafter cited as Schwarzkopf statement), 173–302.

4. Gladys Engel Lang and Kurt Lang, "The Press as Prologue," in W. Lance Bennett and David L. Paletz, eds., *Taken by Storm: The Media, Public Opinion, and U.S. Foreign Policy in the Gulf War* (Chicago: University of Chicago Press, 1994), 49.

5. In Ronald Reagan, *Public Papers of the Presidents of the United States* (Washington, DC: Government Printing Office, 1981) (hereafter cited as Reagan Papers), 873. Also, for a clarification of this statement, see Reagan Papers, 952.

6. President Reagan referred to this lack of military readiness for Gulf contingencies as a "shame" in *Middle East Economic Digest*, November 7, 1980. He later aptly described the RDF as "neither rapid nor deployable and not much of a force." See Reagan Papers, vol. 1, 228, 254, 296.

7. For excellent details, see Schwarzkopf statement, 173–302.

8. Caspar W. Weinberger, "Report of the Secretary of Defense to the Congress on the FY 1988/1989 Budget and FY 1988–92 Defense Programs," 12 June 1987, 36.

9. For more details, see *Strategic Sealift, Report to Congressional Requesters* (Washington, DC: U.S. General Accounting Office, October 1991), 14–15.

10. Lang and Lang, "Press as Prologue," 53–54.

11. Schwarzkopf statement, 58.

12. The discussion of developments in the Saudi infrastructure is based on the author's personal correspondence (August 20, 1994) with Scott Armstrong, who initially broke the story for the *Washington Post*.

13. On the media saturation, see William A. Dorman and Steven Livingston, "News and Historical Content," in Bennett and Paletz, *Taken by Storm*, esp. 67–70.

14. As Fahd told Ambassador Chas Freeman during the crisis. Author's interview with Chas W. Freeman, Jr., U.S. ambassador to Saudi Arabia, Washington, DC, June 26, 1996.

4

President Bush and Saddam Hussein: A Classic Case of Individuals Driving History

> Our hour is marked, and no one can claim a moment of life beyond what fate has predestined.
>
> —Napoleon I, April 1821

Do individuals shape history, or are they defined by it? How much free will do leaders have? Can specific individuals really cause great change? These questions are of central importance across many disciplines, ranging from history to sociology.

This chapter examines the roles of President George Bush and Saddam Hussein in the Gulf War, compares and contrasts their backgrounds, examines the U.S. decision-making process, and argues that the Gulf War is a case in which individuals played a crucial, even defining role in shaping the political environment, nature, and direction of the crisis. George Bush and Saddam Hussein significantly determined how the crisis unfolded through their own personalities and personal decisions. While both men were under a set of domestic and international constraints, they also could have made different choices at critical junctures that probably would have sent history down an alternative path.

In the words of an author and Iraqi dissident whose pen name is Samir al-Khalil, the

absolutism of Saddam Hussein's authority makes his person unusually important in this war. The absence of real pressures from within Iraqi society, from Iran, from the world at large, or even from his own party leaves those of us who would write about the "cause" of this war with nothing to evaluate "objectively" and argue about . . . the whole question of how this war began resolves itself into what was passing through Saddam Hussein's mind.[1]

What is interesting, however, is that Bush, the president of a democratic state who in theory faced greater internal pressures and constraints on his decision-making than did Saddam, also acted in a dominant manner. While Bush, unlike Saddam, did have to consider seriously a number of constituencies in his decision-making, including the public and Congress, he called the shots at critical junctures, and imposed his personal views of history and international affairs on the crisis in a decisive and meaningful manner.

THE NATURE OF DECISION-MAKING DURING THE GULF CRISIS

The decision-making process that guided U.S. foreign policy during the crisis involved five interrelated levels of interaction. The first level involved bilateral discussions between Bush and trusted colleagues, such as National Security Adviser Brent Scowcroft and Secretary of State James Baker. Other officials sometimes did not even know what was going on in these bilateral meetings because Bush, they surmised, shared certain things only with Baker, with whom he had established a thirty-five-year friendship.[2]

The second level consisted of Bush's exclusive group of advisers, the so-called Gang of Eight. This exclusive group included the president plus his closest advisers—Vice President Dan Quayle, White House Chief of Staff John Sununu, Secretary of State James Baker, Secretary of Defense Richard Cheney, Chairman of the Joint Chiefs of Staff Colin Powell, National Security Adviser Brent Scowcroft, and Robert Gates, Scowcroft's deputy, who acted as a link to the Deputies Committee. This elite group helped the president make the critical decisions of the crisis such as the timing and nature of Operations Desert Shield and Storm.

The Deputies Committee, the third layer of decision-making, consisted of six individuals who represented mainly members of the Gang of Eight. Admiral David Jeremiah, for instance, was Colin Powell's deputy and representative on the Deputies Committee. The committee was chaired by Robert Gates, and also involved officials from the Security Council, Chiefs of Staff, CIA, the core agencies of State and Defense, the attorney general, and representatives from the Treasury and Commerce departments and, on occasion, from other departments as well.

The Deputies, who usually met once or twice a day all week long, often through secure video-conferencing, played several roles. They gathered and evaluated the mass of information on the crisis that hit them each day, and in this sense served as information managers. Moreover, they presented options to the Gang of Eight through various briefings on issues ranging from burden sharing to dealing with international terrorism. For instance, they identified what the U.S.-led coalition might do in the event that Iraq withdrew partially or fully from Kuwait, a scenario that Richard Haass, special assistant to the president on Middle East affairs, and others found "quite likely." The committee established a number of tests that Iraq would have to pass even if it withdrew partially from Kuwait, and it was prepared to release these tests publicly. The goal of the committee was to prevent Saddam from changing the political atmosphere by means of a partial withdrawal, thus allowing him to remain in control of most of Kuwait.[3]

In addition, the committee executed the decisions of the Gang of Eight. For example, early in the crisis, the United States wanted to stop Saddam's oil flow, which meant that it had to confront Iraqi ships carrying oil. The Deputies sat around the room deciding how this would be done. As one member described it, "we wondered 'Do we hit the rudder, fire a warning shot across the bow, board the ship?' "[4]

Finally, the committee identified solutions to problems that made sense across agencies and departments. This was critical. By creating common ground for advancing national interests, the committee aimed at avoiding the bureaucratic turf wars and miscommunication that often plagued inter-agency governmental actions.[5]

The fourth layer of decision-making was a smaller group taken from the Deputies Committee, which involved key officials from the departments of State and Defense, the CIA, the Joint Chiefs, plus Richard Haass of the National Security Council, who drafted most of the papers. A separate group led by Lawrence Eagleburger of the State Department focused on the burden-sharing issue.

If the Deputies Committee dealt with day-to-day issues, the smaller group, which engaged in freewheeling discussions in the West Wing conference room of the White House, focused more on bigger conceptual planning questions, such as, How do we take advantage of this fragile time in history to build a better world? How do we pull together elements of the Middle East peace process? After committee meetings, Haass would draw up three- to six-page summaries of the discussions, which he would send to each member, who, in turn, would take it to his boss. Revisions would then be made until an acceptable draft was produced, which might then make its way to the Gang of Eight and the president. Ideas would then come back down to the committee from the Gang for reconsideration or revision.

Other Inputs

Finally, particular members of Congress, Congress as an institution, public opinion, interest groups, and foreign leaders affected U.S. decision-making. Their impact, however, was often limited to a particular issue or time period. For instance, Egypt's Hosni Mubarak and Jordan's King Hussein did persuade Bush to allow time for an Arab solution to the crisis, but after this proved a failure, their role in affecting decisions was negligible.

JUDGING THE POWER OF THE PRESIDENT

In judging the significance of individuals in history, it is useful to examine several questions. Was the nature of the situation such that others would have behaved similarly? Did the individual take initiative? Did the individual overcome opposition or simply follow or build consensus? Was the individual unique in ways that contributed to policymaking?

The Situation

The power of American presidents varies according to several general factors. First, presidents are more likely to exercise influence over military exigencies than over economic issues. This is because many more constituencies become involved in economic issues, where they have a direct, specific interest, than in military questions. National security concerns, moreover, can limit their access in the policymaking process.

Second, American presidents gain power in crisis situations, where time is of the essence and the stakes are often high. They often have to act decisively and with dispatch, before other actors can play a significant role. Finally, presidents are more likely to have power over foreign policy, which is largely the province of the president, than over domestic affairs, which are shared with Congress, the courts, and the public.

Based on these factors, we would have expected any president to play an important role in the Gulf crisis. Indeed, it was a military crisis in a foreign land where the United States had vital interests.

Nonetheless, it is hardly axiomatic that the United States was destined to confront Iraq. History is seductive in this sense. In retrospect, events seem so logical that we sometimes assume that they had to happen that way, or could not have happened in numerous other ways. But history is not so linear. Different individuals and events may send it down other pathways—pathways that remain imaginary because they never occurred, but which could have been very real indeed under different circumstances that are not too difficult to fathom. As one high-level official put it, "I can easily imagine that something else would have happened under another president. Being involved in the crisis, I can say that events seem different when they are in the making than in retrospect."[6] Or in the words of another official who was close to events, "had this been four years earlier, or four years later, it may have come out quite differently."[7]

Initiative

The president took strong initiative during the crisis, displaying the vision that his detractors said he had lost at the domestic level. According to his closest advisers, Bush "clearly set the course for American policy,"[8] and was, according to Colin Powell, both the "spark plug and fuel" for Desert Shield and Storm.[9] In Secretary Baker's words: "His role was absolutely critical. He made a visceral decision to reverse the invasion and he was out in front of all his advisers."[10] Bush contemplated the nature of Iraq's aggression during the weekend following the invasion and then asserted his view in no uncertain terms: "This will not stand."[11] No adviser put those words in his mouth; no script writer fed him those lines. Indeed, at Camp David in the immediate aftermath of the invasion, Bush and his advisers focused primarily on obtaining Saudi cooperation for U.S. entry into the kingdom. Upon returning to the White House Sunday afternoon, the 5th of August, Bush's statement to reporters struck Powell and others who heard this expression on TV for the first time.[12] A younger president would have lacked Bush's historical referent of World War II and, it is reasonable to conjecture, would not have approached the crisis the same way.

From the earliest meetings with his advisers, Bush felt strongly about reversing the invasion by force if necessary, and the real question then became how it would be done. Indeed, Bush, while allowing discussion to flow without his initial interference, was determined at the second major NSC meeting on August 3 to set a serious tone against Saddam, after the first meeting on August 2 appeared too relaxed.[13] The fact that Bush was far more "forceful and convinced" than many of his advisers that the United States needed to take a strong stand decreased the range of debate on how to approach Iraq, and set the parameters of the agenda on the issue.[14] While Bush initially was willing to let Arab leaders find a solution to the problem, he changed course not only because Margaret Thatcher urged him to take a tougher line, but more important, because he thought Saddam was exploiting such diplomatic efforts to consolidate his hold on Kuwait.

"While the president hoped that economic sanctions would work," General Scowcroft notes, "he made up his mind fairly early on that force would be used if necessary and that planning should be based on the assumption that sanctions would fail."[15] This was an independent decision.

The controversial, romantic notion of a new world order of greater peace and cooperation was also hatched by the president on a fishing trip with Brent Scowcroft. The notion referred to a world we had sought since the League of Nations, which the end of the Cold War and the rejection of Iraqi aggression might make possible.[16] The president understood that failing to take a strong stand against Iraq's aggression would make a mockery of the concept of a new world order (discussed in more detail in Chapter 6) and set a bad precedent for the post–Cold War world. While Bush was serious about the notion, it was subsequently distorted by some of the media to mean that the United States would turn over influence to the United Nations.

Bush's message was repeated and clear. Saddam's brutality must be punished because no "nation should rape, pillage, and brutalize its neighbor."[17] It was Bush who decided to up the ante and the rhetoric against Saddam; he did not waffle or mince his words. Indeed, when aides drafted a speech for him to deliver in Rhode Island in August, he rewrote it on Air Force One, for far stronger effect against Saddam.[18] This would occur repeatedly, as he tried to paint Saddam into a corner.

In military matters, Bush set the general parameters of objectives, but by and large let the military develop particular strategies, unlike Lyndon Johnson in Vietnam or Jimmy Carter on Iran. However, along with Scowcroft and Cheney, he sent Schwarzkopf back to the drawing board after seeing the first major strategic plan for the ground war, which called for a direct, head-on, U.S.-led assault on Iraqi forces in Kuwait. Bush, thus, did not hesitate to affect even the military dimension of U.S. foreign policy.

As the months wore on, Bush seemed to personalize the conflict, and Saddam returned the favor. Bush focused on Saddam the individual so much that Colin Powell commented on how much it affected Bush's ad hoc policymaking, characterized by an occasional lack of consultation with others and extreme vitriol against Saddam. Even Secretary Baker expressed concern to aides that the White House was speeding toward an armed confrontation with Saddam.[19] President Bush was clearly willing, even resigned, to use force against Iraq.

The Opposition

Another factor to examine in assessing the role of the individual is the level of opposition the individual had to overcome in making policy. The move toward war was indirectly or directly questioned, but not vigorously opposed, by important people such as Sam Nunn, chairman of the Senate Armed Services Committee, Secretary Baker, General Powell, and General Schwarzkopf. In his church, Bush also met criticism. His own presiding bishop said to him that using force was immoral, even after Bush gave him a report on Iraqi human rights abuses in Kuwait. Such opposition weighed heavily on the president's mind.[20]

The range of views within the Gang of Eight was fairly large. For his part, Schwarzkopf believed that sitting out in the sun for another summer was better than dying in the desert. By contrast, Bush's position was that waiting too long might strengthen Saddam and undermine the coalition. Baker, as well, believed that Iraq was vulnerable to sanctions, and that time was "on the side of the international community," and "patience" was in order.[21] Such differences in view were not insignificant. From his angle, Powell tried to keep options against Iraq open as long as possible, but Bush told him that the United States "couldn't wait forever," which, in Powell's words, "gives you an indication of his 'vital role.' "[22] Other presidents may have been much more open to Powell's initiatives, particularly given that the nation was initially opposed to war.

In late October 1990 Bush began to push for an offensive option against Iraq far sooner than his military officers had wanted. Schwarzkopf responded by arguing that an effort to dislodge the Iraqi army from Kuwait would be too difficult and bloody, and would require much more military capability. If Bush wanted an offensive option, he would have to double U.S. firepower against Iraq. Doubting that UN economic sanctions would affect Saddam's plans, Bush decided in November to double the size of U.S. forces. As Secretary of State Baker recalls, all of Bush's advisers agreed with that decision, and all agreed that it should not be announced until after the midterm elections. The administration should have notified Congress prior to releasing this information to the press. However, as a result of a failure to follow standard consultation practices with Congress, this did not occur, thus causing a firestorm on Capitol Hill.[23]

At a broader level, Baker informed Powell, after Powell contacted him to express concern over the march to war, that the State Department was preparing a report on the advantages of waiting for economic sanctions to work. Powell, for his part, argued against going to war to liberate Kuwait.

He viewed war as nasty business and found the discussion of a potential U.S.-led "surgical" strike against Iraq to be irresponsible.[24] While Bush did not view Powell as "footdragging" on the issue of being tough on Saddam,[25] as others did, clearly Powell preferred a go-slow approach. In the aftermath of the invasion, he tried to redirect the focus in various meetings from liberating Kuwait to defending Saudi Arabia, argued his position with influential members of the broader defense community, and was much more inclined throughout the crisis than was Bush to define U.S. objectives in a limited manner.

Neither Powell, who is perhaps the most notable military man since Douglas MacArthur, nor Schwarzkopf, the four-star general, pushed their views on the president. Both of them recognized that it was the president who was calling the shots. In Powell's words, "In our democracy, it is the President, not generals, who make[s] decisions about going to war. . . . If the President was right, if he decided that it must be war, then my job was to make sure we were ready to go in and win."[26] This, however, raises the interesting question: How powerful should one man be in deciding issues of peace and war in a democracy? It also begs the question of the extent to which advisers should undersell their advice to a determined president, or downplay their views when they know that they conflict with what the president believes.

Opposition in Congress, as discussed in Chapter 1, was strong enough that the Bush administration questioned whether it should send the "use of force" motion to Congress for a vote. Indeed, Secretary Cheney, a former congressman who had never served in the military, argued against the move because in his view the United States would have had to attack Iraq anyway, and it had all the authority it already needed. A "no" vote from Congress, which was dominated by Democrats, would have been an embarrassment.

General Scowcroft also had deep reservations about taking the vote to Congress. Having spent time with the president from the first days following the invasion, he knew that Bush was determined to do what had to be done, which was to force Iraq out of Kuwait if necessary. And if Congress turned the administration down, virtually all of Bush's major advisers would have argued to launch Operation Desert Storm anyway. This raises the question: Is it acceptable in a democratic society to bypass Congress on crucial issues of war if this yields a serious strategic benefit?

Seeking congressional approval was not required by law, but it would have increased national unity and sent Saddam, who doubted American will, a strong warning. While these and other goals ultimately motivated the president to go to Congress, Bush wanted Saddam to know that his determination was unwavering in any event: "I don't think I need [a resolution from Congress]. There are different opinions on either side of this question, but Saddam Hussein should be under no question on this. I feel that I have the authority to fully implement the United Nations resolutions."[27] Later, however, Bush recalled that he also expected impeachment charges to be filed if he did not seek congressional and United Nations approval for launching war against Iraq.[28] In fact, as deputy national security adviser Robert Gates put it, "Bush was going to throw that son of a bitch out of Kuwait whether or not congress and public opinion supported him."[29]

The decision to go the "last mile" in meeting with Iraq's foreign minister, Tariq Aziz, prior to launching Desert Storm was also debated seriously. Cheney and Scowcroft, as well as Gulf Arab officials, were concerned that this would make the United States look weak and send Saddam the wrong message. "But," Scowcroft recalls, "the president felt that to go to war without having a direct meeting with the Iraqis would not be a good idea."[30] The president initiated this idea and saw it through.

At the outset, most Americans as well did not see the crisis as Bush did. In the view of one top U.S. official, "The public was not united behind a strong line against Saddam at the outset; no powerful images of Iraqi brutality were coming from Kuwait because the cameras couldn't get in; and the president faced a range of opinion around him."[31] Bush had to rally the people.

The level of opposition Bush faced, however, did not manifest itself in vitriolic disagreements or in attempts to undermine his decisions. The Gang of Eight eventually fell in line with the move toward war, and each core agency carried out its duties. Even at lower levels of decision-making, the Deputies "were comfortable early on with the notion that force would have to be used if Saddam did not withdraw and believed that sanctions would not work."[32] And the public slowly moved toward strong support for the war effort.

Bush's Characteristics and Background

A number of factors particular to George Bush made his role important, above and beyond what might have been expected. First, Bush's World War II experience was important. Bush remembered how Adolf Hitler had tricked Prime Minister Neville Chamberlain of Great Britain in 1938 into believing that Germany's expansive claims would be limited to the Sudetenland. Hitler's ploy at Munich, which led Chamberlain on his return to England to assure the British naively of "peace for our time," was impressed on Bush's mind. He referred to it often during the Gulf crisis.

Following British foreign secretary Douglas Hurd, who compared Saddam to Hitler on the day of the invasion, Bush repeatedly did the same. On October 23, for instance, he asserted that the United States was faced with "Hitler revisited, a totalitarianism and brutality that is naked and unprecedented in modern times. And it must not stand."[33] In listening to Bush during the decision-making process, his advisers perceived the impact of history on his thinking, and got the impression, as Cheney recalls, "that his formative years had been spent in World War II as a Navy pilot in the Pacific."[34] Scowcroft would later recall that many of Bush's statements comparing the Gulf crisis to World War II came directly from a book that he was reading on World War II.[35]

Second, the president, unlike other U.S. presidents or even some of his key advisers, was familiar with the region. Bush's feeling that he understood foreign affairs, that he had historical experience with aggressors, and that aggression should be checked gave him the confidence and personal mandate to buck his advisers if necessary and to chart the American course through the crisis. His knowledge of the Persian Gulf was critical and evidenced itself in meetings with his advisers and in his interpretation of the level of the Iraqi threat. Dating back to his oil business and interests, his role as director of the CIA, and his lengthy stint as vice president, Bush had started developing a sense of what worked in the Middle East. As one official put it, "He was attached to and aware of Persian Gulf politics and acted on the basis of knowledge."[36]

Third, President Bush had strong, long-standing connections with leaders worldwide. To prevent China from using its UN Security Council veto to torpedo U.S.-led efforts against Iraq, Bush personally and effectively handled relations with Beijing, based on years of experience with the Chinese,[37] and also personally handled President Gorbachev's dogged efforts to save Moscow's ally, Iraq, from destruction. Foreign leaders trusted him, and this facilitated his effort to take a strong stand against Iraq. Although the United States clearly dominated the anti-Iraq effort, allied support was important.

Fourth, Bush enjoyed good relations with his key advisers, with whom he had long-standing friendships. Unlike some other presidents, such as Richard Nixon, Bush trusted a range of key advisers. He did not have to worry so much about being challenged directly or indirectly by individuals or by the bureaucracies they represented. Although there were differences among the members of the Gang of Eight, and although there were instances of questioning who was giving the president bad advice, cooperation on the whole was strong, particularly given the high stakes. As one insider put it,

"The harmony, camaraderie, and rapidity of decisions were amazing and all done so well."[38] Indeed, interviews with the principal actors and those who knew them formally and informally reveal the relative absence of commonplace interagency and interpersonal rivalries.

President Bush in Retrospect

Bush played a critical role in the crisis in that he took the initiative at key points, asserted his position despite (and, perhaps, even because of) a divergence of views among his advisers, and brought to bear unique characteristics based on his background and beliefs. Although the crisis situation required strong presidential leadership, it is not at all axiomatic that any president would have taken as strong a stand against Saddam as did Bush. Other presidents may have let economic sanctions run far longer, thus possibly changing the outcome of the crisis. As Richard Haass puts it, "George Bush's greatest single contribution to history in this crisis . . . was in seeing the reality of this [*sic*] stakes and not blinking. . . . It was not automatic that he or anyone else . . . would have made decisions of that magnitude."[39]

Yet, while Bush drove U.S. policy at critical junctures, he did not dictate how certain American goals should be accomplished. Military policy was largely left to the military brass, their assistants, and Secretary Cheney. As Powell notes, "Bush never told me what to do militarily."[40]

Furthermore, Bush did not interfere much with the work of the Deputies Committee, although he was intensely interested in events. As one committee member put it, "I have a mental image of Lyndon Johnson sitting on the floor of the Oval Office, picking targets during the Vietnam War; I also saw George Bush going over photos, but instead he was looking at post-action bomb damage assessment photos."[41]

CONTRASTING BACKGROUNDS: COMPARING APPLES AND ORANGES

Bush and Saddam Hussein both played critical roles in the Gulf crisis, but their similarity ends there. A journey into their very different backgrounds yields insight into their actions during the crisis.

George Bush was the son of a prominent senator, from a rich and long pedigree, and was groomed in private schools and country clubs. Saddam came from a dirt-poor peasant village near Takrit, Iraq, and grew up in an environment of poverty, degradation, and suspicion.

At Yale, Bush joined the exclusive Skull and Bones Club, where he was tapped last, indicating that he was the top candidate for the club. Saddam might have understood the skull and bones part, but would have fit in at Yale about as well as Genghis Khan. While Bush was excelling as captain of Yale's nationally competitive baseball team in 1948, Saddam, not even in his teens, was struggling in a dysfunctional family environment and learning how to hate and hurt. It is not known whether Saddam's father died about the time Saddam was born in 1937 or whether he abandoned him shortly thereafter, but whatever the details, young Saddam lived under the heel of a crude, abusive, even brutal stepfather. Saddam would later recall how his stepfather often dragged him out of bed at dawn, barking, "Get up, you son of a whore, and look after the sheep."[42]

While Bush, the Ivy League graduate, knew war from experience, Saddam knew it only from imagination and from occasional forays into the battlefield as a self-proclaimed commander-in-chief. Bush had been the youngest Navy pilot during World War II, an eager fighter who flew fifty-eight missions before he was shot down.[43] By contrast, although he entered the Iraqi army at a young age and rose to the rank of colonel, Saddam knew little about military strategy. He certainly did not gain power because of his military credentials; rather, he advanced because of his political savvy, ruthlessness, personal connections, and chance events. Iraq's military, for that matter, was not really involved in the Arab-Israeli wars of the 1960s and 1970s. So, even if Saddam had been a military man, he could not have proven himself in any clear manner until the 1980s, when Iraq slugged it out in the killing fields of the Iran-Iraq war. No doubt Saddam's lack of military experience helps explain his many strategic errors during the Persian Gulf War.

Unlike Bush's, Saddam's rise to power was hardly by the rules. From a very young age, he displayed the brutality, cunning, and duplicity that marked his character and career. In 1956, at age nineteen, he participated in an abortive coup against the monarchy; the following year, he joined the Baath party, which boasted pan-Arab, anti-Western credentials. The Baath party believed that Iraq should be the beating heart of a united and proud Arab world, independent of the West and able to recapture Arab glory for posterity and defeat and destroy the Zionists. In this sense, the Baath party was revolutionary. It sought to chart for Iraq and the Arab world a new course in history toward power and influence in international politics.

During a local election in 1958, the twenty-one-year-old Saddam murdered his uncle's communist rival, and briefly served time in prison as a result. In that same year, a group of nationalist army officers led by General

Abd al-Karim Qassim overthrew King Faisal II of Iraq. Proving his prowess, Saddam was part of a hit team that one year later tried to seize power for the Baath party by machine-gunning Qassim's car. In one widely told version of the story, Saddam was shot and badly wounded in the leg in the devious gamble. While escaping danger by fleeing across the desert to Syria on a donkey, he removed the bullet from his thigh with his own knife, bleeding profusely but forging ahead nonetheless into the sunset. This story became yet another aspect of the cult of Saddam, enlarging him to mythic proportions. Although Saddam played a minor role in the event, he would later, by manipulating the Iraqi press, make it appear that he participated on a grandiose level.[44] In a world where a big ego was a ticket for political survival and where appearing weak was as dangerous as weakness itself, Saddam learned early on to cultivate the image of the strong man who feared nothing. Such talents would serve him well in managing Iraq's police state of the future.

At age twenty-one George Bush was hitting baseballs across fields at Yale. Political intrigue and murder were far from his mind while he pursued the upper-class, privileged existence that would put him on the path to the American presidency. After college, Bush went west to the Texas oil fields to make his own fortune and future. Although he got his political spurs in the bruising and brawling known as Texas politics, Bush traded on his wealth, his Ivy League pedigree, and his father's connections to gain entrance to national Republican circles.

Saddam took a bloodier road to power. When Baathist army and Arab nationalist officers succeeded in ousting and killing General Qassim, Saddam returned from a rare trip abroad to Egypt to take part in this revolution. His position in the new scheme of things was fitting: he became an important interrogator and torturer in the Qasr-al-Niyahayyah, a palace used as a torture chamber for those who were assumed to be enemies of the Baath party and of the state.

Although the Baath were ousted from power in November 1963, Saddam and his Baathist cohorts would seize the helm again in July 1968 and maintain it thereafter. Given his experience in the torture chambers, Saddam was well suited at age thirty-one for his first major position in charge of internal security. His position would help him develop the knowledge and ties to control Iraq's security forces, to maintain his power once he became president in 1979, and to survive the devastation of Desert Storm and the internal uprisings against his rule that followed the Persian Gulf War.

While Bush represented the American people and was entrusted by them to hold great power, Saddam was Iraq. He hijacked Iraq; he represented no one. Indeed, in Iraq, Saddam was number one, and no other number really mattered much. The dictator tolerated little criticism or dissent, and Iraq had no means for an orderly transfer of power should Saddam die or leave office. Succession came by force rather than election. It was no wonder that Saddam refused to back down under U.S. pressure; in his own mind, he was king, monarch, general, legend, and emperor, all wrapped into one. Such people do not allow themselves to lose face easily.

After his official ascent to power in 1979, Saddam tried to return Iraq to the glorious days of ancient Babylon. Portraits of Saddam and Nebuchadnezzar, the Babylonian king who conquered Jerusalem in 586 B.C. and enslaved the Jews, stood under the desert sky. Saddam wanted to see himself and Iraq in that light. In his words: "The glory of the Arabs stems from the glory of Iraq. Throughout history, whenever Iraq became mighty and flourished, so did the Arab nation. This is why we are striving to make Iraq mighty, formidable, able and developed."[45]

Saddam's rise to power was followed by bloody purges in which he executed hundreds of military officers and Baath officials viewed as disloyal or potentially disloyal to him. Saddam's senior officials formed the execution squads. Sometimes he did the honors himself, calling dissenters or incompetent officers out of meetings, summarily executing them with his pistol, and returning to reconvene the meeting. He was "Cool Hand" Saddam. This would be the pattern of his political life thereafter.

For Saddam, the concept of democratic dissent and peaceful exchange of presidential power was foreign. In an interview with Diane Sawyer on *Primetime Live*, he was asked whether it was possible to criticize him in Iraq. With little hesitation, he said no and then asked, with a puzzled look, whether Americans could criticize Bush openly. Sawyer responded that if you did so effectively, you could get your own primetime show. In Iraq, you would be promptly punished at best, and possibly eliminated.

George Bush, of course, conducted politics in a different manner than did Saddam. Bush never told Powell to step outside for "a little chat"; congressional leaders did not have to worry about booby-trapped limousines. In America leaders made policy by means of persuasion rather than intimidation. Coalition-building and cooperation brought legislative and political success. As a former national chairman of the Republican party and as a diplomat at the United Nations and a special envoy to China, Bush learned the politics of patience and resolve. His personal and political heritage anchored his convictions in the rule of law.

HEAD TO HEAD, NOT EYE TO EYE

Given their different backgrounds, beliefs, and styles, it was hardly surprising that when these two leaders clashed in one of the more significant crises of the twentieth century, they found it almost impossible to find common ground for negotiation and trust. Quite the contrary. Bush, a student of Hitler's atrocities in World War II, detested Saddam. Bush led a democratic state that, having freed itself from the shackles of King George's England, loathed autocrats. The United States historically questioned the use of military force, despite resorting to it frequently. It prided itself on the moralistic-legalistic approach to foreign policy, despite often throwing morality to the wind during the Cold War when bigger goals were at stake. From Bush's perspective, Saddam was an international outlaw. And Bush was predisposed to act strongly against him.

Moreover, demonizing Saddam helped Bush rally the American people behind the war effort and made it easier to justify treating Saddam harshly. The story line would be simple and more dramatic if it could be cast in terms of good versus evil. People understood that; great movies were based on it; it worked, and it was a winning theme that Saddam played into as if he were an accomplice in his own demonization.

Unwittingly, however, Bush created a problem for himself by casting Saddam as evil incarnate. If Saddam was so bad, people would later ask, why did Bush leave him in power after the war? Could the Gulf War be successful with Saddam still in power? These questions are addressed in Chapter 7.

BUSH: A LINE IN THE SAND

The course was set—a crash course, that is—for two powerful individuals who were so different that they could not understand each other, even if they really wanted to. Bush drew a line in the sand and warned Saddam not to cross it. Saddam, who could care less about rules, recognized no line. Bush called for Saddam to withdraw from all of Kuwait; Saddam said he would not move an inch. Bush warned of catastrophe for Iraq if Saddam stayed in Kuwait; Saddam, using the great rhetoric of Arabic, warned that rivers of blood would flow if the United States challenged Iraq militarily. Saddam told French diplomats, "I know I am going to lose . . . at least I will have the death of a hero."[46] Bush asserted that the war would be quick and decisive; Saddam called for the "Mother of All Battles." It was a tale suited for a western movie. Two tough characters, brandishing big guns, engaging in brinkmanship, ultimately destined to meet at high noon, ready to go down in battle. Twenty paces. Yet, at the same time, it was all too real, smart bombs and CNN notwithstanding, simply to be a showdown at the OK Corral.

When Bush gave the nod to double the U.S. military force in the region and to create the offensive military option of Desert Storm, he reported to members of Congress in November that he had been reading Martin Gilbert's lengthy history of World War II. Bush, like British prime minister Margaret Thatcher, was from the old school. Aggression must never be rewarded. Thatcher lived up to that line in the Falkland Islands War, and Bush would do the same in the Gulf.

Unlike Powell, Bush was very skeptical about economic sanctions. As discussed in Chapter 2, he thought that keeping economic sanctions in place longer would only strengthen Saddam. Moreover, he did not want to give Saddam the opportunity to withdraw from Kuwait with impunity, with his large army and biological, chemical, and nuclear weapons programs intact. In addition, Bush worried that if given too much time, Saddam might develop weapons of mass destruction and perfect his ability to deliver them. He was also concerned that the U.S.-led alliance against Saddam, which he helped develop and nurture, would unravel over time. Finally, time was a factor for U.S. troops, whose morale was in danger of deteriorating.

Although Bush demonized Saddam partly for American public consumption, he also believed that Saddam was treacherous, deceitful, and aggressive. Saddam, however, was no Hitler, as Bush would have had us believe. Hitler had control over the strongest state in Europe, one with enormous industrial and military capability. By comparison, Iraq was much weaker. While Saddam brutalized Iraq's Kurd and Shiite populations, this was a far cry from Hitler's planned genocide, his "final solution," which systematically murdered at least 6 million Jewish men, women, and children in the Holocaust, and left as many as 4 million other political prisoners dead.

But falling short of Hitler was not exactly a compliment to Saddam, and in some respects, the analogy did resonate. At best, Hitler and Saddam were both brutal, dangerous, dictatorial, overly ambitious, prone to incredible miscalculations, and aggressive in the face of weakness.

Bush, on occasion, offered Saddam a ladder to climb down from his dangerous perch, but more often he used inflammatory rhetoric that made it difficult for Saddam to back down. For instance, Bush told reporters, in a widely disseminated statement, that he would "kick ass," and that there can be "no face saving for Saddam." These words directed at an Arab leader like Saddam clearly decreased prospects for a settlement on anything but Bush's terms. As Secretary of State Baker recalled:

Saddam himself told April Glaspie [U.S. ambassador to Iraq] a week before the invasion, "Do not push us to [war]. Do not make it the only option left with which we can protect our dignity. If Iraq is publicly humiliated by the United States, it will have no choice but to respond, however illogical and self-destructive that would prove." Unfortunately, Saddam was true to his words.[47]

But Saddam also had a few political weapons up his sleeve.

SIX TRICKS IN ONE BAG

While Bush was developing and solidifying his anti-Iraq military alliance, Saddam was struggling to figure out how he might foil Bush's approach and, if necessary, eventually confront the powerful U.S.-led coalition. The Iraqi dictator responded to his self-imposed predicament by playing several cards, some of them simultaneously. Many of the tricks he used to counter Bush and the anti-Iraq coalition were ones he must have first learned in his earlier days at the school of hard knocks.

Human Shields

Shortly after the invasion in August, Western hostages were taken in Kuwait and in Iraq. At least 600 foreigners were held at strategic sites, including approximately 100 Americans, 270 British, 80 Germans, 140 Japanese, and 80 French. Initially, hostages were one of Iraq's most valuable trump cards.

Saddam painted the hostage issue in political terms, arguing that Iraq's possession of hostages would facilitate a peaceful end to the crisis. The idea that he sought to convey was that the hostages would serve as human shields. Placed at critical strategic sites, they would deter Western attack and promote a negotiated withdrawal from Kuwait. Intending to highlight the pain inflicted on Iraqi civilians, Saddam used the hapless hostages to challenge the economic blockade of Iraq, arguing that they would face the same suffering as his people under the UN economic embargo.

The hostages were also used to divert global media attention from the invasion of Kuwait and the atrocities being committed there by Iraqi troops. Saddam's exploitation of the media succeeded in this respect. For several weeks, the media focused great attention on this human dimension of the crisis. At the same time, manipulating human beings in this manner hurt Saddam's already diminished credibility and image.

Over time, Saddam must have realized that the hostage trick was not working. Holding women and children did not play well in the Arab world, much less in the West. Saddam was even accused by some Arab officials of hiding behind the skirts of girls, a major insult in Arab circles.

On August 28, an official statement asserted that the president of Iraq was so moved after meeting with the hostages that he ordered the release of all women and children—an indication that the human shield strategy was failing. After numerous visits from various international figures, such as the Reverend Jesse Jackson and the Austrian president, former Nazi and UN Secretary-General Kurt Waldheim, Saddam began a process of slowly releasing hostages as if to thank these personalities for making their adventuresome trip to Baghdad. As a carrot, Saddam also released the hostages from countries that seemed to be supporting his wish for accommodation, such as Russia and France, his number one and two arms suppliers.

Saddam increasingly focused only on male hostages, and in particular on British and American hostages, who represented the two nations causing him the greatest problems. All in all, about 104 American hostages were held as human shields at various strategic sites. Western leaders, however, asserted time and again that human shields would not deter their attacks on Iraq's facilities. Bush summed up the sentiment, stating on August 30, "We cannot permit hostage-taking to shape the foreign policy of this country, and I won't permit it to do that."[48] Saddam's removal of the human shields nonetheless perplexed Bush, because it simply made the U.S.-led effort to destroy Saddam's strategic facilities easier.[49]

Linking Apples and Oranges

As the hostage card ran its course, Saddam moved to his second ploy. On August 12, he revealed a "peace" initiative that clearly linked his withdrawal from Kuwait to Israeli withdrawal from the occupied territories captured by Israel in the 1967 Six Day War, parts of which the Palestinians sought for their independent state. Saddam sought more than movement on the Palestinian issue when he broached linkage. He wanted the Palestinian problem resolved prior to Iraq's withdrawal from Kuwait, an absurd notion that, if carried out, would have given Iraq a long time to control Kuwait.

Saddam's linkage policy did win him support in some quarters of Europe and the Middle East. The Palestinians in Jordan and in the occupied territories rallied in his favor, even shouting in Arabic on Jerusalem rooftops for their dear Saddam to smash Tel Aviv; demonstrations were also held in North Africa and Yemen.

Despite some support for his linkage efforts, Saddam's policy failed. While he was trying to "Zionize" the conflict, Arab states such as Syria accused him of dividing the Arab world by invading an Arab brother and parading this as concern for Palestinians. Syria and Egypt, after all, had carried the Arab banner during the Arab-Israeli wars, when Iraq hardly contributed at all. Saddam's bravado against Kuwait was not very convincing or inspiring to them.

The Israel Card

Using age-old anti-Semitic and newly developed anti-Zionist lies and distortions, the Baath party had played the Jewish card like a Stradivarius domestically.[50] Somehow, it blamed all its domestic shortcomings on the Jews, and used them as a rallying point for unity. During the Gulf crisis, Saddam widened this approach, using it against Israel at the international level as well.

Napoleon once said that if he had to fight a war, he hoped it would be against a coalition. Saddam perhaps saw the Gulf crisis in a similar manner, because he repeatedly sought to split the coalition. In conjunction with his political approach of linkage, Saddam used a military approach in the form of Scud missile attacks against Israel. Israel had not attacked him, had nothing to do with his fight with Kuwait, and was not even part of the U.S.-led coalition. Nonetheless, Saddam tried to provoke Israeli retaliation and thus splinter the U.S.-led alliance by angering its Arab members such as Egypt and Syria, and generating popular discontent in the Arab world.

But Saddam guessed wrong on two counts. Despite consistently pursuing a policy of retaliation against aggressors, Israel, under pressure from the United States, showed restraint and stayed out of the conflict. In addition, Egypt and Syria, the two most influential Arab states in the U.S.-led coalition, were not at all inclined to fall into Saddam's trap. They understood Israel's right to retaliate in self-defense if attacked. Foreign Minister Farouq al-Shara of Syria as well as President Hosni Mubarak of Egypt asserted that their countries would not be dragged by Saddam into a war with Israel, even if Israel retaliated against Iraq.

A Devout Muslim

Playing another card in his deck of tricks, Saddam passed himself off as part of the Islamic faithful, a devout Muslim leading an Islamic state against the infidel crusaders of the West. The only problem with this story line was that Saddam was not religious, Iraq was a secular state, and the members of the U.S.-led coalition were not crusaders. Unlike Iran, Iraq was not ruled by clerics, did not impose Islamic laws, and did not even promote Islam in the international theater. Rather, Iraq was guided by the secular, pan-Arabist socialist dogma of the Baath party.

The Muslim world was hardly impressed by Saddam's newly found love for Islam. His Muslim charade largely fell on deaf ears. Saddam was no Ayatollah, and most Muslims knew that. King Fahd of Saudi Arabia even went further in describing Saddam's erratic behavior and the possible consequences: "Saddam is a man losing his balance . . . a man with no understanding of morality, a person who disregards every human value accepted by every society. Perhaps Allah has contrived these events to rid us of Saddam."[51]

The Arab Card

In addition to the Islamic card, Saddam played another similar card—the Arab card. Despite having invaded another Arab country, thus violating the Arab League charter and establishing a very bad precedent in the Arab world, he attempted to revive regional hatred for Western colonialism in the Middle East. Suddenly, in this scenario Saddam was not the aggressor. Rather, Western ideas and forces were the threat. Saddam cast himself as the protector of the Arab world against a resurgence of Western imperialism, spearheaded by the sole remaining superpower—the United States.

Saddam's Arab card had potential. Even Arab leaders such as King Fahd feared an eruption of political unrest that could bring down Arab governments. And among the Arab masses, Saddam had some support, particularly in Jordan, Yemen, Sudan, Morocco, Tunisia, Libya, and Algeria, and on the occupied West Bank in Israel. For instance, in Rabat, the capital of Morocco, 300,000 people took to the streets on February 3, 1991, in support of Saddam, despite the fact that King Hassan II sent 5,000 Moroccan troops to join the U.S.-led coalition. Saddam's call for the redistribution of Arab Gulf wealth to the poorer Middle East Arabs and his attack on the "haves" in favor of the Middle East "have-nots" also resonated in Arab streets. The poor Arabs resented the rich Gulf Arabs, who by chance had been so blessed with oil. Saddam, by voicing the concerns of the poor and dispossessed, gave life to their suppressed desires and hatreds and offered them hope of escape from poverty and despair. Never mind that he had brutally crushed a brother Arab state, violating the most basic of norms in the Arab world. Never mind that he was clearly a self-interested, power-hungry dictator. Never mind that even in Iraq, his policies contributed to a blatant division of haves and have-nots. Saddam was now their man because no one else was really carrying their torch.

Buddies with Iran?

Dealing one of the more bizarre tricks from his deck, Saddam sought a rapprochement with Iran, his old enemy. On August 14, 1990, he made an overture of peace to Iranian President Hashemi Rafsanjani, which must have completely taken Iran by surprise. After all, the countries had fought a bloody, horrible war from 1980 to 1988. Why in the world would a street-smart Saddam think that Iran would in any way trust the hated Iraqi dictator who, from Iran's perspective, was responsible for untold death and misery in Iran?

Iraq was technically still at war with Iran when it invaded Kuwait, despite the 1988 cease-fire. However, on August 15, Iraq agreed to Iran's demand that it withdraw from all territory seized during the eight-year war and to exchange prisoners of war. In agreeing to do so, Saddam was now willing to concede virtually all that Iraq had fought over, including bragging rights to a small waterway at the confluence of the Tigris and Euphrates rivers called the Shatt-al-Arab.

Saddam's Iran ploy failed, largely because his success against the U.S.-led coalition would have seriously threatened Tehran, and also because Iran and Iraq remained divided over political, religious, and military issues. To be sure, Iran accepted Saddam's concessions on the Shatt-al-Arab and on exchanging POWs. Later in the Gulf War, it also accepted Iraqi combat aircraft flown to Iran in a desperate attempt to escape allied attacks, but never returned them to Iraq. Iran had no intention of supporting Iraq's adventure in Kuwait or even playing neutral. From its standpoint, it must have been absolutely delighted to see the "Great Satan" and the evil Saddam slug it out to the death, so long as the imperialists went back home after doing their dirty deeds.

The Assassination Trick

After the Gulf War, Saddam vowed to have Bush killed one way or another, and while some people viewed this threat as just more Saddam-esque bravado, in March 1993 Saddam evidently tried to make good his threat. On a visit to Kuwait with his wife Barbara and one of his children, the former president escaped an attempt on his life by what are widely viewed as Saddam-inspired individuals. The Clinton administration responded later with military attacks on key Iraqi targets, but for Bush, who did not view himself any longer as in a personal struggle with Saddam, and who stressed that U.S.-led forces did not aim to destroy Saddam, this was just further evidence of how "crazy" and "evil" Saddam was.[52]

CONCLUSION

Saddam remains in power after virtually every one of his Gulf War adversaries, including George Bush, Margaret Thatcher, François Mitterrand, and Turgut Ozal, have left office. However, in the face-off between the presidents, George Bush had Saddam politically outmaneuvered, militarily outgunned, and diplomatically outclassed. Had Saddam faced a president who did not have Bush's background, experience, contacts, and strong beliefs against tyrants, he probably would have fared better in his gambit to seize Kuwait and its riches.

NOTES

1. Samir al-Khalil, *Republic of Fear: The Politics of Modern Iraq* (Berkeley: University of California Press, 1989), 271–72.

2. Author's interview with General Colin Powell, Chairman, Joint Chiefs of Staff, Alexandria, VA, May 30, 1996.

3. This paragraph is based on author's interview with Richard Haass, Special Assistant to the President for Near East and South Asian Affairs, phone interview, June 13, 1996.

4. Author's interview with David Jeremiah, Vice Chairman, Joint Chiefs of Staff, Washington, DC, June 26, 1996.

5. Ibid.

6. Author's interview with Richard Haass, 6/13/96.

7. Author's interview with Sandra Charles, Deputy National Security Adviser for Near East and South Asia, Washington, DC, June 5, 1996.

8. Author's interview with Secretary of State James Baker III, Washington, DC, June 4, 1996.

9. Author's interview with Colin Powell, 5/30/96.

10. Author's interview with James Baker III, 6/4/96.

11. Author's interview with Colin Powell, 5/30/96.

12. *Frontline* interview with General Colin Powell, broadcast January 9 and 10, 1996.

13. Author's interview with General Brent Scowcroft, National Security Adviser, Washington, DC, June 26, 1996.

14. Author's interview with Lawrence Eagleburger, Under Secretary of State, phone interview, July 23, 1996.

15. Author's interview with Brent Scowcroft, 6/26/96.

16. Ibid.

17. News conference remarks, November 30, 1990. In *Weekly Compilation of Presidential Documents, Administration of George Bush*, 1990, 1948.

18. Ann Devroy, "President on Inexorable Course," *Washington Post*, February 24, 1991, A1.

19. Jean Edward Smith, *George Bush's War* (New York: Henry Holt, 1992), 89–90.

20. George Bush, interview with Bernard Shaw, CNN, March 2, 1996.

21. James A. Baker III, Secretary of State, "U.S. Policy in the Persian Gulf," Hearings Before the Senate Foreign Relations Committee, 101st Congress, 2nd Session, September 5, 1990, 9–11.

22. Author's interview with Colin Powell, 5/30/96.

23. Author's interview with James Baker, 6/4/96.

24. See Bob Woodward, *The Commanders* (New York: Simon and Schuster, 1991), 220, 299–303.

25. George Bush, interview with David Frost, PBS, January 16, 1996.

26. Colin Powell, *My American Journey* (New York: Random House, 1995), 480.

27. "Statement During White House News Conference," January 9, 1991, *Congressional Quarterly*, January 12, 1991, 71.

28. George Bush, interview with Bernard Shaw, 3/2/96.

29. *Frontline* interview with Robert Gates, rebroadcast January 27, 1997.

30. Author's interview with Brent Scowcroft, 6/26/96.

31. Author's interview with Richard Haass, 6/13/96.

32. Ibid.

33. Quoted in *New York Times*, November 13, 1990.

34. *Frontline* interview with Richard Cheney, Secretary of Defense, broadcast January 9 and 10, 1996.

35. *Frontline* interview with General Brent Scowcroft, broadcast January 9 and 10, 1996.

36. Author's interview with Sandra Charles, Deputy National Security Adviser for Near East and South Asia, June 5, 1996.

37. Author's interview with James Baker, 6/4/96.

38. Author's interview with Sandra Charles, 6/5/96.

39. *Frontline* interview with Richard Haass, broadcast January 9 and 10, 1996.

40. Author's interview with Colin Powell, 5/30/96.

41. Author's interview with David Jeremiah, 6/26/96.

42. Judith Miller and Laurie Mylroie, *Saddam Hussein and the Crisis in the Gulf* (New York: Random House, 1990), 26–27.

43. On Bush's life, see Fitzhugh Green, *George Bush: An Intimate Portrait* (New York: Hippocrene Books, 1989).

44. Quoted in Elaine Sciolino, *The Outlaw State: Saddam Hussein's Quest for Power and the Gulf Crisis* (New York: John Wiley and Sons, 1991), 31.

45. Quoted in Miller and Mylroie, *Saddam Hussein*, 41.

46. Sciolino, *The Outlaw State*, 59–60.

47. James A. Baker III, *The Politics of Diplomacy: Revolution, War and Peace, 1989–1992* (New York: G. P. Putnam's Sons, 1995), 274.

48. "The President's News Conference on the Persian Gulf Crisis," August 30, 1990, in George Bush, *Public Papers of the Presidents of the United States*, vol. 2 (Washington, DC: U.S. Government Printing Office, 1991), 1179.

49. George Bush, interview with David Frost, 1/16/96.

50. Al-Khalil, *Republic of Fear*, 248–49.

51. Quoted in Baker, *Politics of Diplomacy*, 300.

52. George Bush, interview with Bernard Shaw, 3/2/96.

5

The West Arms a Brutal Dictator: Can Proliferation Be Controlled in the Post–Cold War World?

Nuclear, biological, and chemical (NBC) weapons are an issue of great international importance and one in which an eager Saddam has dabbled extensively. The Middle East, a tinderbox of underlying conflicts and tensions, is the most heavily armed region in the world, and many states, including Iraq, are attempting to develop NBC capability. This is of particular concern because the information-technology revolution in the world is likely to facilitate such efforts in the future. As technological knowledge and materials spread, it will be easier for states to develop and deliver horrible weapons of death to distant sites, including the U.S. mainland.

The case of Iraq raises a number of troubling but intriguing questions for further thought. How close was Iraq to developing nuclear weapons? Was Saddam just one decision away from using chemical and biological weapons during the Gulf War? Is it possible to prevent a rogue state, one that bucks international laws, from obtaining NBC weapons? Is a world of many nuclear states inevitable? This chapter examines how the West armed Iraq in a way that almost came back to haunt it, and reminds us that such questions are real and that the consequences of ignoring them may be severe.

NBC ALMOST ON CNN

The Persian Gulf crisis was one of the few wars since World War II in which the full range of NBC weapons could have been used. The defections of Saddam's sons-in-law in August 1995 (discussed in more detail in Chapter 7) pushed Iraq to reveal aspects of the size and nature of its NBC programs.

General Hussein Kamel, who presided over the NBC programs, threatened to tell all to United Nations inspectors, thus pushing Saddam to preempt the revelations, probably figuring that if the information was to be divulged anyway, at least he could earn some points with the UN for being "forthcoming." Information released in August 1995 by Iraqi authorities to UN inspectors showed that Iraq was prepared for chemical and biological warfare. Iraq had placed chemical and biological agents in Scud warheads and was ready to use them. Prior to the defections, the West did not know that Saddam had loaded such dangerous weapons on bombs and warheads during the Persian Gulf War, and that his program was so developed and deadly.

Iraqi documents released in August 1995 showed that Iraq had at least twenty-five missile warheads carrying about 11,000 pounds of biological agents, including the germs that cause anthrax, and botulin poisons, highly deadly potions that kill by destroying the ability to breathe. An additional 33,000 pounds of biological agents were placed in bombs to be dropped by airplanes or to be delivered by other means. UN experts also revealed that Iraq conducted flight tests of chemical and biological weapons, in one case actually launching a real chemical warhead aboard a Scud missile. Prior to the defections, Iraq had stated that it had never developed or tested missiles to launch weapons of mass destruction. Later, in early 1996, the UN speculated that Saddam was still hiding missile launchers and warheads capable of delivering weapons of mass destruction.

Had Iraq launched such weapons during the Gulf War, and had these weapons caused serious casualties, it might have provoked a nuclear response from Israel or the United States and escalated the crisis to enormous proportions. Indeed, Israel suffered a significant nerve weapons scare during the war when Iraqi Scuds hit key Israeli cities.

At a minimum, NBC weapons added an unpredictable, volatile element to the Persian Gulf crisis. While U.S.-led forces facing Saddam's vaunted army were confident in their superior conventional firepower, they were less certain about how to deal with Saddam's chemical and biological capability. Such doubts were well founded. Five years after the war, we would discover that allied military equipment used to detect chemical weapons during the Persian Gulf War was really inadequate and unreliable. Antibiological warfare also was not dependable in that no system existed to warn quickly of biological agents. The systems in place, according to the twelve-member Presidential Advisory Committee on Gulf War Veterans' Illnesses, measured only toxic levels of mustard gas that could cause death or acute symptoms. This finding was startling, given the confidence U.S. forces had in these systems.[1]

THE SCUD: CRUDE BUT DANGEROUS

In one of the paradoxes of the modern age, the Scud missile, ancient compared to allied technology, would cause much more concern than even the tantalizing wizardry of the radar-evading Stealth bomber. The Scud, shot with great inaccuracy, could make possible the death of tens of thousands of people from biological attack.

Iraq had two types of Scud missiles that, hypothetically, could have been armed with conventional, nuclear, chemical, or biological warheads. The first type fired a 500-pound warhead approximately 400 miles, to an area within about one-third of a mile of its intended target. This inaccurate but nonetheless terrorizing weapon was used against Israel and Saudi Arabia. The second type of Scud missile had a range of approximately 210 miles, carried a 1,000-pound warhead, and was much more accurate. Both types were made to be launched from a highly mobile, hard-to-find Scud launcher, fixed on a large truck that resembled a tractor-trailer or eighteen-wheeler.

Prior to the actual outbreak of war, a great deal of attention focused on Iraq's NBC capabilities. But it was never very clear whether Iraq could construct or deliver a chemical or biological warhead. While allied troops were in theory trained to absorb a chemical attack and were outfitted with chemical gear, serious doubts also existed about Iraq's will to use such weapons in the face of a possible nuclear response.

The biological program, in particular, clearly gave Saddam a potential trump card. Botulin toxin, for instance, is 10,000 times more powerful than the paralyzing nerve agent sarin, which was used with deadly effect by radical groups on Japan's transit system in 1995. A 1993 study by the U.S. Office of Technology Assessment concluded that 220 pounds of anthrax spores released from an airplane over Washington might kill as many as 3 million people. One Iraqi Scud could carry twice that much. Had Iraq chosen to use such weapons against Israel and U.S.-led forces, the result could have been disastrous for both sides.

THE WEST AND SADDAM: STRANGE BEDFELLOWS?

If NBC capability was not troubling enough, an even more perverse element of the situation was that the Western allies had helped Saddam develop the very NBC weapons and massive conventional arsenal that were endangering their troops. Regarding U.S. efforts, this would later become part of what would be referred to as the Iraqgate scandal. Between 1981 and 1988, Iraq bought at least $46.7 billion worth of arms and military equipment from foreign actors,[2] far exceeding Iranian arms purchases. Saddam squandered much of his country's vast resources to develop an enormous military-industrial complex, which included the intellectual infrastructure for developing weapons of mass destruction.

It appears that during the Gulf crisis Saddam ultimately chose not to use his biological and chemical weapons, although he may have had greater difficulty delivering these weapons than is now understood. Yet, if he made this choice freely, it may very well have been because he expected a nuclear response from Washington.

To be sure, the Bush administration was quite reluctant to resort to tactical nuclear weapons against Iraq. Using such weapons would have transformed the nature of the crisis, and, in addition, would have posed some strategic problems. Indeed, Defense Secretary Cheney asked Colin Powell for a briefing on the use of such weapons. "What do we do if we had to use them," Cheney queried, "because we have never used such weapons before?"[3] Powell showed Cheney that such weapons would have to be dropped close to Iraqi forces to cause the intended effect on hardened tanks and other targets, and thus "a lot of tactical nuclear weapons were needed."[4] A continued and intensified bombing campaign using conventional weapons would probably have made more sense, which, according to General Scowcroft, was what was decided early on.[5]

Nonetheless, neither Cheney nor Baker ruled out a nuclear option. Had Saddam used any weapons of mass destruction, Cheney would have clearly considered recommending the use of tactical nuclear weapons. Even Secretary of State Baker, who warned Aziz at Geneva against biological or chemical weapons, asserted that if "we lost a lot of men, all bets were off on not using these weapons."[6] Other high-level officials confirmed that if many Americans were killed in chemical, biological, or possibly a crude nuclear attack by Iraq, Washington would have considered a nuclear response.[7]

While President Bush appeared to rule out the use of nuclear weapons, his letter to Saddam, which Aziz received from Secretary of State James Baker in Geneva on January 9 when they met prior to the war, also warned of doom. Iraqi defectors later seemed to confirm that Saddam did indeed consider the potential of a U.S. or Israeli nuclear response.

While American threats probably deterred Saddam and averted catastrophe, this still left an important question unanswered. Saddam had developed incredibly destructive weapons and could have used them against U.S.-led troops. How did he get his hands on such dangerous weapons? This issue captured American public attention during and after the Persian Gulf crisis and motivated a congressional investigation. The heightened concern over the proliferation of NBC weapons would become one of the principal legacies of the Gulf War. People worldwide would become sensitized to the frightening prospect that aggressive dictators had a potential range of deadly weapons at their disposal, which they could deliver through conventional or unconventional means.

THE UNITED STATES AND SADDAM: NOT FRIENDS FOR LIFE

During the 1980s the United States and Iraq had developed a relationship of necessity. The two states realized that despite their dislike for each other, they both wanted Ayatollah Khomeini's revolutionary Iran checked. In 1982, after Iran reversed Iraqi war gains, King Hussein of Jordan pressed Washington to send arms to Saddam. But this proved problematic. Congress had embargoed arms to Iraq because of Saddam's atrocious human rights record. By 1984, however, U.S.-Iraqi diplomatic relations were restored, primarily because both states feared Iran more than they disliked each other.

Revolutionary Iran's threat to the region, particularly after its significant military victory at the Faw peninsula in February 1986, left Washington with few good options but to tilt toward Iraq in order to balance against Iran. It appeared possible at the time that Iran would defeat Iraq and dominate the region politically and even militarily. Iranian regional domination in 1986–1987 probably would have been as threatening to American and regional interests as Iraqi domination in 1990 had Saddam successfully absorbed Kuwait.

The U.S. reflagging of Kuwaiti tankers in 1986–1987—an effort to use U.S. naval force to prevent Iran from attacking Kuwaiti oil tankers—indirectly helped Iraq against Iran. This is because Iran had been retaliating against Kuwait for its support of Iraq, and now the United States was cutting Iran off in this regard by casting a protective shield over Kuwaiti tankers. U.S. forces also clashed with Iran's naval forces and imposed punishing air strikes, while at the same time limiting Iran's room for strategic maneuver. This further benefited Iraq. Washington also helped Iraq by selling arms through third parties and by providing it with satellite intelligence information about Iranian movements.

Furthermore, American companies provided Baghdad with technology that would allow Iraq to test nuclear weapons and to develop missile guidance and radar systems. Between 1985 and the start of Desert Shield, American companies delivered $500 million worth of high-technology equipment to Iraq, with the approval of the Department of Defense. This equipment later became cause for scandal as some members of the media described American soldiers being targeted by American technology.

The American technology included such things as $2.8 million in computers for the Iraqi Atomic Energy Commission in 1987; materials that could be used in weapons research, including computers useful in the development of missiles and warheads; and manufacturing equipment for jet engine repair. In some cases, the Department of Defense objected to the sales but was vetoed by the Commerce Department.[8] The Commerce Department even allowed the Consarc Corporation of New Jersey to sell Iraq sophisticated high-temperature furnaces that had a clear potential to be used in Iraq's nuclear program, even after the corporation indicated its own concern about the sale.[9]

American support also included loan guarantees. From 1983 to 1990, the Department of Agriculture's Commodity Credit Corporation provided over $4.5 billion in loan guarantees to Iraq, including a precedent-setting $1 billion one-time loan in 1987. The Department of Defense suspected that Iraq had used the loans not for agricultural development but for weapons purchases and military development, although it still remains unclear to what extent, if any, Iraq accomplished this difficult maneuver. Investigations into loan fraud by the departments of Justice and Agriculture, however, did lead to the indictment in 1991 of a number of bankers and four Iraqi officials.

U.S. support of Iraq's military buildup came under enormous fire during Desert Shield and Storm. This support may have been reasonable when Iran appeared able to dominate the Persian Gulf in February 1986, but it made less sense after the 1988 cease-fire in the Iran-Iraq war, when the threat from Iran had diminished and Iraq began flexing its regional muscles. In this period, Saddam chose to rebuild Iraq's war-ravaged country through a strategy based on force, power, and brinkmanship, while at the same time advancing his own inflated political agenda.

FRANCE AND IRAQ'S NUCLEAR PROGRAM

If the United States went too far in supporting Saddam, France made a pro-Iraqi policy the centerpiece of its Middle East diplomacy. While the United States supported Iraq in the 1980s to check Iran, the French had different motivations. Historically, France was interested in the Persian Gulf largely for purposes of protecting its colonial possessions in Indochina and for economic reasons. In more recent times, the French, who became Iraq's number two arms supplier after the Soviets, have consistently defended Iraq, proclaimed its "progressive" nature, and taken a strong pro-Arab line against Israel. The Iraqi connection would prove a great embarrassment to Paris after Iraq's invasion of Kuwait.

The pro-Arab French approach was driven largely by economic reasons, although Paris also argued that it sought to lure Iraq out of the Soviet orbit. For its support of the Arab cause, France was rewarded with preferential treatment in joint oil exploration after Iraq nationalized the Iraq Petroleum Company in June 1972. During the 1973 Arab oil embargo, France escaped being targeted and was even entitled to prewar levels of oil supply.

By the 1970s, the French were heavily involved in developing Iraq's military capability. In 1984 alone, nearly half of France's total arms exports went to Iraq. Iraq obtained a fleet of French Mirage F-1 fighters, one of the world's most sophisticated planes, capable of carrying Exocets, the missile that killed thirty-seven American soldiers aboard the USS *Stark* in 1987. French companies also sold Iraq a variety of weapons, such as sophisticated air-to-ground and air-to-air missiles that included the AS-30 laser-guided bombs and R-530s and R-550 magics, Super Frelon helicopters, advanced radar systems, navigation systems, and laser-guided bombs.

Perhaps the most troubling fact was that Paris helped Iraq develop its nuclear program, a program that came close to producing a nuclear weapon prior to Desert Storm. Through a deal that Saddam himself had helped strike in a rare trip abroad to Paris in 1976, France helped build Iraq's $275 million Osirak nuclear reactor near Tuwaitha, over the objections of the United States. During Desert Storm, Iraq possessed about 12.4 kilograms of French-supplied uranium, which France had sold to Iraq to run the Osirak reactor.

In June 1981, Israeli aircraft destroyed the Osirak reactor before it "went hot," or, in other words, became radioactive. The world community condemned Israel for interference in the internal affairs of another state. But behind closed doors, many states, probably including France, which was reportedly notified of the raid before it occurred, heaved sighs of relief. In response to Israel's successful attack, Baghdad reorganized its air defense, partly by purchasing and employing the French C3 I system called the KARI during 1986–1987.[10] This system was also used against allied forces in Operation Desert Storm, although without great effect, and then rebuilt after the Gulf War.

Even during the Gulf crisis, France remained interested in maintaining some ties to Baghdad. Indeed, at first France declined to join the air attack, arguing that it needed to husband its planes and bombs for the ground war. In Schwarzkopf's view, however, the French wanted to have their cake and eat it too. They wanted to be part of the coalition, while at the same time leaving the door open for postwar arms sales and interaction with Iraq. In the postwar period, France, still eager for a big role in arms sales to Iraq, pushed to have UN economic sanctions against Iraq lifted.

THE GERMAN CONNECTION:
BUSINESS AS USUAL

The Germans took up where the French left off on Iraq's nuclear program. After Israel's 1981 Osirak attack, the French refused to rebuild Iraq's nuclear reactor, despite the pledge by King Fahd of Saudi Arabia to finance the reconstruction. Iraq, however, had in its possession uranium from several countries, including France and the Soviet Union. Instead of using a nuclear reactor such as Osirak to "breed" weapons-grade material out of natural uranium, Saddam chose another route by which to make uranium suitable for nuclear weapons. For this purpose, he began an extensive, "money is no object" shopping spree for technology to developed centrifuges. These machines could do exactly what Saddam wanted—separate the unstable U-235 atoms in uranium from the stable U-238 atoms, thus providing weapons-grade uranium. Enter Germany.

German suppliers sold Iraq critical equipment for making centrifuges, and Iraq hired German engineers to install and run these machines. From 1987 up through 1990, when Iraq invaded Kuwait, German firms, in many cases with the knowledge of the German government, led the Western world in the dubious category of building Saddam's nuclear centrifuges.

The West Germans also helped Iraq build major military facilities, including the Saad 16 military research and development complex in the mountains near Mosul. They were also the chief supplier to at least six Iraqi plants making deadly nerve and mustard gas, and built Saddam's reputedly nuclear-proof bunker.

Members of the world community found the German connection to Iraq's chemical and biological weapons program troubling. The Nazis had killed millions of Jews using such agents, and yet Germans were helping arm Iraq, an actor committed to Israel's elimination, with weapons of mass destruction. Clearly embarrassed by revelations of the role of German companies in such trade, the German government, which has endeavored to make amends with the Jewish people, offered allied forces chemical gear during the Gulf War. German soldiers, however, were absent from the front line against Iraq. Until 1996, when its constitution was reinterpreted by a German court, German troops were prohibited from deploying outside Europe.

CONCLUSION

Iraq's NBC program could not have been developed so effectively without the support of Western companies and governments. Although Desert Storm did deal Iraq's NBC capability a serious blow, this masked the danger of the conflict. The outcome of the crisis could have been far worse. Saddam evidently had the ability to make and deliver chemical and biological weapons that could have cost tens of thousands of lives, if not many more. Such an outcome may have been just one decision away. We may never know for sure.

It is, of course, unclear what the future holds for Iraq's NBC program. Iraq retains thousands of scientists and immense knowledge and experience to develop NBC weapons. It probably has hidden significant materials and machines, and it may very well be back in business once the United Nations lifts economic sanctions fully and Iraq is free to sell oil on international markets. That is a disconcerting prospect for the other Arab states, Iran, and Israel, and for the rest of the world, which depends on stability in the oil-rich Persian Gulf.

Indeed, the case of Iraq raises critical questions for all to ponder: Is it inevitable that rogue states will develop weapons of mass destruction with which to threaten the global status quo? Can the major industrialized states join together to stop the proliferation of NBC, despite the strong economic incentives attached to arms sales and transfers? Or are we condemned to repeat history with Iraq or another state that this time around unleashes its NBC weapons and triggers a regional nuclear confrontation?

NOTES

1. Jim Abrams, "Chemical-Warfare Detectors Were Unreliable in Gulf War, Report Finds," *Philadelphia Inquirer*, February 1, 1996, A9.

2. Richard F. Grimmett, *Trends in Conventional Arms Transfers to the Third World by Major Supplier, 1981–1988* (Washington, DC: Congressional Research Service, 1989), 51.

3. Author's interview with General Colin Powell, Chairman, Joint Chiefs of Staff, Alexandria, VA, May 30, 1996.

4. Ibid.

5. Author's interview with General Brent Scowcroft, National Security Adviser, Washington, DC, June 26, 1996.

6. Author's interview with Secretary of State James Baker III, Washington, DC, June 4, 1996.

7. Numerous interviews with American officials, Washington, DC, June–October 1996.

8. Elaine Sciolino, *The Outlaw State: Saddam Hussein's Quest for Power and the Gulf Crisis* (New York: John Wiley and Sons, 1991), 142.

9. See ibid., 153.

10. Anthony H. Cordesman, *After the Storm: The Changing Military Balance in the Middle East* (Boulder, CO: Westview Press, 1993), 209.

A close-up view of a map used during Operation Desert Shield, depicting the location of King Faisal Naval Base. *Official U.S. Army photo.*

An F-117A Stealth aircraft from the 37th Tactical Fighter Wing (37th TFW) moves in for a midair refueling during Operation Desert Shield. *Official U.S. Air Force Photo.*

Four soldiers from the 82nd Airborne Division walk around their camp wearing rain suits, gloves, and M-17A1 protective masks as they try to acclimate their bodies to the heat of the Saudi summer during Operation Desert Shield. *Official U.S. Air Force photo, F. Lee Corkran.*

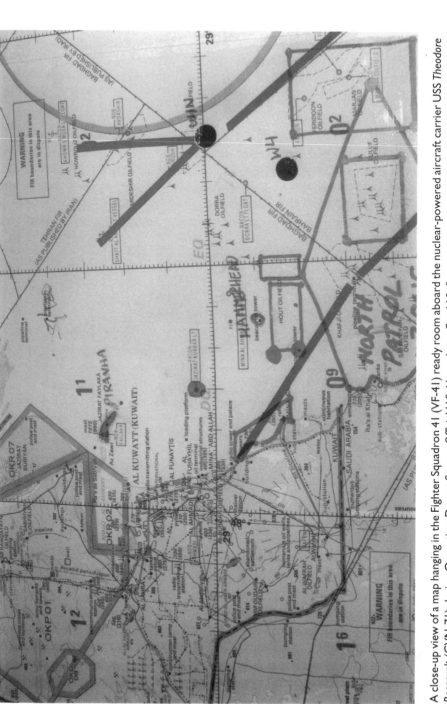

A close-up view of a map hanging in the Fighter Squadron 41 (VF-41) ready room aboard the nuclear-powered aircraft carrier USS *Theodore Roosevelt* (CVN-71) during Operation Desert Storm. *Official U.S. Navy photo, Gerald B. Parsons.*

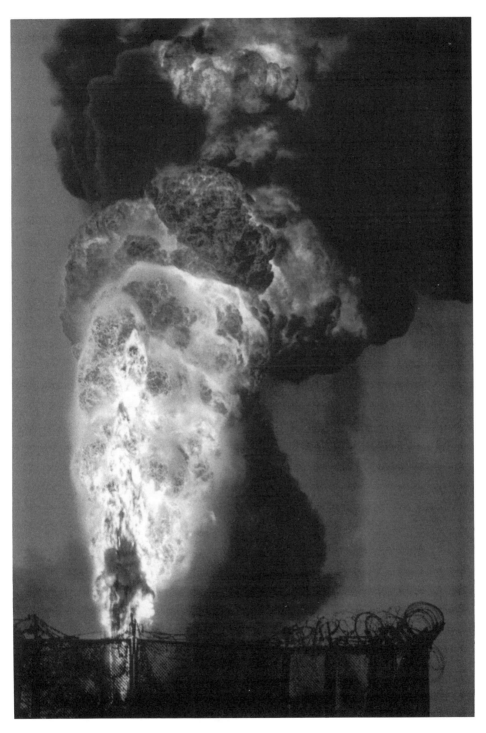

A burning oil well spews flame and smoke into the air after it was set afire by retreating Iraqi forces during Operation Desert Storm. *Official U.S. Navy photo, Ed Baily.*

Two reinforced concrete aircraft hangars at the Ahmed Al Jaber Airfield show the results of a coalition bombing strike during Operation Desert Storm. The hangars had been suspected of housing Iraqi aircraft. The photograph was taken from a Fighter Squadron 84 (VF-84) F-14A Tomcat aircraft using the tactical air reconnaissance pod system (TARPS). *Official U.S. Navy Photo.*

A Fighter Squadron 114 (VF-114) F-14A Tomcat aircraft flies over part of Al Jaber Airfield. The airfield was heavily damaged during Operation Desert Storm. *Courtesy U.S. Navy, Steve Gozzo.*

A view of damage to concrete munitions bunkers and hardened aircraft shelters at Al-Salman Air Base caused by Allied bombing during Operation Desert Storm. *Official U.S. Air Force photo, Dean Wagner.*

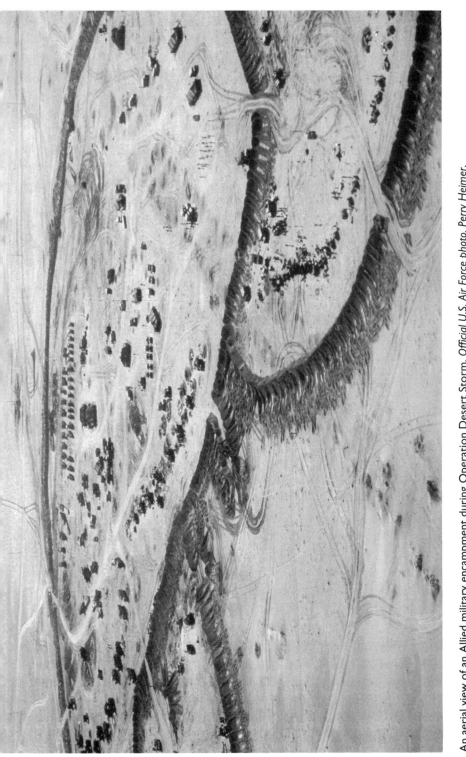

An aerial view of an Allied military encampment during Operation Desert Storm. *Official U.S. Air Force photo, Perry Heimer.*

M-60A1 main battle tanks of the 1st Tank Battalion, 1st Marine Division, advance toward Kuwait City during the third day of the ground offensive phase of Operation Desert Storm. *R. Price.*

Ships of Task Force 155 gather in the Red Sea during Operation Desert Storm. Clockwise from the bottom are the guided missile destroyer USS *William V. Pratt* (DDG-44), the aircraft carrier USS *John F. Kennedy* (CV-67), the guided missile cruiser USS *Thomas S. Gates* (CG-51), the aircraft carrier USS *Saratoga* (CV-60), the guided missile cruiser USS *San Jacinto* (CG-56), the aircraft carrier USS *America* (CV-66), the guided missile destroyer USS *Preble* (DDG-46), and the guided missile cruisers USS *Philippine Sea* (CG-58) and USS *Normandy* (CG-60). In the center is the nuclear-powered guided missile cruiser USS *Mississippi* (CGN-40). *William A. Lipski.*

Demolished vehicles line Highway 8, the route that fleeing Iraqi forces took as they retreated from Kuwait during Operation Desert Storm. *Official U.S. Air Force photo, Joe Coleman.*

Military personnel work at the site where a warehouse was hit by an Iraqi Scud missile February 25, 1991, killing 27 U.S. Army Reserve personnel and wounding 100 others during Operation Desert Storm. The building housed the 475th Quartermaster Group (Provisional). *Official U.S. Air Force photo, F. Lee Corkran.*

Gen. H. Norman Schwarzkopf, commander in chief, U.S. Central Command, and Lt. Gen. Khalid Bin Sultan Bin Abdul Aziz, far right, commander of Joint Forces in Saudi Arabia, sit across the table from an interpreter and an Iraqi general to discuss cease-fire conditions during Operation Desert Storm. *Official U.S. Army photo, Jose D. Trejo.*

6

The United Nations and Collective Security: Was the Gulf War a Model for the Future?

The Persian Gulf crisis shattered the euphoria that erupted after communist regimes collapsed in Eastern Europe in 1989 (and were liberated from Soviet military control) and the Soviet Union disintegrated. These events had signaled a change in world politics: the coming of an era of greater cooperation between nations, an era in which in theory they would move away from the use of aggressive force and of rule by fiat and toward the development of an international society. Indeed, it was a break with the past that some observers put on a par with 1492, when the Europeans "discovered" the New World. Then came Saddam.

Iraq's invasion disrupted all of these hopeful and romantic visions, and proved an inescapable, blatant reminder of the unpredictable, dangerous, and sometimes brutal nature of world politics. Almost overnight, the world turned its attention away from Europe and what was viewed as human progress and liberation, toward the dog-eat-dog Persian Gulf. If Saddam could get away with hijacking Kuwait, he could make a mockery of any notions of a new era in world politics. The invasion thus had meaning well beyond Kuwait.

Saddam's naked aggression, however, met with nearly unanimous world-wide condemnation and generated almost unprecedented cooperation between states. This cooperation helped reinvigorate the idea of a new world order. Indeed, two hours after Desert Storm began, while smart bombs were raining on Baghdad, President Bush told the American people that the world was at a historic moment. We have in this past year made great progress in ending the long era of conflict and Cold War. We have before us the opportunity to forge for ourselves and for future generations a new world order, a world where the rule of law, not the law of the jungle, governs the conduct of nations.

When we are successful, and we will be, we have a real chance at this new world order, an order in which a credible United Nations can use its peacekeeping role to fulfill the promise and vision of the U.N.'s founders.[1]

Was Bush's statement prophetic? Did collective security work during the crisis? Could it work in general? Was a new world order upon us? This chapter argues that while collective security worked during the crisis with a little help from Uncle Sam, and although the Middle East peace process held some promise of a better Middle East, collective security as a general mode of protecting international peace faces serious obstacles in the future.

In the immediate aftermath of Desert Storm, Saddam's military machine was seriously weakened, Iraqi troops withdrew into Iraq or surrendered by the thousands, the allied coalition dictated postwar terms, and the UN appeared for perhaps the first time since the Korean War to be credible in enforcing collective security. In Bush's stern words, Desert Storm was "a victory for the United Nations, for all mankind, for the rule of law, and, for what is right."[2] A new era appeared to be in the offing.

Desert Storm demonstrated to would-be aggressors the hazards of aggressive force, and revived, at least in theory, the viability of the moribund notion of collective security. Saddam's invasion proved to be not only the first serious crisis in the post–Cold War world, but also the first serious test of the UN's ability to exercise collective security in that world. The UN passed this test with flying colors, backed by the power of the U.S. military.

The UN authorization to wage war against Iraq, passed on November 29, 1990, was the first such authorization since 1950, when the absence of the Soviet Union at the Security Council made it possible for the UN to effectuate collective security against North Korea in defense of South Korea. The success of collective security raised hopes for a future in which significant international cooperation could enforce peace in the world. The idea of collective security was reborn.

COLLECTIVE SECURITY IN THEORY

In the minds of key leaders worldwide, collective security stood at the center of the new world order. In this sense, it was vital to prospects for creating a more stable, predictable, safe world.

The idea of a new world order was a profound and abstract one, pregnant with assumptions about, and implications for, the conduct of international relations. It was based on the idea that world politics was evolutionary, that human beings and the nations that they formed could learn and better themselves, that progress between nations was possible, and that, contrary to skeptics, international relations was not simply a recurring struggle in which force and war were inevitable. In other words, the new world order was based on a fundamental faith in human beings, leaders, and nations. To realist theorists of international relations, this notion was simply too optimistic and naive; to liberal theorists, it offered an alternative to the otherwise brutal, often anarchic realm of world politics.

The idea of collective security, like that of a new world order, was popularized by President Woodrow Wilson after World War I. That war, like World War II and, to a lesser extent, the Gulf War, shocked leaders and citizens worldwide into embracing more cooperative forms of international interaction. World War I shattered the false notion that war could be glorious, cleansing, and triumphant. Rather, the war killed off a generation, as vast armies slaughtered one another in brutal, blood-filled trench warfare.

In January 1918, as part of its rationale for entering the war, the United States issued a fourteen-point statement explaining how the "Great War" might be transformed into "the war to end all wars." In his fourteenth point, the optimistic Wilson called for a "general association of nations to be formed under specific covenants for the purpose of affording mutual guarantees of political independence and territorial integrity to great and small states alike." Collective security became a central concept of this soon-to-be League of Nations, a precursor to the United Nations. While the League was spearheaded by an enthusiastic Wilson, it was roundly rejected by a vote of 98 to 2 by his own Senate. Wilson's internationalism ran ahead of American public opinion. The United States remained too isolationist in 1920 to embrace a notion such as a world league or collective security, which violated warnings by the founding fathers against getting the United States stuck in "entangling alliances." The isolationist spirit, a core view in U.S. foreign policy, continued to dominate the American approach to world politics until World War II.

Collective security was based on several principles. Foremost was the belief that unprovoked aggressive use of force by one nation against another was illegal; actors using it would be checked by collective action. This action would come under the auspices of a world organization—the League of Nations initially, and later, the United Nations. Security, in other words, was a collective responsibility.

Article 10 of the League of Nations Charter, which formed the legal heart of collective security, pledged to protect all members against aggression. Under terms of the United Nations Charter, all states who joined the UN agreed to accept responsibility for punishing egregious violators of international law. The UN Charter included a series of articles that outlawed the threat or use of force except in cases of self-defense or for purposes of collective security, and which called on member nations to contribute to collective security. Articles 39–46 of the UN Charter required all members to make available to the Security Council, "on its call and in accordance with a special agreement or agreements, armed forces, assistance and facilities, including rights of passage, necessary for the purpose of maintaining international peace and security."

Collective security had failed under the League of Nations, first of all, because the United States had refused to join the League even though Woodrow Wilson had initiated and sustained it. The League did not check Japan's invasion of Manchuria in 1931 or Italy's invasion of Ethiopia in 1935. The League of Nations lacked the means, as well as the collective political will, to deal with such aggression. The great powers essentially flaunted the League's mandate any time it conflicted with their national vital interests. In the short run, dictators such as Italy's Benito Mussolini learned that aggression paid, a lesson not lost on Adolf Hitler.

Second, under collective security, alliances would not be formed in advance to stop potential aggressors, but would be activated only after aggression had taken place. This set collective security apart from the unique balance of power politics that characterized nineteenth-century European affairs. After Napoleon of France sought (and ultimately failed) to dominate Europe in the years following the French Revolution (1789– 1793), other European nations joined at the Congress of Vienna in 1815 to assure that no nation would again try to dominate all others. To meet this goal, they tried to produce a balance of power between themselves and to engage in shifting alliances against any state that appeared to be rising in power. Balance of power politics in pre–World War I Europe allowed the stronger European states—Britain, Austria-Hungary, Russia, France, and Germany (after 1871)—to balance each other even when no clear threat had manifested itself. But, more important, it also allowed them to dominate and exploit weaker nations in world politics. Indeed, while they cooperated to create a balance among themselves, they sanctioned European domination of others who were viewed as second-class citizens of the world and fit for subjugation. Wilson, for his part, viewed balance of power politics as secretive, manipulative, and power-dominated, and held it in disdain.

Third, collective security involved a community of nations whose norms were challenged by an aggressor. This also set it apart from balance of power politics, which often involved only a few self-interested actors rather than a community of nations and was guided by power and force rather than by international laws and organizations.

COLLECTIVE SECURITY IN PRACTICE

Although collective security had a checkered past in the interwar period from 1919 to 1939, it worked against Iraq. But its success resulted from an interesting combination of circumstances, which raised serious doubts about whether it could succeed so well again.

First, to work effectively, collective security requires agreement among the members of the UN Security Council. To Saddam's great misfortune, the end of the Cold War made it possible for Security Council members to agree on a general approach to Iraq. This is important because under Chapter 7 of the UN Charter, the five great powers on the Security Council—the United States, Great Britain, France, the Soviet Union (now Russia), and China—all have veto powers. Any of them could have torpedoed the U.S.-led effort to enforce collective security.

During the Cold War, the collective security system was largely ineffective, with the "police action" against North Korea during the Korean War being the exception. The superpowers could scarcely agree on what constituted aggression, much less on how to punish it when it involved one of their allies or proxies. Consensus on the Security Council could not be achieved because of the great rivalry among its members—namely, the two superpowers. They could, and did, veto any collective effort, when it ran against their vital national interests.

The end of the Cold War significantly changed the prospects for successful collective security. Under the reform-minded President Mikhail Gorbachev, the Soviet Union improved its relations with the United States, sought Western technology and economic support, and attempted to develop cooperative relations generally. This approach spilled over into the Gulf crisis.

On the whole, Moscow supported Washington in the effort to check Iraqi aggression. This was not easy for the Soviets. The USSR was reluctant to support Desert Shield and Storm and to damage ties to Iraq, which was its closest ally in the Arab world. Iraq also owed Moscow billions of dollars for arms, and several thousand Soviet oil and military technicians and advisers were in Iraq at the time of the invasion. Moreover, Iraqi and Soviet elites had had an established rapport since the early 1970s.

Nonetheless, the USSR, not wanting to antagonize its new Western friends, and seeing that Saddam had gone too far, voted in the Security Council to condemn the invasion. Furthermore, Gorbachev joined President Bush on September 9 in Helsinki, Finland, to call for Iraqi withdrawal from Kuwait and for the return of the legitimate government. The Gulf crisis set a precedent in this regard. It represented the first time that the Soviet Union cooperated with the United States against a former regional ally, as well as the first time the United Nations provisioned the use of military force by individual nations against another sovereign nation, the case of Korea perhaps notwithstanding.

Second, the success of collective security also is related to the aggressor in question. Iraq committed blatant, brutal, and unabashed aggression. There was nothing ambiguous about it. Not only did Iraq invade, pillage, and occupy Kuwait, it also sought to erase it from the map by making it Iraq's nineteenth province. Saddam's unambiguous aggression facilitated collective security efforts by decreasing the potential for divisive debate over how to deal with Iraq. In the past, collective security was more difficult to exercise in part because disagreements arose over what constituted aggression. Not this time.

Iraq's invasion and occupation of Kuwait triggered numerous UN resolutions that defined the collective security effort of over thirty states party to the U.S.-led anti-Iraq coalition (see "Primary Documents of the Crisis"). From Desert Shield through Desert Storm, the allies were guided by these resolutions and laws under the auspices of the UN. In this sense, this was classic collective security.

Third, Iraqi control or influence over Kuwaiti and Saudi oil would have given Saddam enormous power. He could have increased oil prices and used the funds to develop further his military capability. Since most of the world was in one way or another dependent on the region's oil, Saddam's actions against Kuwait posed a broad threat to the international economy, and even to distant Third World nations that depended directly on oil or indirectly on the economic health of Western lenders. This also facilitated collective security efforts.

Fourth, Iraq's nuclear program proved a serious concern, particularly for the American public. If Saddam were allowed to engage in such aggression and to continue to develop his nuclear capability, he would become nuclear-capable. The dictator from Takrit was threatening enough with his pistol in pocket and army in waiting, even without any nuclear capability. By threatening U.S. interests directly, Saddam motivated the United States to be the author of and impetus behind broader collective security. He made it sensible for the United States to use its political resources and leverage to coax other nations into climbing on the collective security bandwagon.

Fifth, the small nations of the UN identified with Kuwait, because some of them had disputed boundaries with larger nations. If Saddam could attack Kuwait with impunity, then other big actors might also engage in territorial aggression against weaker nations. This would be a dangerous precedent indeed. Small nations around the world thus had a vested interest in seeing that Saddam was taught a very painful lesson. This is perhaps ironic, because Saddam tried to portray his fight with the U.S.-led coalition as that of the weak (read Iraq) against the powerful, the rightful indigenous nation protecting the downtrodden against the imperialists.

COLLECTIVE SECURITY AND THE FUTURE

The success of collective security during the Gulf crisis raised the interesting question of whether it could succeed elsewhere in the post–Cold War world. Was the Persian Gulf crisis a model for the future? Much attention turned to this issue, because the answer to this question would affect how countries viewed international security as well as their own national security. Some leaders and observers believed that the end of the Cold War, the increasing cooperation between Russia and the United States, the possible discrediting of aggressive force, and the development of international norms suggested that collective security could work. But, in reality, the circumstances of the Persian Gulf crisis were so unique that they are unlikely to be repeated elsewhere.

Since the Gulf War, the UN has not fared so well in dealing with other world hot spots. The heart-wrenching Bosnian crisis, which erupted after the Persian Gulf War and which seemed to send Europe back several decades, raised serious doubts about UN effectiveness. Time and again, the defiant, determined Serbs bucked the UN and even attacked its personnel. Whereas in the Persian Gulf context, the UN, with American military backing, met its goals in controlling Iraqi aggression, the record in Bosnia was far more mixed.

The Bosnian problem confounded the NATO allies, which until 1995 took no serious military action to bring peace to the region and seemed to waffle diplomatically as well. If anything, Bosnia seemed to support the notion that collective security worked during the Gulf crisis not primarily because the world had embarked on a new world order of cooperation against aggression, but rather because of the particular context and character of the crisis.

Blatant aggression by an overambitious, brutal dictator, a clear threat to numerous states worldwide, a strong, determined American military and political role, and the international importance of protecting world oil supplies—most of these features were more or less absent in Bosnia. It was not fully clear who the aggressors were, although Serbian atrocities received great media attention. Moreover, the Bosnian problem did not pose a worldwide threat, and while the United States played an important role, it was not nearly as determined to restore peace in Bosnia as it was in the Gulf because the stakes were far lower. NATO bombing of Serbian military sites did move the sides toward a negotiated settlement. But this was not collective security per se, and it was unclear how long the whole edifice would endure.

One possible lesson from the Gulf and Bosnian crises is that the success of collective security depends largely on the peculiar set of circumstances in each case. That is, it may not be possible to make a sweeping judgment as to whether it is the wave of the future, based on any one case. At a minimum, the great powers on the UN Security Council must have a similar view of the aggression that has taken place and of how to address it for collective security to work, or must be willing to compromise their views in order to generate cooperation. Such a set of circumstances is not very common in world politics.

THE PEACE PROCESS

While the fate of collective security remains unclear, one movement toward a type of better world was the Middle East peace process. The Gulf War is linked to the peace process in several ways that need to be understood, particularly by individuals who view the Gulf War as a failure.

First, by enhancing U.S. credibility, the war put Washington in a position to broker the peace process. It reinforced America's ability to convince Arab states that it could influence Israel to make serious concessions for peace, and made peace potentially more rewarding for Arab states. At the same time, U.S. power gave Israel more confidence that its concessions for peace would not compromise its security. U.S. influence could help ensure Arab compliance with a peace agreement, or assure Israel of effective U.S. support in the event that peace collapsed after Israel had made territorial concessions. Arab Gulf states also felt indebted to the United States for checking Saddam's growing regional influence, remained dependent on U.S. security support, and did not want to be viewed as undermining the peace process.

Second, by weakening Iraq, the war also made it safer for Israel to make concessions for peace. Moreover, Iraq's Scud missile attacks on Israel convinced some Israelis that territorial depth was less significant in the ballistic missile age than it had been before, thus making territorial concessions more palatable.

Third, Desert Storm stripped Arab nationalist and radical states of a military alternative to the peace process. Iraq and Syria had been the only actors that could seriously fight Israel. However, by weakening Iraq militarily and discrediting it politically, Desert Storm removed Iraq, in the near term, as a serious antagonist and political force in the Arab world. Meanwhile, Syria's involvement in Desert Shield made it more likely to assume a role in the peace process. This was not only because Syria joined the U.S.-led alliance, but also because cooperation with the West, as opposed to steadfastness with the Arab radical front, made more sense after the military success of Desert Storm.

Fourth, for the first time, excluding Egypt's threat to Saudi Arabia in the 1960s, Arab Gulf states and Israel had similar interests. Iraq was and remains a common threat. The war clearly improved the Arab attitude toward Israel and made the Arab Gulf states more willing to join the peace process.

Fifth, the war has illustrated to Arabs and Israelis the dangers of conflict in the twenty-first century. While no weapons of mass destruction were used in the Gulf War, Iraq did deploy chemical weapons, and fears did exist that Israel would retaliate with nuclear weapons if Iraq used nerve or chemical weapons in its Scud attacks. Given the spread of information and technology, states of the Middle East will become even more heavily armed in the future. This makes peace and communication between them even more important. One Scud missile filled with botulin toxin could kill hundreds of thousands of people—that is something to think about.

The peace process is, of course, still vulnerable to breakdown, as suggested by repeated terrorist attacks on Israelis by the Islamic militant group Hamas and by the election in Israel in May 1996 of Likud party hard-liner Benjamin Netanyahu. But the peace initiative may still prove resilient over the longer run. In such a case, the Gulf War, unfortunate as it was, may go down in history as the event that finally made regional peace possible.

CONCLUSION

The Persian Gulf crisis at once shattered and reinvigorated the concept of collective security embedded in the broader, idealistic notion of a new world order. In some respects, the Gulf War did inaugurate a new era in the

Middle East, and did enhance the status of the United Nations. However, it did *not* establish a model for future collective security efforts—witness the lengthy Bosnian war. The UN did show that, with significant direction from a great power like the United States, it could punish aggression and check an international menace. At the same time, collective security succeeded in this instance because of a peculiar combination of circumstances that may not so easily arise again. While this does not mean that the United Nations cannot be useful in future crises, it does suggest that its potential usefulness can only be judged on a case-by-case basis.

NOTES

1. Excerpted from the president's address to the nation announcing allied military action in the Persian Gulf, January 16, 1991, in George Bush, *Public Papers of the Presidents* (hereafter cited as *PPP*), vol. 1 (Washington, DC: United States Government Printing Office, 1992), 43–44.

2. Transcript of President Bush's February 27 address, "Kuwait Is Liberated," February 27, 1991, in Bush, *PPP*, vol. 1, 187–88.

7

The Impact of the Gulf War: The Operation Was a Success but the Patient Lived

Soon after the guns fell silent, scholars of world politics, as well as armchair analysts and policymakers, began to evaluate the success of the Persian Gulf War. To some of them, the Gulf War either failed or was not very successful, and certainly was not the stunning victory that the Bush administration portrayed it to be. The critics pointed to such things as the festering Kurdish problem, Saddam's longevity, Iraq's remaining military capability, its likely resurgence as a producer of weapons of mass destruction, the absence of regional democracy, the regional arms race, and the financial and human cost of the war.

For instance, military analyst Jeffrey Record, a seasoned observer, argued at a general level that while the Gulf War was a great military victory, it was a political failure.[1]

Adding to the criticism, Roger Hilsman argued that Saddam Hussein not only remained in power, but may very well have been strengthened by the war, and that in this sense Saddam won out over President Bush.[2] And one widely cited book opined that Desert Storm was a "triumph without victory."[3]

While great attention is focused on what causes war, much less attention is devoted to what war causes. This chapter examines the major economic, political, military, social, and environmental consequences of the war for the Middle East and world politics, and, in the process, seeks to draw attention to these questions: Did the Gulf War succeed? Is the Middle East a better place after the war? Did the war fulfill U.S. policy goals?

THE MAJOR CONSEQUENCES OF THE GULF WAR

Although the impact of the Gulf War on human beings was insignificant compared to the disasters of World War I, World War II, Korea, and Vietnam, many people did lose their lives, were displaced, and suffered postwar trauma. At the same time, Desert Storm produced a number of successful consequences for world politics and for the Middle East, some of which are only now maturing.

In brief, President Bush outlined the following American goals during the crisis:

- the unconditional withdrawal of all Iraqi forces from Kuwait;
- the restoration of Kuwait's legitimate government;
- the protection of the security and stability of the region; and
- the protection of the lives of Americans abroad.

The United States accomplished the first two goals and, with some recent exceptions, the fourth. To some extent, it also protected regional security and stability. But at the same time, the elusive Iraqi strong man has remained in power, has restructured and rebuilt an important part of his military, and thus has continued to pose a regional threat. Washington would have preferred Saddam's elimination, but, for several reasons, was unwilling to march on Baghdad to accomplish this implicit goal. Getting rid of Saddam, in any event, raised the question of whether any post-Saddam leader would be better for regional security. The answer to that was unclear.

U.S. POWER AND INCREASED WESTERN INVOLVEMENT

At the global level, the war created three primary effects. As discussed in Chapter 3, it increased the power, prominence, and role of the United States in the Persian Gulf region and in world politics. The war also lifted the influence of Russia and European states in the Persian Gulf. Although these actors took a back seat to the United States, they did play a role during the war and after it. Great Britain and France participated fully in Desert Storm, and their military contributions, although dwarfed by Washington's, were rewarded in the postwar period. Both states signed defense accords with Kuwait (as did Russia), increased their lucrative arms sales to the region, and obtained valuable contracts for postwar reconstruction.

Furthermore, prior to Desert Storm, the UN presence in the region was limited to a small peacekeeping mission aimed at keeping Iran and Iraq apart after their eight-year war. During the Gulf crisis, the UN condemned and sought ways to punish Iraqi behavior. In the postwar period, it continued to be involved by maintaining economic sanctions and ensuring that Iraq made serious efforts to destroy its weapons of mass destruction. While the United States was responsible for driving elements of UN actions, the UN was also a bona fide actor in and of itself at certain junctures.

ARAB STATES AND GULF SECURITY AFTER THE STORM

By underscoring regional dangers, the war generated increased interest in security, as well as political and economic cooperation among members of the Gulf Cooperation Council (GCC), composed of Saudi Arabia, Kuwait, Oman, Qatar, the United Arab Emirates, and Bahrain. King Fahd of Saudi Arabia, expressing broader sentiment, claimed that Iraq's invasion revealed the failure of "those who covet the territory of other states," and brought the GCC states closer together.[4] However, the idea of developing a serious GCC military force, an idea bandied about in the past, went nowhere. GCC members regarded it as overly ambitious and allowed discussions of the proposal to lapse.

Regional collective security efforts in the military form of the so-called Damascus Declaration also failed after Desert Storm. This declaration was issued on March 6, 1991, and called for strategic collaboration between the GCC states, Egypt, and Syria.[5] In exchange for security support in the form of Egyptian and Syrian military contingents permanently stationed in the Gulf region, the GCC states would provide much-needed capital for the Syrian and Egyptian economies. In theory, it all sounded like a good deal. However, while the Gulf states thought that Egypt and Syria were angling to get maximum money for minimal security, Egypt and Syria believed the Gulf states wanted maximum security for minimal money. In part because of this dynamic, the Damascus formula collapsed.

In the wake of its failure, regional players redoubled their efforts to secure and solidify the backing of outside players—primarily the United States. Kuwait, the least secure regional player, was in a position vis-à-vis Iraq similar to that of France vis-à-vis Germany after World War I. In both cases, the weaker player, fearing a resurgence of its nemesis, aimed to sign defense accords with various powerful players. As noted earlier in this chapter, an eager Kuwait managed to sign defense accords with Great Britain, France, and Russia, intended to preserve regional peace and to deter further aggression through defense cooperation, training and exercises, and arms sales. In the years following the Gulf War, Kuwait and those external players would engage in sporadic joint maneuvers as a deterrent signal to Iraq and also as a means of maintaining military readiness against a reinvigorated Saddam. Likewise, the Saudis continued to link their military readiness to joint maneuvers with U.S. air, naval, and army forces and to purchase sophisticated weapons from the United States and other suppliers.

IRAQ CONSTRAINED BUT DEFIANT

Although Desert Storm devastated Iraq's military, it did not destroy it. Even after Desert Storm, Iraq remained a political and military threat to the region. This made enforcement of UN sanctions critical to regional security. U.S. policy under President Bill Clinton aimed to force Iraq to comply with all UN resolutions and to stand firmly behind the security and integrity of the states in the area against any future aggression.

UN Resolutions 687 (see Document 3) and 707, which called for critical UN sanctions against Iraq, seriously impeded Iraq's ability to restore its military capabilities, despite its attempts to circumvent the resolutions. Referred to as the "mother of all resolutions" for its record length, Resolution 687 was passed by the Security Council on April 3, 1991. It forced Iraq to accept a UN demarcated border with Kuwait, the inviolability of Kuwaiti territory, and UN peacekeepers on the Iraq-Kuwait border. It also mandated full disclosure of all of Iraq's ballistic missile stocks and production facilities (for missiles with a range exceeding 150 kilometers) and of all nuclear materials, chemical and biological weapons and facilities, as well as cooperation in their destruction. Paragraphs 10 through 12, furthermore, required that Iraq "unconditionally undertake not to use, develop, construct, or acquire" weapons of mass destruction. Iraqi compliance with Resolution 687 was a prerequisite for lifting or reducing sanctions against it.

The ban on the sale of its oil deprived Iraq of an estimated $15–25 billion per year with which it could rebuild its conventional capabilities and develop nonconventional weapons. UN sanctions prohibiting arms transfers and related materials further hindered Iraq's ability to restore its conventional capability to prewar levels. And the ban on the sale or supply of commodities and products added to Saddam's problems by generating some internal discontent and forcing him to divert funds from reconstruction toward providing goods for important domestic constituencies.

Saddam resorted to various tricks and disguises to avoid full compliance, while lobbying for an end to the sanctions. Iraq simply did not forthrightly obey UN sanctions. Rather, it assumed a two-pronged approach of blatant duplicity. On the one hand, it accepted Resolution 687, acted to or pretended to meet some of its obligations, and then called for the lifting of the UN embargo. On the other hand, Saddam left little doubt about his enduring ambitions. Although the Iraq-Kuwait border dispute was settled in legal terms in the postwar period, Iraq did not accept the result as final.

The UN did not look kindly on Iraqi defiance and deceit. The UN commission designated to redraw the border did so in a manner that favored Kuwait. Kuwait received a larger portion of the Rumaila oil field over which Kuwait and Iraq lay joint claim, and retained control over Warba and Bubiyan islands. Sovereignty over these islands allowed Kuwait to control Iraq's only current access point to Persian Gulf waters. Kuwait considered the area its rightful possession, one usurped by Iraq in 1932 and 1973.[6] This infuriated the Iraqis, because they had felt prior to the war that Kuwait was stealing from the Rumaila oil field and was thumbing its nose at Iraq, which had just staved off the Iranian threat to the whole Arab world.

Not surprisingly, Iraq continued to assert that it would eventually conquer Kuwait. Despite warnings from the United Nations Iraq-Kuwait Observer Mission (UNIKOM), the Iraqi army mocked UN authority by repeatedly violating Kuwaiti territory and threatening the Saudi border as well. For instance, on July 1 and 3, 1993, Iraqi forces shot machine guns along the Saudi border, which alarmed the royal family.

As another act of defiance, until mid-1996 Saddam also refused to allow the UN to control Iraq's overseas oil sales and to use proceeds for humanitarian purposes and for funding UN operations in Iraq. This put tens of thousands of Iraqi lives in danger from malnutrition and disease. Furthermore, Iraq displayed no intention of giving up its efforts to develop weapons of mass destruction. Rather, it engaged in sporadic concealment and pretended cooperation. At times, it simply refused to allow UN inspectors into certain buildings for days, with the apparent goal of moving critical documents or materials from the buildings in the meantime.

SADDAM'S MANY DOMESTIC PROBLEMS

Iraq's defiance of the UN and the world community was generally unsuccessful. At the political level, the United States and other actors, particularly the Saudis, worked to isolate Baghdad. At the economic level, UN sanctions deprived Iraq of oil revenues and a role in affecting decision-making in global oil markets. Saddam not only had to quell the troublesome Kurds and Shiites, but also had to keep his own officers content. Iraq's living standards were cut to half the prewar level, inflation reached 250 percent over prewar levels, and the Iraqi dinar was devalued repeatedly between 1990 and 1993. Economic deprivation also exacerbated Saddam's internal problems, resulting in deep dissatisfaction with the regime among the Iraqi people, the army, and even within Saddam's Tikriti ruling family. Nonetheless, Saddam, seemingly defying fate and logic, continued to hang on to power.

The Kurds in the North

Saddam's problems even extended to maintaining sovereignty over Iraqi territory in the period immediately following the war, from March 1 to March 7, when civil unrest erupted in fifteen Iraqi cities, until April 2, when the rebellion was suppressed. In northern Iraq, Kurdish rebels succeeded for the first time in history in taking several major urban centers, including the oil facilities at Kirkuk, and, at the height of the rebellion, a majority of Kurdistan territory. Although Saddam crushed the rebellion, it sapped Iraq's energy and created nearly 2 million refugees in early April 1991, concentrated primarily on the Iranian and Turkish borders. This human tragedy ultimately generated support for an international relief effort launched between April 6 and April 10, code-named Operation Provide Comfort, and led the coalition allies to create safe havens against Iraqi attacks.

A no-fly zone was created above the 36th parallel in northern Iraq in 1991 to bar Iraqi military aircraft from attacking the Kurds. Yet, in late August and early September 1996, Iraqi forces on the ground seized Irbil in northern Iraq from Kurds, thus forcing the United States to enhance its military presence in the region.

Saddam was probably motivated by three factors in invading Kurdistan. First, he wanted to check Iranian influence. Iran, Iraq's archenemy, was supporting the Patriotic Union of Kurdistan (PUK) against another Kurdish faction, the Kurdish Democratic Party (KDP). The KDP called on Saddam to seize Irbil, an important city, in order to strengthen it in its ongoing rivalry with the PUK.

Second, Iraqi military forces killed political opponents who were cooperating with the Kurds and undermined CIA efforts to oust Saddam. It is important to note that in the weeks prior to the September invasion of Kurdistan, regional sources reported much unrest in Iraq's armed forces, power struggles within the country's hierarchy, continuing problems in Saddam's divided family, and bloody government purges after a failed coup attempt by Iraqi officers was uncovered in May. Moreover, reportedly a bomb in mid-August narrowly missed Saddam at one of his palaces. By attacking the Kurds, Saddam was nipping opposition in the bud and keeping his armed forces focused on the Kurds rather than on ousting the dictator.

Third, by taking strong action in the north, Saddam improved his credibility with his people as well. The United States responded with two sets of cruise missile strikes on Iraqi military targets in southern Iraq, but did not do much damage. Saddam painted this attack as aggression and tried to rally his people behind him.

Washington also moved the line in the south beyond which Iraq's aircraft and ground forces could not move (the 32nd parallel discussed in the next few paragraphs) much closer to Baghdad. This further restricted Iraq's movement toward the really critical targets in the south—the region's oil supplies.

Iraq initially defied this zone and even fired a few hapless surface-to-air missiles at U.S. aircraft patrolling this southern zone. This prompted Washington to send the USS *Enterprise*, eight Stealth fighters, and several hundred F-15s and F-16s, as well as other forces, to the region.

In the short term, Saddam appeared to win a victory. He increased his influence in northern Iraq, decreased the power of his opponents and of the CIA, and checked Iran. Moreover, the lackluster allied support of U.S. action revealed that the Gulf War coalition had a few cracks.

However, Saddam did set back Iraq's ability to have economic sanctions lifted, because his invasion of the north violated UN Resolution 688, which protected the Kurds. Moreover, Washington refocused its energies on Iraq and cut off the latter's movement in the south, thus posing a potential longer-term humiliation for Saddam and creating a basis for further punishing strikes by U.S. air power.

The Shiites in the South

In the south, Saddam met the postwar Shiite uprising in 1991 with an unprecedented crackdown. He used helicopter gunships, which American generals, having been duped by the Iraqis at cease-fire talks, agreed to let Iraq fly for purposes of "transporting" officials around the country. Although they had been suppressed, repressed, and abused for years, the Shiites of southern Iraq seized on the moment of Saddam's military retreat in 1991 to make their own bid for autonomy and to hasten Saddam's end. President Bush, glowing in the aftermath of Iraq's devastating military defeat at the hands of the U.S.-led coalition, encouraged the postwar uprising by Iraq's Kurds and Shiites against Saddam but decided not to engage the United States in this effort. He would later be severely criticized for having failed to support the brave efforts of Iraq's disaffected groups.

American concern with Iraq's gross human rights violations against the Shiites, however, did lead the United States, Britain, and France to declare a no-fly zone over southern Iraq in August 1992, which applied to Iraqi fixed-winged aircraft and helicopters south of the 32nd parallel. Saddam's forces were also restricted from moving south on the ground. The three Western powers enforced this no-fly zone—which seriously limited Saddam's control over nearly one-third of Iraq—with threats of force when Saddam moved soldiers toward Kuwait in October 1994, and then when he reputedly was considering another foray south toward Kuwait in August 1995, after the defections of his sons-in-law to Jordan.

The Defectors: All in the Family

The August 1995 defections of Lt. General Hussein Kamel Hussan Majeed, the architect of Saddam's war machine, and Lt. Col. Saddam Kamel Hassan Majeed, the head of his personal guards, added another dimension to Saddam's domestic problems. When they threatened to divulge Baghdad's secrets while in Jordan, Saddam was forced to reveal previously concealed facts about the extent of Iraq's biological and chemical programs, so as to preempt the defectors and gain favor with the UN. The defections were serious, particularly in light of a coup attempt in March 1995. This revolt did not involve the entire Dulaym clan, but rather the Albunimr tribe, one particular tribe within the Dulaym clan from the city of Ramadi, which heretofore had largely supported Saddam. The Albunimr really had no chance of unseating Saddam. Saddam crushed the small revolt within three weeks. Still, shock waves rippled through Iraq. For the first time since the rise of Saddam's Baath party in 1968, a Sunni tribe traditionally loyal to Saddam had attempted a coup.

Three scenarios could help explain the defections to Jordan. Under scenario one, Saddam's minister of defense, Hussein Kamel, who had plenty of Iraqi blood on his hands, committed a political "mistake." He then fled to save himself from Saddam's wrath. Once in Jordan, he conveniently assumed the noble role of overthrowing Saddam. Given Iraq's Byzantine politics, he might even have left based on a rumor of impending doom. We do know that Saddam freely let Kamel leave for Bulgaria prior to his defection. Although Kamel never made it past Jordan, this suggests that Saddam did not expect him to defect.

In scenario two, Kamel left because Saddam's sons, Uday and Qosai, eclipsed him in power or annoyed him. The corrupt Uday, known, among other vices, for identifying beautiful women on the streets of Baghdad and having their husbands killed and the women brought to him, reputedly often interfered with and even usurped Kamel's responsibilities, with Saddam acquiescing to strengthen his loyal son at Kamel's expense. At one family celebration in August 1995, a drunk Uday reportedly even killed several dancing girls and a male guest after shooting his uncle, an event that contributed to the defectors' interest in leaving Iraq. Uday would later be shot, although not killed, in December 1996, possibly in retaliation or for various other reasons.

Under scenario three, Kamel left Iraq because Saddam subordinated Iraq's national goals to his own obsession with defying UN sanctions. From Jordan, Kamel would launch a glorious coup in conjunction with internal forces, to regain the credibility that Iraq had lost on the international and Arab scene. The defections seemed to confirm the weakening of Saddam's Sunni power base and to indicate despair within Saddam's inner circle. But far more than two high-level defections were needed to bring Saddam down.

The Iraqi political and military elite, whatever their doubts about Saddam's stability, had to be convinced that a post-Saddam Iraq would not be worse than Saddam himself. This was no small point. The Iraqi elite, the Baath party, and elements of the Iraqi military all had stakes in Saddam's Iraq and risked losing their prestige, positions, wealth, and possibly their lives if Saddam died or was driven from office. A host of unpleasant post-Saddam scenarios kept these actors from bringing about Saddam's fall. Only when such actors could be assured that such worst-case scenarios would not occur *might* they conspire against Saddam.

For them, a first frightening post-Saddam scenario is the prospect of a total breakdown of Iraq. Under Ottoman rule prior to 1918, Iraq was not a unified or independent state. It consisted of three disparate provinces: Mosul, Baghdad, and Basra. When Iraq achieved independence, these three areas came together into one state. Saddam, through brute force, kept them unified, despite pressures in the north from the Kurds and in the south from the Shiites to tear Iraq asunder along ethnic and religious fault lines. Would-be coup plotters must consider that a post-Saddam Iraq might bring civil war and chaos.

Second, in a post-Saddam Iraq, Shiite influence might rise. Iraq, like most other Gulf states, is predominantly Shiite. In Iraq, however, Sunnis who come mainly from Saddam's small town of Takrit rule the state. While Shiites currently lack political influence, Saddam's demise could empower them and very likely embolden them to seek a larger role in Iraq. Such a prospect poses a grave and even lethal threat to elements of the current Sunni regime, and is a strong disincentive for Sunnis to eliminate Saddam.

Third, aspiring coup plotters must worry that with Saddam gone, and Iraq in possible chaos, Iran and Syria might gain influence. Syria, like other regional states, has created a special committee to rid Iraq of Saddam, and has cultivated political contacts within Iraq. Iran, which is 93 percent Shiite, would delight in affecting Iraqi internal politics. It has done so in the past and would relish the prospects offered by the demise of its archenemy, Saddam. Iraqi elites fear such an outcome.

Fourth, most of Iraq's elite do not want American influence over Iraq to increase significantly. While Saddam is unpopular and vulnerable, Iraqis may perceive, as many Arabs do, a U.S. conspiracy in the making. If would-be coup plotters feel that Washington wants to exploit Saddam's fall either to impose a pro-Western regime or to gain strategic benefit, they may very well resist efforts to unseat Saddam. For its part, the United States does not want to, and should not, get stuck in the quagmire of Iraqi internal politics, about which it knows little in any case.

THE GULF WAR AND SADDAM'S LONGEVITY

Although no crystal ball can give a definitive answer, Saddam's fate seems to hinge on five interrelated factors. When considered together, they suggest that he is far weaker than he was prior to the Gulf War, but still resilient in the near term.

The first factor that affects Saddam's fate is the extent to which he can control his personal security forces, which total over 10,000 men. Although a coup or assassination attempt could come from these forces, Saddam has controlled them effectively since the war through a combination of purges, executions, and overlapping security groups that spy on each other. Despite the near assassination of his son Uday, which may suggest a problem with the security forces, Saddam appears to be in full control. Indeed, in response to the Uday hit attempt, he successfully rounded up 600 suspects, which would have been difficult unless he were in control of the security apparatus.

A second factor is Saddam's need for continued support from the Sunni elite, which forms his second important base of support. Two major events suggest that his position among the elite has diminished. The unprecedented March coup attempt by the Albunimr tribe of the Dulaym clan, heretofore very loyal to Saddam, revealed a serious fissure in the once unified Sunni elite as did the surprising August 1995 defections of high-level Iraqi officials from Saddam's family. Saddam responded to both events with brutal force and bloody purges.

Indeed, this would be the gruesome fate of his sons-in-law, who, believing they had been exonerated by Saddam for their defections, were killed upon returning to Iraq in February 1996. Additional purges followed. Perhaps this was Saddam's way of sending any future defectors or challengers an unambiguous warning: If you challenge me and fail, I will kill you, your family members, and quite possibly your friends. While this has worked in preserving his power—for now—it has also cut down his cadre of talented, experienced people to the bone, and reflects his weakening internal position.

Another factor is Saddam's control over Republican Guard divisions—his third major base of support and his best fighting forces. Early indications suggest he has retained sufficient loyalty here, despite the Gulf War disaster. Although some soldiers have defected, the Guard played a critical role in suppressing the postwar Shiite and Kurdish uprisings against Saddam, in containing the March 1995 coup attempt, and in recapturing Irbil for pro-Saddam Kurdish forces in September 1996.

The fourth factor that will determine Saddam's fate is his level of control over Iraq's complex system of propaganda and terror. At present, he seems to be in full control. Elections in Iraq in 1996, which yielded him nearly 100 percent of the vote, were a farce given that the threat of banishment or death hung over the heads of voters. Nonetheless, such an outcome required coordination and domination of Iraq's propaganda machine and security forces. After all, it is no easy task to rig an election on a national scale. Strong public dissension, which occurs in Iran nowadays, remains rare in Iraq. It is still too risky to challenge Saddam openly; rather, effusive, even obsequious praise, makes more sense to many common Iraqis and elites alike.

A fifth factor is that Saddam's power is linked to financial resources without which he cannot keep key individuals and groups satisfied. UN sanctions banning sale of oil by Iraq deprive it of $15–$20 billion per year. By imposing hardship on Iraq's people, these sanctions are probably weakening Saddam's hand.

Six years after the war, we can say that Saddam has proven adept at the art of survival in Iraq's Byzantine, dangerous political arena. However, the destabilizing economic and political forces that he put in motion by invading Iran in 1980 and then Kuwait in 1990 are still in motion. And they may yet unseat him.

CONTAINING IRAQ'S WAR MACHINE

At the strategic level, Desert Storm and postwar UN sanctions weakened Iraq in the conventional military arena, impeded its nuclear program, and damaged to some extent its biological and chemical weapons programs. Prior to Desert Storm, Iraq had a formidable conventional force, which enabled it to affect events in the Persian Gulf region and the broader Middle East.

Furthermore, postwar UN sanctions decreased Iraqi capabilities by reducing the operational readiness of forces that survived Desert Storm. Although seriously weakened, Iraq did retain about 50–60 percent of its prewar conventional military capability and reconstituted a total of twenty-eight of its fifty-seven prewar divisions. As a result, on paper at least, it remained the strongest military in the Persian Gulf region, although it was so constrained by political and economic sanctions that Iran became the more influential regional state.

Despite suffering severe and perhaps irreparable damage, Iraq's nuclear program remained potentially viable. Baghdad retained the human intelligence capability to support a major nuclear program, including substantial dual-use technology and working designs for a centrifuge system. Such human intelligence also existed in the form of thousands of well-trained nuclear scientists and support staff whom Saddam kept intact even after the Gulf War.

Furthermore, some analysts speculated that Iraq retained an underground reactor or centrifuge cascade, despite the failure of UN inspectors to identify such facilities. A more likely risk is that Iraq could buy nuclear fuel and technology, or even a nuclear weapon, from former Soviet republics starved for capital. At a minimum, Saddam's continuing interest in obtaining nuclear weapons has necessitated long-term monitoring, as described in UN Resolution 715, to prevent Iraq's program from taking off again.

Prior to the Gulf War, Iraq had the most advanced chemical warfare program in the Arab world. After Desert Storm, Iraq retained the ability to produce chemical and biological weapons, despite the severe damage imposed by allied air forces on its principal chemical agent facility at Samarra and its main biological warfare research complex at Salman Pak. Were UN sanctions to be lifted, Iraq could restore its former chemical weapons production in less than one year (it may be able to do so even with sanctions in place) and produce biological weapons within weeks. Permanent monitoring by the UN, mandated by the cease-fire accord and UN resolutions, nonetheless makes it difficult for Iraq to resume business as usual in these areas.

THE RISE OF IRAN

By weakening Iraq, Desert Storm raised Iran's relative power in the region significantly and turned U.S. attention to Tehran. Iraq's defeat gave Iran more room for strategic and political maneuvering, despite the fact that the Iran-Iraq war (1980–1988) had left Tehran economically devastated and militarily weak. Iran proceeded to impose its sovereignty on the Arab Gulf islands of Abu Musa and the Upper and Lesser Tunbs in August 1992, which caused regional and international alarm. Abu Musa had been jointly administered by Iran and the United Arab Emirates (UAE) under an agreement concluded in 1971, until Iran took control of it.

Iran also engaged in other actions that concerned Arab Gulf states and Washington. It embarked on a major five-year defense buildup, continued its pursuit of nuclear capability, developed the ability to produce tanks and other weapons indigenously, and increased its ability to deliver ballistic missiles. It also opposed the Middle East peace process, supported the Islamic militant group Hamas, which engineered numerous suicide bombings in Israel, and called for Israel's outright destruction as a state. Indeed, in October 1995, tens of thousands of Iranian soldiers shouted "Death to America, death to Israel" in conjunction with Iranian military exercises and with support of high-level Iranian officials. This was reminiscent of the days of the Iranian hostage crisis, when the Ayatollah Khomeini fueled the passions of the faithful against the "Great Satan."

Fears of Iran in 1995, however, were exaggerated in the press. The Ayatollah was dead (in 1989), Iran was economically supine, and its power remained dubious. The Saudis, after all, spent more on defense than Iran, and Iran's military was more "smoke and mirrors" than an effective machine. Iran, nonetheless, did loom as potentially powerful over the long run, especially if Iraq remained shackled by the effects of the Persian Gulf War.

THE MIDDLE EAST PEACE PROCESS

Iran's efforts to torpedo the peace process, which reportedly even included plans to assassinate PLO chairman Yasser Arafat, were not successful in the short term. The actors pushing for peace, as well as the incentives for peace, were strong, and motivated the Jordanian-Israeli peace accord and the signing on September 28, 1995, of the Israeli-Palestinian Interim Agreement on the West Bank and the Gaza Strip.

As discussed in Chapter 5, the Middle East peace process was, in part, a by-product of the Gulf War. At the intraregional level, war was the midwife of the Middle East peace process. From the Arab perspective, Israel became less of a liability in America's effort to forge stronger relations with Gulf states, and from Israel's standpoint, American relations with GCC states became less worrisome. Whether or not peace would stick was a troubling question. It was one thing to make peace and another to maintain it.

THE HUMAN DIMENSION AND THE GULF WAR SYNDROME

Four key consequences of the Persian Gulf War are worth noting at the human level. First, during the war, Kuwaiti citizens and Third World and Western hostages became pawns in Saddam's struggle to retain Kuwait. Used as human shields, they were at the mercy of chance and of their Iraqi captors. Many of them suffered severe postwar trauma.

Second, the Kuwaiti population was terrorized by the invasion. The Iraqis arbitrarily arrested, brutalized, and detained thousands of Kuwaiti civilians and military personnel. Hundreds of civilians, including children, were tortured and executed. As many as 10,000 Kuwaitis may have died from direct and indirect effects of the war. Between August and November 1990, 850,000 third-country nationals and 300,000 Kuwaitis fled Kuwait. And in next-door Saudi Arabia over 800,000 Yemenis who had had a stable life and lucrative jobs in the kingdom were expelled by the royal family in retaliation for Yemen's support of Iraq.

Third, the war produced casualties. Prior to Desert Storm, predictions of American war dead reached as high as 10,000. In reality, American casualties were incredibly limited. Total battlefield deaths for the U.S.-led coalition numbered 243 (many from friendly fire), and between 450 and 750 soldiers were wounded in action. The United States lost 148 killed in action, with 458 more wounded. In the postwar period, however, many soldiers developed health problems. Indeed, a fraction of the 700,000 Americans who served in the crisis developed headaches, joint pain, fatigue, diarrhea, and other ailments. These problems were collectively dubbed the "Gulf War syndrome," a problem that gained enormous media attention in the years following the 1991 Gulf War.

The Pentagon said on December 13, 1993, that a study of more than 1,000 ailing Gulf War veterans showed that 85 percent had unknown diseases, probably resulting from more than one cause.[7] By 1994 U.S. officials began taking the mystery illnesses very seriously and set up an interagency board to deal with the problem. The Pentagon, hoping to avoid a repeat of the mysterious illnesses, began requiring medical personnel to monitor closely troops sent to the Gulf; and in March 1995, President Clinton announced the formation of an independent panel that could improve the government's treatment of Gulf War veterans. Researchers would later find that some of the symptoms of the Gulf War syndrome were possibly caused by a medication called Pyridostigmine, a drug administered to U.S. troops for anti–chemical warfare purposes.

After asserting from 1991 to 1996 that U.S. soldiers did not encounter Iraqi chemical weapons, the Pentagon announced in June 1996 that at least one chemical weapons facility was hit and did contain two highly toxic gases, sarin and mustard gases. This site contained 122mm nerve-agent rockets and 155mm mustard gas shells, which were found by UN inspection teams in May 1996. Their belated search was prompted after a report filed in October 1991 by UN inspectors resurfaced during an interagency review of the Gulf War syndrome ordered by President Clinton in March 1995. In that earlier report Iraqi officials indeed confirmed the presence of chemical agents at the site. This report seemed to suggest that Gulf War syndrome was linked to chemical poisoning. Although the Department of Defense found no clinical evidence that U.S. troops were exposed to chemical weapons, speculation arose that this was possible. In September 1996, the Pentagon announced that perhaps thousands of veterans may have been affected by chemical poisoning—four times the number previously discussed. By November 1996, about 70,000 of the 650,000 U.S. troops who served in the Gulf had requested special examinations to determine if they were affected.

Over time, the Pentagon investigations of Gulf War syndrome came under fire. In early November 1996, a special White House panel, the Presidential Advisory Committee on Gulf War Veterans' Illnesses, released a draft report that called the Pentagon's investigation "superficial," asserted that many more veterans could be affected than is currently believed, and called for more serious research on the subject. Some observers even hinted at a Defense Department cover-up. This allegation was fiercely denied by the Pentagon and by General Schwarzkopf, who invited Senate investigators in January 1997 to examine his private logs of the Gulf War. While recognizing that the illness was real, Schwarzkopf asserted that there were no reports of chemical weapons exposure or of any cover-up.

In fact, as of January 1997, the cause of Gulf War syndrome remains unknown. The fourth report from the Department of Defense in April 1996, as well as a study by the National Institutes of Health Technology Assessment Workshop Panel, concluded that no single disease or syndrome is apparent, but rather that multiple illnesses with overlapping symptoms and causes may be at play. Moreover, the final report of the Presidential Advisory Committee submitted in December 1996 found no proof of a chemical cause for the illness or of a Pentagon cover-up, and called for further study. That is precisely what has taken place. Not only did the president extend the work of his Advisory Committee, but also, eighty federally supported research and evaluation projects are underway on the syndrome to examine general health and environmental effects. Clearly, U.S. soldiers have suffered greatly from the syndrome, but it may take some time to discover precisely why.

Yet, while American soldiers suffered from postwar illnesses, Iraqi soldiers took a far more serious pounding during the actual war. Estimates of Iraqi soldiers killed during the war are sketchy, but they have been placed at between 5,000 and 200,000, with the U.S. Department of Defense estimating in May 1991 100,000 dead, 300,000 wounded, and 150,000 deserters. Subsequent estimates, which may be more reliable given the passage of time, place the number of Iraqi war dead at around 10,000.

Fourth, the war hurt civilians. Several hundred Iraqi civilians were killed during the war, and thousands more would die of malnutrition and disease, largely as a result of Saddam's refusal to cooperate in order to have UN economic sanctions lifted. And in the postwar period the human suffering continued.

THE ENVIRONMENT

While Saddam's troops were suppressing uprisings in the immediate aftermath of the Gulf War, Iraqi oil fires were still burning. Iraq's environmental mischief was not new to warfare. During both world wars, oil fields were destroyed in order to impede the adversary's progress. However, it was unclear whether Saddam's environmental terror had a military purpose, other than to exact punishment on his enemies. This earned Iraq even greater disdain in the world community.

During the war, Iraq sabotaged approximately 700 Kuwaiti oil wells and twenty collecting centers. The oil well fires, struck by Saddam's army, burned for months and spewed tons of pollutants into the atmosphere. A number of scientists predicted radical changes in weather patterns. A U.S. Defense Nuclear Agency report warned that oil fires would cause "a massive and unprecedented pollution event. It would impact the ecology of the Persian Gulf, and fall out on a wide swath across Southern Iran, Pakistan, and Northern India."[8]

Flying over the disaster, Secretary of State James Baker, disgusted by the horrid spectacle, was struck by the eerie darkness of billowing smoke from over 600 oil well fires. He would later cable the president to say that he had just seen "a colossal waste and a colossal environmental disaster. Iraq should pay for it."9

During the war, Iraqi troops also dynamited five oil tankers, and released oil from wellheads at three major Kuwaiti ports. This allowed oil to flow unchecked over land and sea. While the environmental damage appeared less severe than expected, Iraq's actions produced an oil spill estimated at thirty times greater than that of the *Exxon Valdez* in Alaska, damaging the marine environment, ecology, and wildlife habitats along the Gulf coast.

While the oil fires did pollute air for hundreds of miles, atmospheric problems did not arise to the extent expected. The Kuwait Oil Company claims that 3 percent of its prewar oil reserves of 100 billion barrels were lost in the fires. One study showed that by mid-March 1991, clouds of toxic smoke were stretching from Romania and Bulgaria to Afghanistan and Pakistan, and another reported that black snow had fallen in the Himalayas;[10] a third study found that the oil fires could well have caused rain contaminated with crude oil in Turkey.[11] The long-term impact remains unclear.

KUWAIT: THE POSTWAR HANGOVER

One of the most interesting questions is how the Gulf War has affected the small, vulnerable state over which it was fought. In some ways the impact was tremendous; in other ways, however, not a great deal changed.

Prior to the war, Kuwait underestimated the threat from Iraq and acted in an overconfident manner. Although they had faced threats from Iraq before in history, and from Iran in the 1980s, Kuwaitis seemed confident after the Iran-Iraq war. The Gulf War shattered this world of comfort and impressed upon them in a brutal fashion just how vulnerable their cosmopolitan, rich sheikdom was to the lion from the north. Kuwaiti foreign policy adjusted to this reality. In the 1980s, Kuwait had been perhaps the most pro-Soviet Gulf state after Iraq. After the Gulf War, it embraced the United States as its principal non-Arab friend. Portraits of Bush were commonplace in Kuwait, U.S. forces were welcome there, and Kuwait's ruling family paid tribute to their new protector—the United States.

At the domestic level, Kuwaiti demography changed considerably. The significant Palestinian population in Kuwait was virtually gone—war retribution for their support of Saddam Hussein. A major crackdown followed the war to punish any other Kuwaitis who may have sympathized with the Iraqis. Torture and murder were not uncommon in this retaliatory process.

Democracy was much talked about in the press during the crisis and in small commonplace gatherings in Kuwait called *Diwaniyas*, but never really moved beyond the display of parliamentary freedom allowed by the royal family in the past. Rather, the emir sought to control such aspirations and to take any liberalization moves quite slowly. He remained concerned about Iraq both as an external and an internal threat to his regime. While liberals hoped for broader participation after the Iraqi invaders were expelled, in reality only about 25,000 males over the age of twenty-one who could establish that their families had resided in Kuwait since 1920 were eligible to vote in October 1992, out of a permanent population about eight times that size. Kuwait had made greater moves toward democratization than any Arab Gulf state, but many groups remained outside the reorganized, legal political process.

The social fabric of Kuwait, while torn by what was perceived as Palestinian betrayal, and while ripped at the edge by memories of Iraqi brutality and torture, remained resilient. No wide-scale uprisings occurred against the regime, which had learned long ago how to keep its people happy and to maintain tribal unity. Rather, political and social ferment was kept under control, and the state, having been pillaged and ransacked, rebuilt itself rapidly with eager support from Western contractors. The plush stores were reconstructed and refurbished; the damaged high-rise buildings were restored; the military was strengthened; and the cultural and civic centers were enhanced.

However, the long-term impact of the war on Kuwaiti domestic politics remains unclear. In some ways, the war unleashed political and social forces that have not yet run their course. Certainly, many of the thousands of Kuwaitis who served in the resistance against Iraqi occupation feel that they deserve a bigger role in postwar Kuwaiti domestic politics. Some of them resented the flight of upper-class Kuwaiti families when the Iraqis came and the return of those same families to privilege and power when the Iraqis left. A nascent Kuwaiti nationalism emerged from the war and made heroes of resistance fighters. How one acted during the crisis earned one political and cultural capital in Kuwait. In rebuilding Kuwait, the royal family could not be blind to the new political aspirations of those who had stayed to fight for Kuwaiti freedom. In the past, Kuwait had enjoyed elements of democracy absent in other Gulf Cooperation Council states. Whether or not the Gulf War will accelerate this democratization process may not be known fully for some years.

A TROUBLED BUT STABLE SAUDI ARABIA

Like Kuwait, Saudi Arabia rebounded from the war, but not without some turbulence. The bombing of American personnel in Dhahran, Saudi Arabia, in June 1996 shocked Americans and raised serious questions about the violent Persian Gulf: How stable was the royal family? Could it go down in flames, as did the once invincible Shah of Iran, thus undermining vital U.S. interests in the region?

Media reports lead one to believe so. In reality, the Saudis faced serious problems, but also possessed the ability to deal with them. It is important to understand the sources both of trouble and of stability in the kingdom to have a balanced view of the longer-run impact of the war.

What were the sources of Saudi problems? First, as strange as it sounds to Americans, to whom the words "Saudi" and "big bucks" go together, the Gulf War temporarily bankrupted the oil-rich royal family. The Saudis spent $55 billion in direct monies to support U.S.-led troops and much more indirectly. In the past, the royal family could use such monies to keep its domestic allies and adversaries happy. But with the money spigot temporarily dry, domestic discontent is on the rise. This is a relatively new problem for the royal family.

Second, the Gulf War accelerated social and political turmoil in the kingdom. In December 1990, King Fahd received a "Secular Petition" from forty-three religious and secular leaders, which was followed three months later by "The Religious Petition" from scores of top religious leaders. The religious forces expressed strong concern over royal family corruption, nepotism, and monopoly control over decision-making. Liberal democratic forces pushed for reforms as well, although more in terms of opening up the political system to a broader base of views.

While most political groups in the kingdom simply want the Saudi regime to reform itself, others want it overthrown. But in either case, most of these extremist elements do want the U.S. regional presence curtailed or elimi-nated, in part because the kingdom is the home to Islam's two holiest sites at Mecca and Medina, and the presence of U.S. troops is viewed by some as an affront to Islam.

Since 1990 a small but increasingly voluble and growing Islamic reform movement has developed, which has sought more influence over policy-making. In 1995 the Committee for the Defense of Legitimate Rights of Saudi Arabia, a group that came into being mainly after the Gulf War, organized a mass demonstration against the royal family at Buraydah. It was quite significant in defying the Fahd regime and further generating social ferment, and involved individuals who usually support the king and who come from his tribal and cultural hinterland. These are the people that King Fahd is most concerned about; some of them are elder tribal leaders with whom he regularly consorts as an equal among many (they call him simply "Fahd"), and with whom he needs to play careful politics in order to maintain his rule and credibility. While Fahd is concerned about bombings in the kingdom, he is far more concerned with his standing among these tribal leaders.

Third, the Gulf War heightened the American profile in the region. Saddam Hussein, while cut down to size, still possesses the strongest regional army. Without a strong U.S. military deterrent in the region, he would surely wreak revenge on the vulnerable Kuwaitis and Saudis. The Saudis know they need the United States against Saddam, but the Catch-22 is that the greater the U.S. role against Saddam, the more annoyed become anti-American groups in the kingdom and beyond. Until now, the Saudis have balanced these goals fairly well, but now they are starting to reconsider their options.

However, while the Saudis face these troubles, it is also important not to exaggerate their plight—at least, not yet. The Saudis have faced internal turmoil and political pressure in the past. In 1962, for instance, they were under domestic pressure to establish a Consultative Council of commoners appointed by the king, which could help advise him on various policies, and they promised to do so, a promise that would be fulfilled only after Desert Storm in 1992. In November 1979, the Grand Mosque in Mecca was seized by armed zealots, and demonstrations erupted in the predominantly Shiite eastern oil province that same year. Many observers thought it was the beginning of the end for the kingdom. In 1987 Iran reportedly instigated a riot at the Haj, the annual pilgrimage to Mecca that Muslims are supposed to undertake at least once in a lifetime. This nearly put the two states in physical confrontation. The Saudis bounced back from these domestic problems by appeasing opponents, playing tribal politics, and cooperating with other states where appropriate.

To be sure, the present Saudi domestic climate differs in kind from that of the past. This is largely because domestic instability has been compounded by unprecedented economic strains, a potential succession struggle that is likely to take place between 1996 and 2002, and a growing disparity between the beliefs of the ruling family and those of the educated middle class, especially the younger Saudis. Yet the royal family still sits above the world's largest proven oil reserves. While it faces short-term economic problems, it can count on these reserves down the road to balance its yearly budgets, and then some.

Moreover, King Fahd has taken effective steps to shore up his relations with the other tribal leaders from the Nejd, his historical base. Whether he can meet their varying demands for such things as a less corrupt, more

Islamic regime over the long run remains to be seen. For that matter, no one can really rule out the fall of the royal family in the next decade.

However, the longevity of the regime—enviable by almost any stand-ard—has invested it with a very good sense of self-preservation. Fahd also knows how to adapt to changing political realities.

Opponents and even lukewarm supporters of the Fahd regime also must consider that toppling it could leave them even less able to realize their goals. They could face internal chaos, be outmaneuvered by other forces filling the void, and lose present contacts with the regime. This creates a serious logic of vested interests that works against significant shifts in the status quo.

In the future, we are likely to see more bombings in the kingdom. The forces of extremism are afoot and are getting better organized. But regimes are not overthrown by terror alone. Thousands of foot soldiers are needed for revo-lution, or military officers must coordinate if the deed is to be done by coup. Yet, the military is controlled by the royal family, and serious foot soldiers of revolution do not yet exist in the kingdom. Saudi Arabia is not Iran.

For now, the royal family remains very much in control, despite appear-ances. That is of vital importance to the United States. Indeed, no matter how much it may want to do so in the coming years, Washington cannot easily replace the Saudis as allies in the Persian Gulf region.

THE MILITARY DIMENSION: LESSONS

Like any war, the Gulf War gave U.S. armed forces a testing ground for weapons and strategy, and to some extent it proved useful in this regard. At the same time, the war was unique, in the sense that U.S.-led forces had so much preparation time and overwhelming force, so that drawing any lessons needs to be done cautiously. With that in mind, several points command attention.

First, the role of electronic warfare (EW) tactics, systems, and operations cannot be overemphasized. They were critical to the success of the war. They were heavily integrated into all phases of the war, and literally made Iraq blind and deaf to the reality befalling it. The electronic warfare spectrum ranged from GPS (Global Positioning System), which allowed troops to identify their position in three dimensions, to the complex array of radar and communications jamming weapons. EW allowed the coalition to fight the war with a thinking, adaptive "brain," while Iraq was left to guess where U.S.-led forces might attack and where its own forces were. Without such a sophisticated level of electronic warfare, allied losses would have been far higher, accuracy far lower, and the war probably much longer.

The application of EW was part and parcel of what would be viewed as a high-tech revolution in the art of military statecraft. In the words of Defense Secretary Cheney, "The war demonstrated dramatically the new possibilities of what has been called the 'military-technological revolution in warfare.' "[12] In 1994 U.S. Secretary of Defense William Perry concurred, noting that in the Gulf War "a new class of military systems . . . gave American forces a revolutionary advance in military capability."[13]

The war also demonstrated clearly the benefits of air superiority. The bombing of Iraqi targets after the first week of the war would have been much more difficult without such supremacy. At the same time, such dominance would have been much more difficult under conditions where the odds were not so heavily stacked in favor of the allies. Air superiority gave the allies the ability to cut off Iraqi ground troops from their supplies, disrupt communications, and pin down large numbers of men. By gaining control over the air, the allies gained the initiative on the ground. Air power did not determine victory, but it did make it possible.

Third, as discussed in Chapter 2, the war did raise the question of the dominant role of air power in modern warfare. It is not as though the question had never been explored before. The United States has attempted to achieve air superiority in almost every war it has fought. But during the Gulf War, prominent military officials and academics seriously argued, for perhaps the first time, that air power alone could win the war, and that a ground war was unnecessary. The debate on this issue carried over into the postwar period and will be studied by U.S. policymakers, the nation's military colleges, and academic historians for years to come. While it is not fully clear what the Gulf War taught us on the issue of dominant air power, the very fact that it became such an important issue is relevant and important in and of itself.

The successful air campaign in the Gulf War had an effect on subsequent U.S. policy. It is no surprise that the United States and other NATO members engaged with confidence in air strikes on Serbian targets in 1995. U.S. military officers repeatedly stated their belief, as did President Clinton, that air strikes could impose severe punishment on the Serbs, despite the mountainous terrain of the former Yugoslavia, which, unlike the desert, complicated such air attacks. The inability of air strikes alone to check Serb aggression brought some sober reality to the limits of air power, but the Gulf War success still lingered in many policymaking minds, as military appropriations priorities attest.

The air campaign also highlighted the effectiveness of nonlethal weapons, smart bombs, and antiseptic tactical approaches which made the war seem clean and blood-free. While some observers saw "surgical war" as a future possibility, others cautioned that this was a mere chimera created by the media, perpetuated by the U.S. government, and reinforced by Iraq's inability to put up a serious fight. Some critics worried that the high-tech success in the Gulf War might make Americans more likely to seek military solutions to political problems, believing that technological know-how could win the day without loss of American or innocent lives.

Third, the now famous Patriot missile, which the United States deployed to Israel and used to protect its position in Saudi Arabia, seemed to do miracles during the war. The Patriot was such a sensation that people worldwide would marvel at its ability, captured on CNN and carried on nightly newscasts, to identify a Scud missile and fly in a trajectory that would ultimately shoot the Scud out of the sky. Poof! It was magic. The only problem was that it really was just magic. Indeed, the Patriot served the political-strategic goal of keeping Israel out of the war far better than it served any tactical goal. It missed its target almost all the time. Nonetheless, Iraq's Scud attacks focused great attention on antiballistic missile capability, and in the postwar period armies around the world sought to develop such capabilities. The Patriot itself was also improved so as to make it more likely to hit its target.

Fourth, the war proved the great effectiveness of unmanned aerial vehicles (UAVs). These planes helped determine enemy positions and identify fast-moving friendly troop movements. In the postwar period, the world's armies may very well invest upwards of $5 billion in UAVs, a fraction of what manned flight would cost. These low-cost, high-tech vehicles may be able in the future to stay aloft on spying missions for a day or even weeks, photographing hundreds of targets in detail and thereby perhaps saving thousands of lives with pinpoint targeting that hits military sites rather than civilian populations.[14]

Fifth, special forces played an important role during the war, in ways that did not receive much publicity. U.S. Navy SEALs, for instance, were instrumental not only in anti-mine warfare at sea and on land, but also in helping fool Iraq into believing that the allied ground attack would come from the Persian Gulf waters. British and U.S. special forces busted Scuds, and U.S. forces helped blind Iraq to the U.S. attack on January 16 by sabotaging Iraqi border surveillance posts. On the whole, the Gulf War boosted the status of special forces as an element of modern warfare, while at the same time elevating high technology. On its face, this seems ironic, because special forces were age-old, human-based capabilities, while high tech represented the opposite thrust, but special forces succeeded by using high-tech finding aids, detonation devices, and antipersonnel weapons.

Sixth, while cooperation among the U.S. armed forces was good, top-down intelligence sharing could have been better. As Admiral David Jeremiah, a key member of the Deputies Committee, put it:

The war required integrated information that could be distributed across thousands of miles and up and down chains of command, and we were not set up for that. We need to learn better how to integrate information for a single picture of a crisis situation. Schwarzkopf criticized the intelligence community for intelligence problems but it had more to do with how intelligence was integrated and disseminated.[15]

Finally, in the years following Desert Storm, the need for U.S. quick-reaction forces was made apparent, particularly when it appeared in October 1994 that Saddam might yet again invade parts of Kuwait. By 1996 the Air Force was seriously testing and refining a new, quick-response capability composed of several Airpower Expeditionary Forces (AEF) of thirty F-15s and F-16s, plus four KC-135 tankers, in Jordan. It had already established sites for such forces at Bahrain and Qatar, and the State Department was negotiating for two more sites. The idea is that with these sites in place, the AEF could be dispatched from stateside bases within twenty-four hours of receiving orders from the Pentagon. They could then join U.S. forces already in the region to impose punishing attacks on Iraq, a capability U.S. defense planners say was fairly absent when Iraq again threatened Kuwait in October 1994 and Washington was caught unprepared, but which was used in September 1996 when Saddam invaded Kurdistan.

While the AEF idea is not altogether novel, it does allow for U.S. forces to engage the Iraqi military more quickly and with more effect, and it also raises questions about the relative importance of aircraft carriers. While some observers argue that carriers perform a similar job at much higher expense, others may argue that the two forces can complement each other. Future conflicts will show whether the AEF spurs interservice rivalry or cooperation on and off the battlefield.

THE U.S. ARMED SERVICES AND THE U.S. PUBLIC

H. Norman Schwarzkopf, the emotional and sometimes overly frank general, had a goal going into the Gulf War, which really had been hatched after the Vietnam War. He wanted to help revitalize a demoralized and publicly humiliated military. Upon the shoulders of other generals and admirals who shared and advanced this goal since the Vietnam War, he helped realize that personal objective in the sands of a desert far from the tortuous jungles of Southeast Asia.

Vietnam had convinced him of the lack of leadership among the U.S. officer class, a class of individuals that to Schwarzkopf was out of touch with their men, too passive in battle, and too cynical to generate any serious motivation in their fighting forces. But it wasn't just Schwarzkopf who was affected by the Vietnam experience. Virtually all the major Army, Navy, and Air Force generals of Desert Storm were as well, including, of course, Colin Powell. The Gulf War was really a second chance for some of these Vietnam veterans to rid themselves of the horrid ghosts of that American tragedy. And they did so.

Desert Storm clearly raised the status of the U.S. armed forces, and stood in sharp contrast to the Vietnam experience. News reports from Vietnam of massive civilian suffering, of U.S. armed forces unable to meet their objectives, and of dissembling American politicians had left the American public doubtful of the effectiveness and moral fiber of its armed forces. The Gulf crisis, however, painted a contrasting portrait of the military; it was viewed as professional and efficient. Unlike in Vietnam, the military was very concerned with civilian casualties, and thus seemed to take and maintain the moral high ground, which is difficult to do in wartime.

Desert Storm troops came home to a hero's welcome, big flamboyant parades, and accolades from Congress, the president, and the media. They were not shunned, ridiculed, ignored, and forgotten.

The contrast with Vietnam could not have been more stark. Americans wanted to forget Vietnam and all that accompanied it, including to some extent the many soldiers who fought there. The Gulf War, by contrast, reminded many Americans of what was good about the United States, about diligence, resolve, bravery, and competence. It is no surprise, then, that Colin Powell, the then chairman of the Joint Chiefs of Staff, became so popular with the American people. He embodied values that had been lost in Vietnam but recaptured in the Gulf. Powell's successful leadership, dignity, and well-spoken manner, and the effective role of other African Americans in Desert Storm, such as Commander General Calvin Waller, also elevated the position of blacks in the military and won the military new stature as a vehicle of opportunity for African Americans. At all ranks, they contributed heavily to what would be one of the military's finest hours. Their joint contributions were most reflected in one man—Colin Powell—who had reached great heights in the collective American mind as a result of his role in the war.

The Desert Storm victory also put the military in better stead on Capitol Hill. Some military programs slated to be cut before the Gulf crisis were reinstated. Evidence strongly suggests that the Persian Gulf helped stave off the significant budget-cutting plans that were in motion in the post–Cold War era, certainly in the short term. Saddam Hussein was exactly what the doctor ordered for the Pentagon. Whether this made sense, given competing needs for such monies, was another question. On the whole, the military appeared to be back in vogue with the American people.

WOMEN IN THE GULF WAR

While the roles and numbers of women in the military have expanded significantly since 1970, the Gulf War brought this home in stark relief and paved the way for women to serve in more serious combat roles. Indeed, approximately 40,000 American women served in the war; 2 became POWs, and 11 were killed in action. Many women flew helicopters and reconnaissance aircraft during the war, but were restricted from other roles. In December 1991, however, the 1948 law preventing women from flying in combat was repealed. Thereafter, women took on new combat roles in the Gulf. By 1994 women were regularly serving on combat ships in the region. And when Iraqi forces attacked the Kurds in northern Iraq in early September 1996, the United States responded with missile strikes on Iraqi targets. On the destroyer USS *Laboon*, for the first time ever a woman targeted and fired Tomahawk missiles in a combat situation.[16] The Gulf War clearly marked a watershed in the evolution of efforts by women to play serious roles in the military. The experience they gained in the Gulf is likely to open even more doors in the future.

INTERSERVICE RIVALRY

The various elements of the American military were not united prior to the National Security Act of 1947, which created an integrated Department of Defense. After 1947, however, the integration of the services did not necessarily bring them together in the pursuit of U.S. national security. Quite the contrary—serious interservice rivalry was as common as significant interservice cooperation. In Vietnam, for instance, the U.S. armed forces ran many separate air wars and only occasionally engaged in joint air operations. The Army and the Air Force competed for influence and often had separate goals and limited communication in the field. The Gulf War represented a real change in this approach. "When I was flying from

Thailand into Laos," remembers one Air Force flier, "we hadn't the slightest idea what the Navy was doing. We just hoped we never ran into them." In Desert Storm, by contrast, Schwarzkopf's air commander, Air Force Lt. General Charles Horner, heavily integrated the air operations, which involved all the services. "Navy and Marine pilots worked in concert to destroy Iraq's integrated air defense system and command and control infrastructure." Each service knew what the other was doing. "Air Force F-15s and Navy F-14s helped the Marines provide combat air patrol and mine sweeps. Another Air Force–Marine–Navy amalgam jammed enemy radar installations and then attacked them with antiradiation missiles."[17] The air war in the Gulf operation succeeded in large part because the services coordinated, synchronized, and integrated their operations.

To be sure, the Gulf War was not without rivalry among the services. Elements of the Air Force, as previously noted in this book, believed the war could be won from the air, an assertion that angered many in the Army and Navy and that was rejected by both Powell and Schwarzkopf. The Gulf War showed an overall decrease in interservice rivalry as compared with past wars, however. Interservice rivalry is built into the American military system, but the success that came from interservice cooperation in the Gulf War and more rigorous congressional reviews of military spending might encourage more coordinated planning and operations among the military branches.

MEDIA

The electronic and print media were important during the Gulf War because they, and in particular CNN, provided information to a worldwide audience that may very well remember the Gulf War as the first day-by-day television war, and, much more important, to both the U.S.-led coalition and Iraq. Indeed, U.S. divisions in the field carried with them CNN satellite dishes and portable televisions for up-to-date reports, and both President Bush and Saddam Hussein—who got CNN in his bunker—were avid watchers. In the fog of war, CNN's human intelligence on the ground often got to the news story before the military did.

The role of CNN and other media also raised difficult questions about national security being jeopardized. In some circles, the reporting from Baghdad of CNN's Peter Arnett on the impact of the bombing civilians was even viewed as giving support to Iraq and putting checks on the allied coalition. His news analysis of the unfortunate U.S.-led attack on the famous "Baby Milk Factory," which the coalition believed was a biological facility, caused President Bush "great grief."[18] In front of a worldwide audience,

Arnett held up a packet with baby milk powder in it, indicating that the facility indeed was as innocuous as could be. Although Bush and others assailed Arnett for what they believed were actions benefiting Saddam, Arnett stuck to the story when later queried about it.

Arnett's coverage of the allied bombing of the Amiriya bunker, in which 300 civilians were killed, also embarrassed the military, which believed (based on hard evidence that top-level Iraqi officials had been seen entering and exiting it) that the bunker was a military post. As it turned out, this was true, but these officials were keeping their families in the bunker, at least at the time of the bombing. Arnett, however, painted the attack as reckless and immoral.

Schwarzkopf, for his part, viewed Arnett's coverage of the incident as a "deceitful" action that benefited the enemy.[19] Senate minority whip Alan Simpson, of Wyoming referred to Arnett as a "sympathizer" and as one of those journalists who lost the Vietnam War for us; other critics went even further to suggest that Arnett was a traitor. This was a big issue, because a worldwide audience was riveted to the television and clearly affected by CNN coverage of the war. The larger question that emerged was whether Arnett, representing the media, was simply doing his job or taking sides and creating his own news. Naturally, this was an issue about more than the Gulf War, and it ignited international debate.

At the domestic level, the role of the media in light of national security concerns also arose. By and large, during the war the military had the support of the public in checking the media. Later, Powell would recall the day when he knew the military had won the battle for public opinion. Watching *Saturday Night Live*, Powell was treated to a hilarious shot in which a mythical "Lieutenant Colonel Pierson" appears in desert camouflage at a press conference and is bombarded with highly sensitive questions such as, "Colonel, where would you say our forces are most vulnerable to attack? On what date are we going to start the ground attack?" To Powell, who was always concerned about communicating too much information to the enemy and who viewed the press as trying at times to overstep its bounds, the *Saturday Night Live* spoof rang somewhat true and was certainly funny.[20]

During the Gulf War the Pentagon controlled the media to the extent possible on grounds of national security. In the field, the media had expected to be able to roam the battlefields, as a small number of reporters had done in Vietnam, but in fact, the importance of secrecy made this unacceptable from the military's standpoint. Instead, the military developed an ad hoc system of combat pools controlled by the military in conjunction with the media, which were taken to particular areas for news coverage. While the American people believed they received good news coverage of the crisis, the media felt that the use of pools controlled by the Defense Department actually impeded their ability to report stories. Indeed, Secretary of Defense Richard Cheney received a letter from fifteen bureau chiefs of various major newspapers and television outlets lambasting the Pentagon's system of pools. Most of the 186 journalists in the combat pools, however, had far fewer complaints about the system.

The Pentagon used pools not only for purposes of secrecy but also because the Saudis were reluctant to have journalists running around looking for stories. Indeed, King Fahd did not want reporters in his country at all until he learned that Saddam Hussein watched CNN, and even then he didn't quite understand the concept.

In a *Times-Mirror* poll taken January 25–27, 1991, eight of ten Americans who responded gave the press a positive rating for its coverage of the war, and in subsequent polls virtually all respondents believed they had seen the best war coverage in history. Nonetheless, complaints by the media led to negotiations with the Pentagon that produced a new "Statement of Principles—News Coverage for Combat"; adopted in 1992, it gives journalists greater leeway in future wars, so long as they respect national security concerns.[21]

The Pentagon also controlled the news by providing information to the American people through carefully orchestrated daily "press briefings." These briefings made stars of Colin Powell and Norman Schwarzkopf, whose robust frame and confident demeanor filled the room. The briefings were carried on network and global news, thus achieving almost virtual domination of the public imagination regarding the nature, course, and success of the war. This was certainly not going to be Vietnam all over again. No left-leaning journalists were going to make the U.S. armed forces look like the bad guys. No Dan Rathers were going to earn their spurs by thrusting microphones into the mouths of writhing soldiers on their deathbeds. The military brass, all too familiar through firsthand experience with the media intrusion of Vietnam and the impact it had on the confused, torn American public, made efforts to produce an antiseptic treatment of this war.

The Gulf War and changes in the ability of the media to report news, changes that are of relatively recent origin, hit head-on in the Arabian desert in 1990–1991. The technical capacity to cover rapidly and with great precision critical global events for a global audience has made television a much more powerful force than ever before. U.S. policymakers and Iraqi leader Saddam Hussein used CNN not only for propaganda purposes, but also as a diplomatic back channel for sending messages, floating ideas, and communicating positions on issues.[22]

Clearly, policymakers were affected by the media. In one set of interviews of senior defense and foreign policy officials during the Gulf War, researchers found that 87 percent of the interview respondents could recall cases in which the media were their only source of information for decision-making, and 65 percent agreed that the media were frequently their fastest source of policymaking information. The media clearly helped shape their views of the crisis, particular actors in it, and the broader world environment in which it took place.[23]

CONCLUSION

As a military victory, the Gulf War is textbook material for the efficiency with which U.S.-led forces defeated the vaunted million-man Iraqi army. But the war was much more than that. Like the many wars that litter world history, the Gulf War painfully made us think. It introduced cultures to each other and raised questions about the media, the environment, human nature and progress, the future of world politics, the meaning of victory, the morality of war, and the power of the United States after the Cold War.

The Gulf War reversed the military aggression of a totalitarian state ruled by a brutal dictator who sought to punish a recalcitrant, vulnerable former ally while in the process of dominating the Persian Gulf and possibly world oil supplies. The U.S.-led international response, culminating in the massive use of military force, pushed Iraqi forces out of occupied Kuwait, severely crippled Iraq's military, and left Iraq under the influence of allied forces who imposed severe international sanctions. The nearly eight-month-long crisis produced innumerable consequences, but the few discussed in the following concluding paragraphs stand out.

By generating international cooperation against Iraq, the war raised the ironic prospect of a better world, a world in which cooperation could prevail over conflict, in which collective security could keep aggressors in check, and in which the United Nations could play an important role. Indeed, the UN role in generating sanctions against Iraq, in legitimizing war against Iraq, and in inspecting and destroying Iraq's weapons of mass destruction in the postwar period, greatly enhanced its credibility. Polling data worldwide showed that the role of the United Nations was respected and considered important. In 1991 the UN's popularity reached an all-time high with Americans. In June 1991, polls showed that 66 percent approved of the job being done by the United Nations; by November, that number jumped to 78 percent.[24]

At the same time, the war also raised serious questions about whether such a world was even possible. Was aggression an inevitable part of the human condition? Did Iraq's invasion simply represent one more war in a string of wars stretching back to time immemorial? Could states in the future once again stop an aggressor, under less favorable circumstances than Saddam gave the U.S.-led coalition? These questions deserved careful thought.

In global politics, the war elevated the power of the United States. The United States was clearly the only state that had the political and military ability to protect international security. The Persian Gulf War erased post-Vietnam doubts about U.S. resolve.

At home, George Bush, the military victor, was a political loser to a young, telegenic southerner from Arkansas, William Jefferson Clinton, who promised change in America. Domestic politics rather than international affairs determined the outcome of the 1992 presidential race. While Bush failed to recapture the White House, he did leave behind an America proud of its armed forces. Indeed, the Gulf War helped some Americans heal lingering wounds from the Vietnam debacle, elevated the reputation of the U.S. armed forces at home, and restored pride in American efficiency and ingenuity.

Halfway around the world, the war also produced significant effects. Saddam Hussein tried to paint the war as a victory, based on the notion that he and Iraq survived, while most of his adversaries—Bush, Thatcher, Prime Minister Shamir of Israel—were bygones. Perhaps in his own mind he was the victor. But in fact, Saddam devastated his country, its people, and its economy, and undermined its very future. By attacking Kuwait in 1990 and by pumping large amounts of money into military efforts instead of nation-building projects, Saddam set Iraq's development back years and perhaps decades, and damaged its ability to become a truly great, rich, influential Arab state in the Middle East and the world. What would Iraq have been had Saddam not been so war-prone? Is merely surviving a war a sign of victory when the costs are so high?

If the war damaged Iraq's future, it did the opposite for the Middle East as a whole. While a new world order was not in the offing, the Middle East did embark on a bumpy road to peace. Syria, to be sure, dragged its feet in the peace process. And the election of Israeli hard-liner Benjamin Netanyahu as prime minister in May 1996 made Israel less likely to compromise its security than it would have been under the more dovish Shimon Peres, who replaced his slain comrade, Prime Minister Yitzhak Rabin. However, the peace process had already reaped benefits. Israel and Jordan signed a historic peace accord; the PLO and Israel made serious headway as well; and Israel and Arab Gulf states improved their relations.

While the war itself was fundamentally about organized violence between massive armies, the crisis in general also produced clashes between various cultures, the media and the military, and individual personalities. The Saudis, for their part, were forced to interact very closely with more American troops than they thought they would ever see, and this brush of cultures produced some interesting results. Indeed, in one rare defiant act, Saudi women, representing the Westernized business class, drove cars to express their agenda of reform and were summarily punished for it. Subsequently, Saudi Islamic authorities made the prohibition on women driving, up to then a matter of custom, a formal legal violation. Change and repression were in the air at the same time.

King Fahd, for his part, was encouraged by Washington and some of his own citizens to open up the political system, to democratize, Saudi style; political opposition to the royal family increased after the war, spurred by more difficult postwar economic times and by the shock of Western intervention in the region. Bombing attacks by Islamic extremists in Riyadh in November 1995 and then in Dhahran in June 1996 sent chills down the royal family's spine.

How stable was the royal family? Should the U.S. military presence in the kingdom be reduced? Did democracy make sense for Saudi Arabia? for Kuwait? Was it right for the United States to encourage these states to adopt democratic ways? Were individual rights inalienable and God-given? Or were these just ideas that made sense in the West but not elsewhere? These issues were raised by the war and its aftermath, and will probably remain salient for many years as the Middle East tries to deal with modernity while at the same time preserving age-old traditions.

While Saudis were grappling with things Western, the international media were fighting their own fight with the U.S. military. Differences in goals and philosophy were surely at play. That is, the media seek to know as much as they can; the military seeks to divulge only what it wants. While the media wanted greater access to the war, the military wanted such access restricted.

The war generated much debate about the role of the media. How far should the media go in covering war? When do national security concerns override the public's right to know? Is it constitutional to restrict media coverage in wartime? To what extent should the media affect the course of events, rather than just report events? In the postwar period, the U.S. military and the media had a series of discussions aimed at sorting out these thorny questions, discussions which will continue and resurface the next time American forces find themselves at war.

The war, and the massive, unprecedented worldwide coverage it received, also produced a little-noticed effect. It educated people the world over on such diverse subjects as environmental warfare, the role of the United

Nations, the danger of chemical, biological, and nuclear warfare and usage, the stunning capabilities of modern warfare, and the potential for a better world. Indeed, the Gulf War was one of the few in which environmental warfare—in the form of oil spills and fires—was used blatantly and received great attention; it was the first war, moreover, in which UN collective security worked with all five permanent members of the Security Council present. Furthermore, rarely in the past had the potential use of nuclear, chemical, and biological warfare been so distinct; and never before had the world seen firsthand a combination of technologies—Stealth bombers, cruise missiles, laser-guided bombs, radar-seeking missiles—that allowed for strategic surprise and accuracy at such a high level.

Yes, in the process of being glued to their TV sets, people learned about their world, thus possibly making them more thoughtful citizens. That wars were bad needed no elaboration; that some were necessary seemed unfortunately clear; but that war could educate people all the while was an interesting philosophical, sociological, historical, and political issue.

To be sure, the full impact of the Persian Gulf War has not yet been felt. Like any major event, its effects will continue to spiral through history, producing additional consequences and perhaps significant developments. This is inevitable; it is the nature of politics, of time, of history. And we can only wait for time to tell us the rest of the tale that has unfolded in the sands of Arabia.

NOTES

1. Jeffrey Record, *Hollow Victory: A Contrary View of the Gulf War* (Washington, DC: Brassey's, 1993).

2. Roger Hilsman, *George Bush vs. Saddam Hussein: Military Success! Political Failure?* (Novato, CA: Lyford Books, 1992).

3. U.S. News and World Report, *Triumph Without Victory: The Unreported History of the Persian Gulf War* (New York: Times Books, 1992).

4. For King Fahd's view of postwar security, see *Saudi Arabia, The Monthly Newsletter of the Royal Embassy of Saudi Arabia* 9, no. 2: 1–2.

5. The text of the Damascus Declaration appears in *Journal of Palestine Studies* 20 (Summer 1991): 161–63.

6. On Kuwait's position, see *Cairo MENA*, in FBIS: NES, April 24, 1992, 13. Also see *Cairo MENA*, in FBIS: NES, May 7, 1992, 15–16.

7. Marlene Cimons, "Pentagon Takes Steps to Prevent Mysterious Gulf War Illness," *Los Angeles Times*, October 13, 1994, A6.

8. Saul Bloom, John M. Miller, James Warner, and Philippa Winkler, eds., *Hidden Casualties: Environmental, Health and Political Consequences of the Persian Gulf War* (Berkeley, CA: North Atlantic Books, 1994), 82.

9. James A. Baker III, *The Politics of Diplomacy: Revolution, War and Peace, 1989–1992* (New York: G. P. Putnam's Sons, 1995), 411.

10. Bloom et al., *Hidden Casualties*, 83.

11. Hunay Evliya, "Black Rain in Turkey: Possible Environmental Effects of the Gulf War," *Environmental Science and Technology* 26 (May 1992): 873–75.

12. Quoted in Eliot A. Cohen, "The Mystique of U.S. Air Power," *Foreign Affairs* 73 (January-February 1994): 110.

13. Quoted in ibid.

14. David A. Fulghum, "Gulf War Successes Push UAVs into Military Doctrine Forefront," *Aviation Week and Space Technology* (9 December 1991): 38–39.

15. Author's interview with Admiral David Jeremiah, Washington, DC, June 26, 1996.

16. For a good, brief piece on women, see Heather Wilson, "Women in Combat," *The National Interest* 32 (Summer 1993).

17. Katherine Boo, "How Congress Won the War in the Gulf," *Washington Monthly* (October 1991): 36.

18. George Bush, interview with Bernard Shaw, CNN, March 2, 1996.

19. Schwarzkopf interview with Sir David Frost, PBS, April 3, 1991.

20. Colin Powell, *My American Journey* (New York: Random House, 1995), 529.

21. This paragraph is based on Frank Aukofer and William P. Lawrence, *America's Team: The Odd Couple* (Nashville, TN: Freedom Forum First Amendment Center, 1995), 19–20.

22. See L. A. Friedland, "Democracy, Diversity, and Cable: The Case of CNN," unpublished manuscript, University of Wisconsin, cited in W. Lance Bennett and David L. Paletz, eds., *Taken by Storm: The Media, Public Opinion, and U.S. Foreign Policy in the Gulf War* (Chicago: University of Chicago Press, 1994), 12.

23. See Patrick O'Heffernan, "A Mutual Exploitation Model of Media Influence in U.S. Foreign Policy," in Bennett and Paletz, eds., *Taken by Storm*, esp. 234–38.

24. John O'Loughlin, Tom Mayer, and Edward S. Greenberg, *War and Its Consequences: Lessons from the Persian Gulf Conflict* (New York: HarperCollins, 1994), 188.

Biographies: The Personalities Behind the Crisis

Tariq Aziz (1936–   ), Foreign Minister of Iraq
Tariq Aziz, cultured in the ways of the West, proved to be an important bridge to the United States and Europe for the more insular Iraqi dictator. His rhetorical skills helped in Iraq's attempt to put a good face on its invasion of Kuwait and in its effort to argue its case globally. The assertive, cigar-smoking chief Iraqi diplomat would become one of Saddam's most loyal allies in the Baath party movement, and an unusual leader because he is a Christian Arab in a predominantly Sunni regime.

Aziz and Saddam seemed worlds apart in style and appearance. Saddam brandished a gun and rarely left Iraq, while Aziz cultivated a smooth, cosmopolitan manner and traveled widely. Of all things, Aziz majored in English literature at Baghdad University. Appearances aside, however, they shared common roots of poverty and a common vision about Iraq's place in the Arab world. Aziz was born in 1936, presumably in the northern Iraqi city of Tell Kaif, near Mosul, into a poor family. Like Saddam, the polished Aziz had a cold and calculating side. Although he wore fancy Western business suits on foreign trips, he often also sported military clothing and a pistol, and had no problem understanding Saddam's brutal policies on the home front.

Aziz rose from a Baath party organizer and propagandist to become editor of the party newspaper, *al-Thawra*, which in Arabic means "the revolution." After the fall of General Qassim in 1968, the Baath party seized power in Iraq, with Aziz as one of its leaders. As a master negotiator and a loyal Baathist familiar with Western history, mores, and culture, Aziz was a natural to become Iraqi foreign minister, and was named to that post in 1983. He played an important role in improving U.S.-Iraqi relations and in 1984 helped the two nations restore diplomatic relations, which had been severed in 1967 after the Arab-Israeli Six Day War. Aziz was also instrumental in gaining Iraq military and economic support during the Iran-Iraq war, in getting the United Nations to broker a peace agreement in that war in 1988, and in developing Iraqi relations with Western Europe.

During the Persian Gulf crisis, Aziz, widely viewed as Saddam's mouthpiece, represented Iraq in front of the world. Perhaps his most noted moment came when he met with U.S. Secretary of State James Baker in Geneva prior to the U.S.-led attack on Iraq. Displaying his loyalty to Saddam, Aziz refused to take a letter from George Bush to Saddam that Aziz viewed as insulting to his president.

Like Saddam, Aziz survived the war and continued in his role as Saddam's voice to the world. Appearing on a CNN special report in February 1996, Aziz emphasized just how well Iraq had rebounded from the war. He dedicated himself in the postwar period to the task of having UN economic sanctions on Iraq lifted.

James Baker (1930–), U.S. Secretary of State

James Baker, President Bush's close personal friend for over three decades, played a critical role in organizing the U.S.-led alliance during the Gulf crisis, guiding U.S. diplomacy at the United Nations, securing financial support for Operations Desert Shield and Storm, and convincing the American people of the importance of the U.S. stand against Iraq. Baker and Bush shared a similar view of the U.S. role in the world. They saw it as a great power, an enforcer of peace against aggression, and an engine for a move toward a better world. Against Saddam, Bush and Baker sought to make this vision come true.

In his memoirs, Baker notes that as a young Texas lawyer, he never intended to "become involved in either politics or diplomacy," but like Bush, he slowly became a beltway insider. Born April 28, 1930, into a prestigious family in Houston, Texas, Baker served in the Marine Corps as a second lieutenant. But politics soon became his life. He later served in several key governmental positions under three presidents. He was under secretary of commerce for Gerald Ford (1975–1976), White House chief of staff and treasury secretary for President Ronald Reagan (1985–1988), and White House chief of staff for Vice President George Bush (1981–1984), and also managed presidential campaigns for all three Republican presidents he served. His distinguished record, which included numerous honors ranging from the Presidential Medal of Freedom in 1991 to the Department of State's Distinguished Service Award, gave him unusual credibility as secretary of state.

Under Reagan, Bush and Baker became even closer friends and allies, commonly seeing eye to eye on trade and defense. They had a similar background as Texans with Ivy League credentials, Baker having gone to Princeton, where he was a classics scholar, and Bush to Yale. But while friendly and cooperative, Bush and Baker did not agree on all things during the Gulf crisis. Unlike Bush, Baker was much more optimistic that economic sanctions, backed by the threat of the use of force, would push Iraq to withdraw from Kuwait. Baker, known for being diplomatically astute, clearly favored the option of letting economic sanctions run their course, and questioned the faster move toward war.

In one of his more famous diplomatic encounters, he met with Iraq's foreign minister, Tariq Aziz, in Geneva on January 9, 1991, to attempt to avert war. Although the meeting accomplished nothing, it did make Baker wonder if Aziz, as if "plagued by some inner demon of national inferiority . . . felt compelled to insist that Iraq was not governed by fools."[1] Did Iraq have something to prove? In one tense moment, Baker, who was then over sixty years old, tried to make a joke that didn't go over very well. Aziz had just reminded Baker, as if to establish the credentials of Iraq's leadership, that the Iraqi regime has "been leading our country for twenty-two years. The average age of our leadership is in the fifties. I'm fifty-five, my President is fifty-four. I believe you would agree that this is a mature age." Baker, being clearly the elder, observed in jest, "That's quite young," to which Aziz, mistaking Baker's reply for an insult, took apparent umbrage.[2] The meeting with Aziz made it clear to Baker that war was likely.

After the war, Baker oversaw the effort to bring peace to the Middle East. Bush's election defeat left Baker a bit disillusioned with politics, and he assumed a key position in the law firm of Baker and Botts, which originated in Houston but also had offices in Washington, D.C. But his interest in politics did not wane altogether. Indeed, for a short period, he was prominently featured as a possible Republican presidential nominee and vice presidential running mate for Senator Robert Dole in 1996, and when Iraqi forces invaded Kurdistan in September 1996, Baker became a frequent media commentator.

Prince Bandar bin Sultan (1949–   ), Saudi Ambassador to the United States

Despite being familiar with Iraqi brutality, Prince Bandar was shocked by the invasion of Kuwait. The threat it posed to Saudi Arabia pushed him into action on the Washington front, where he proved to be a critical player in coordinating political and military affairs between the United States and Saudi Arabia after the invasion. While Bandar at first questioned U.S. resolve against Saddam, plans for the immense American rapid deployment convinced him of the strong, urgent need to cooperate with Washington against Saddam.

The gregarious Prince Bandar, born March 2, 1949, in Taif, Saudi Arabia, is Fahd's nephew, son of the Saudi defense minister, Prince Sultan, and a possible long-shot contender for the throne down the road. A King Bandar would likely be a good outcome for the United States, because he is more pro-American than Crown Prince Abdullah. Bandar supports U.S.-Saudi strategic ties, the U.S. military presence in the region, and the Middle East peace process.

Like many members of the royal family, Bandar earned his spurs in the armed forces. After having graduated from the British Royal Air Force College in Cromwell, England, in 1968, he was commissioned in the Royal Saudi Air Force as a second lieutenant. He was a fighter pilot for seventeen years, survived the crash of an F-5, and later learned how to fly the more sophisticated F-15.

Bandar, who sometimes acts as interpreter when King Fahd meets foreign officials, has a strong set of connections in Washington, where he is accepted in elite circles. Bandar became ambassador to the United States in 1983, after having been the Saudi defense attaché in Washington. He benefited from long-term friendships he cultivated with Bush, Powell, Cheney, Baker, and Scowcroft—the key U.S. policymakers during the Gulf crisis. Naturally, this access enhanced the Saudi royal family's reach and influence in Washington. When William Casey, Ronald Reagan's CIA director, sought to give the Iraqis sensitive satellite information regarding Iranian movements, Bandar made his Washington home available for the meeting.

Colin Powell recalls one of his meetings with Bandar during the Gulf crisis:

Later that day, President Bush and Scowcroft spoke with Prince Bandar, my old racquetball partner, now Saudi ambassador to the United States. . . . On his arrival at Cheney's office, Bandar played his usual Americanized, jaunty fighter-pilot role, drinking coffee from a foam cup and stirring it with a gold pen. Ordinarily we addressed each other in terms bordering on the obscene, with my printable favorites including "Bandar the Magnificent" and "Bandar, you Arab Gatsby" while he called me "Milord."[3]

In the postwar period, Bandar continued to play a critical role as a liaison between Washington and Saudi Arabia, often shuttling back and forth between the countries. Bandar has remained heavily involved in all facets of Saudi decision-making.

George Bush (1924–), U.S. President

George Bush, born on June 12, 1924, in Milton, Massachusetts, was the individual most responsible for drawing a "line in the sand" after Iraq invaded Kuwait, for organizing UN resolutions against Iraq, and for initiating Operation Desert Shield. After consulting with the military brass and his chief advisers in the "Gang of Eight," Bush chose to double U.S. troops in the region in November 1990, to give Saddam the ultimatum to withdraw from Kuwait by January 15, 1991, or face war, and to launch the air and ground wars against Iraq.

In contrast to some other American presidents, Bush was hardly a novice at foreign affairs. His interest in world politics in younger years was related to oil; he had made his fortune in the 1950s by running an oil-drilling firm in Texas.

At the official level, Bush had a stunning resumé that included U.S. ambassador to the UN (1971–1973), director of the CIA (1976–1977), and in particular vice president under President Ronald Reagan (1981–1989). His eight-year stint in the Reagan White House was critical because it familiarized him with the Middle East. From the 1979–1980 Iranian hostage crisis, the 1983 Beirut intervention, and the Iranian arms-for-hostages controversy, Bush learned that U.S. failures in the Middle East could produce embarrassing results that seriously hurt U.S. credibility abroad and created political problems at home.

When Bush was elected president, the expectation was that he would focus attention on his favorite subject, foreign affairs. While few political observers believed that Bush would approach the job with the "Cowboy, knock 'em dead" flair of President Reagan, they did expect a hands-on management style and personal immersion in the foreign policy-making process. Essentially, this is what they got. In 1990–1991, Bush brought his hard-working, energetic, focused personality to bear on an unsuspecting Saddam Hussein. Never before was Bush so consumed by one event.

Bush was once heard to say that presidents became great when they were tested by fire and proved their mettle. He sometimes would refer to Abraham Lincoln and the difficult times of the Civil War in thinking about what he must do in this crisis. While the Gulf War was not the Civil War, it did provide some fire for Bush. Reaching into his stock of memories about World War II, Adolf Hitler, territorial aggrandizement, and failed appeasement, Bush was predisposed to act strongly in 1990–1991. While the Gulf War was a spectacular military victory that elevated Bush's personal prestige and that of the United States, even he was puzzled at the fact that Saddam stayed in power and that the afterglow of the Desert Storm victory did not secure his own reelection in 1992.

Like Winston Churchill, who failed to hold on to political office after World War II despite his wartime heroics, Bush was unable to win reelection in 1992, despite his enormous popularity during the Gulf War, because the election turned on domestic and economic issues rather than foreign policy. After a disappointing defeat by Bill Clinton, Bush retired to Houston, Texas. Although he would thereafter occasionally dabble in politics, make trips to Kuwait and Saudi Arabia to receive awards for his valor during the war, and even address the Republican National Convention in August 1996, Bush would stay far from the limelight to which he was so accustomed most of his life.

Richard Cheney (1947–), U.S. Secretary of Defense

Secretary of Defense Richard Cheney was one of the most hawkish of Bush's small cadre of trusted advisers. Cheney, who was born January 30, 1941, in Lincoln, Nebraska, placed a high premium on American freedom of action against Saddam. He did not believe that the United States should allow the allies to affect American determination to undermine Saddam, and, unlike some of Bush's other advisers, cautioned the president against asking Congress for its consent in launching war against Iraq. The straightforward Cheney argued that economic sanctions were unlikely to remove Saddam from Kuwait, and that Iraq's military capabilities needed to be weakened. For Cheney, Saddam's withdrawal from Kuwait would have presented problems. Indeed, he argued that Saddam himself should be removed from power so as to safeguard U.S. long-term goals in the region. Secretary Cheney also played a critical role, along with General Scowcroft, in pushing for the allied flanking plan that ultimately proved so effective.

A former White House chief of staff under President Gerald Ford (1975–1977) and later a Republican congressman from Wyoming, Cheney was one of the most likable figures on the Washington scene. He effectively won allies on Capitol Hill and in the press, and by so doing gained much influence inside the Bush administration.

After having attended Yale for some time, Cheney earned his B.A. in 1965 from the University of Wyoming. He got his big break when, as a Ph.D. candidate at the University of Wisconsin along with his wife Lynne, he won a one-year fellowship that brought him to Capitol Hill. During that time, he met Donald Rumsfield, director of President Richard Nixon's Office of Economic Opportunity, who gave Cheney a job. When Ford named Rumsfield his chief of staff in 1974, he brought Cheney to the White House as his deputy.[4]

The ambitious Cheney made his way into politics as a hard-driving, diligent worker, but his health suffered as a consequence. Although he was still in his forties during the Gulf crisis, he had already had three heart attacks, having undergone a quadruple bypass operation just one year before Iraq's invasion. Saddam's action in Kuwait threatened to put Cheney under even more pressure. But he rose to the occasion and in ways almost relished the opportunity to set aggression back, and to make the national security process, which he believed had gotten mired at times in useless infighting and power plays during the Ford years,[5] work.

After the Gulf War, Cheney returned to Dallas, Texas, to pursue private business interests as president of Halliburton Corporation. While he occasionally consented to an interview about the Gulf War, and while Gulf War books piled up on his desk gathering dust, he remained outside the public arena until 1996. Like James Baker, he surfaced briefly as a potential vice presidential running mate for Republican nominee Robert Dole in August 1996.

Javier Pérez de Cuéllar (1920–), Secretary-General of the United Nations

In the course of his career, Javier Pérez de Cuéllar has been decorated by some twenty-five countries for promoting peace and cooperation. Born in Lima, Peru, on January 19, 1920, de Cuéllar attended Catholic schools and then earned a law degree from the Catholic University in Lima. He joined the Peruvian Ministry of Foreign Affairs in 1940 and the diplomatic service in 1944, serving subsequently as secretary at the Peruvian embassies in France, the United Kingdom, Bolivia, and Brazil, and as counsellor and minister counsellor at the embassy in Brazil. He has been the Peruvian ambassador to Switzerland, the Soviet Union, Poland, and Venezuela. De Cuéllar has served as professor of international law at Peru's Academia Diplomatica and professor of international relations at Peru's Academia de Guerra Aérea. He is the author of *Manual de Derecho Diplomático* [Manual of Diplomatic Law] (1964).[6]

After holding a number of diplomatic posts, he was appointed permanent representative of Peru to the United Nations in 1971, and he led his country's delegation to all sessions of the Assembly from then until 1975. In 1979 he was appointed United Nations Under Secretary General for Special Political Affairs. From April 1981, while still holding this post, he acted as the Secretary-General's personal representative regarding the Soviet invasion of Afghanistan. De Cuéllar assumed office as Secretary-General of the United Nations on January 1, 1982.

When Iraq invaded Kuwait, this placed the UN and de Cuéllar in a difficult position. The UN had to respond strongly to naked aggression by one of its member states. Yet de Cuéllar wanted to avoid a major war in one of the world's most sensitive regions. Thus, as Secretary-General of the UN, his role during the crisis was to condemn and contain Iraq, while also trying to reach a peaceful resolution to the crisis.

James Baker would later write that he had heard that "de Cuéllar was miffed that the U.N. bureaucracy wasn't calling the shots on the Gulf crisis." But from Baker's perspective and that of the United States, the Gulf crisis from the outset "had been our show; we had assembled the coalition, and the President had sent America's sons and daughters into the Gulf."[7]

In the final analysis, de Cuéllar had far less to do with the nature and direction of the crisis than President George Bush. While the UN responded positively to American initiatives against Iraq, the anti-Iraq coalition was essentially an American undertaking. UN resolutions against Iraq were organized by the United States, and the nature of discourse at the UN was shaped by U.S. representatives. Even so, de Cuéllar did not agree with all U.S. positions. He would have pursued economic sanctions against Iraq longer than Bush wanted to do.

After the war, de Cuéllar oversaw the United Nations' effort to force Iraqi compliance with UN resolutions, especially 687. In 1992 he stepped down as Secretary-General, and Boutros Boutros-Ghali of Egypt assumed the post.

King Fahd (1922–), Saudi Monarch

Of all actors in the Middle East other than Saddam Hussein, King Fahd, born in 1922, was most critical to the outcome of the Gulf crisis. After Iraq invaded Kuwait, Fahd at first hesitated to give U.S. forces the right of entry into Saudi Arabia. But he became quickly convinced by U.S. officials that Saddam presented a serious threat to the kingdom, and therefore gave the critical go-ahead.

King Fahd is the eleventh of forty-three sons of Abdul Aziz Ibn Saud, who founded the far-reaching desert kingdom of Saudi Arabia through brute force and outright conquest. Fahd saw the kingdom evolve from a backward, irrelevant desert outpost to a modern, rich nation influential in world politics. This fast-paced modernization process has brought great rewards but also social and political turbulence to its traditional society.

While Fahd has witnessed, and even encouraged, so much change, he also has tried to preserve Bedouin customs and Islamic culture amid this great transformation. He has done so in his own life, in which he often departs for the desert to pray, and in the life of his nation, which prides itself on being the leader of the Muslim world.

Fahd, who played a critical role in shaping Saudi foreign policy in the 1970s and who had earlier served as interior minister (1962–1975), ascended the throne in 1982 at the age of sixty, after the death of his half brother, King Khalid. This was a difficult time for the kingdom because the Iran-Iraq war was raging and the Iranian revolution was still a domestic-level threat to Saudi stability.

The invasion of Kuwait crashed into Fahd's world like a meteorite. Not only was his rich, serene kingdom imperiled by Iraq, its Islamic ways were also endangered by the influx of hundreds of thousands of U.S.-led soldiers. The kingdom had never before seen such a thing, and the mere presence of these forces caused some political and social dislocation. After the Gulf War, Saudi Arabia would be rocked by two terrorist bombs (one of which killed nineteen U.S. soldiers at Dhahran in July 1996) and increased challenges to royal family control. The ailing Fahd himself would temporarily turn over power to his half brother, Crown Prince Abdullah.

King Hussein ibn Talal (1935–), Jordanian Monarch

King Hussein, born in 1935 in Amman, Jordan, has played an important role in the Middle East for decades. He has ruled Jordan since 1953, succeeding his father, who was declared mentally ill that year, and his grandfather, King Abdullah, who was killed by a Palestinian assassin in 1951. At times, he has sided with the forces of moderation, pushing for peace and reconciliation with Israel; at other junctures, he has supported aggressive actors such as Saddam Hussein. Depending on the international and domestic climate, his policies have varied from bellicose to extremely accommodating. But on the whole, the king, who was educated in England, has been viewed as a moderate and reasonable force in the region.

When Iraq invaded Kuwait, the king was in a difficult spot. On the one hand, Saddam was popular in Jordan, Iraq provided Jordan with cheap oil, Iraq and Jordan had historical ties as part of the Hashemite family, and Iraq was next door to Jordan, thus posing a potential military threat. On the other hand, Saddam had clearly gone too far in Kuwait, was facing a formidable U.S.-led coalition, and did not appear very inclined to withdraw from Kuwait peacefully.

The king, in the final analysis, chose to side with Saddam. Perhaps this was because he knew that his population, 70 percent of which was Palestinian, tilted toward Iraq; perhaps it also had to do with the resentment in the Arab world of the rich Kuwaitis, who often came to Amman for a good time, flaunting their riches.

Because of Jordan's support of Iraq, Saudi Arabia and Kuwait cut their financial support to Jordan and distanced themselves from King Hussein, as did the United States. In the postwar period, however, King Hussein's critical participation in the peace process put his relations with Washington back on track. Moreover, the king moved away from supporting Saddam and even allowed Iraqi defectors to seek refuge in Amman for several months.

Saddam Hussein (1937–   ), Iraqi President

Saddam Hussein, who was born in 1937 in a small village near Takrit, Iraq, became a household name after Iraq invaded Kuwait. Prior to his rise to power, Saddam was vice chairman of the Revolutionary Command Council. He was also effectively the head of the Baath party, the ideological group that argued for Arab unity and pride and promoted socialism. Strangely enough, Saddam helped bring about a détente with Iran in 1975, only to launch a war against that nation five years later. Saddam also tried to move Iraq toward an independent course and further away from its alliance with Moscow.

Shortly after becoming president in 1979, through power politics rather than by election, Saddam arranged to have himself named lieutenant general, and later promoted himself to field marshal. Invested with this grand title, he then sought to dominate Arab world politics through his Baathist pan-Arab charter. He spearheaded attempts to isolate Egypt for its peace with Israel, to decrease U.S. influence in the region, and to keep Shiite Iran in check. He focused ruthless attention on getting big money with which to rebuild Iraq. At a summit of Arab leaders in February 1989, Saddam blatantly asserted to fellow Arab leaders: "I need $30 billion in fresh money.

Go and tell them in Saudi Arabia and the Gulf that if they don't give it to me, I will know how to take it."[8] Saddam, who rarely minced words, often carried out his open threats.

In Saddam's Iraq, torture and terror became instruments of state policy. They were used to breed mistrust, inspire fear, and divide and conquer. They were intended to break the very spirit of dissent and to suppress any creative, nonconventional energies that might break Saddam's self-created world of unreality. Citizens were subordinated to the state; the state was subordinated to Saddam; and anyone even suspected of challenging the hierarchy could suffer a horrid fate.

In September 1980, Iraq launched an attack on revolutionary Iran which would ignite the bloody eight-year-long Iran-Iraq war and, as discussed in Chapter 1, set the stage for the Iraqi invasion of Kuwait in 1990. The war did not accomplish much, other than to predispose Iraq to invade Kuwait, thus triggering the Persian Gulf War. The Gulf War, a military and economic disaster for Iraq, could have been avoided by Saddam. His strategy, however, may have been to impose casualties on U.S. troops, thus pushing the United States, whose credibility he doubted, to withdraw from the Gulf. But the U.S.-led coalition was so formidable that Iraq's forces could not accomplish this goal. Furthermore, Saddam clearly underestimated just how determined George Bush was to reverse his aggression against Kuwait.

Iraq remained in a political, economic, and military box after the war. But the irrepressible Saddam Hussein not only retained power, unlike many of his Desert Storm adversaries, but lived to suppress uprisings against him, purge his opponents, and somewhat reconstitute his army. Saddam continued to threaten Kuwait verbally in the following years and even sent 80,000 troops toward Kuwait again in October 1994, posing a significant invasion threat. By May 1996, the United Nations allowed Iraq to sell oil for purposes of buying food and medicine for its people, but the broader economic embargo remained in place. And when Iraqi forces invaded Kurdistan in September 1996, thus violating UN resolutions, Saddam lost this right as well.

François Mitterrand (1916–1996), President of France

A veteran politician and a man highly knowledgeable in foreign affairs, Mitterrand understood the implications of Iraq's invasion of Kuwait. However, he did not take the same line as George Bush toward Saddam. While France did send 16,000 soldiers to support Desert Shield forces, Mitterrand was reluctant to go to war against Saddam. The French were Iraq's number two arms supplier after the Soviets, consistently defended Iraq, underscored its progressive nature, and took a strong pro-Arab line against Israel. By the 1970s, the French were heavily involved in developing Iraq's military capability, including the conventional and nuclear dimensions. In 1984 alone, nearly half of France's total arms exports went to Iraq. France also helped Iraq build its $275 million Osirak nuclear reactor near Tuwaitha, against the objections of the United States.

During the Gulf crisis, Mitterrand consistently argued for allowing Saddam a face-saving retreat from Kuwait and even backed Saddam's wish to link the Palestinian issue to Iraqi withdrawal. Bush viewed this as rewarding Saddam's aggression and rejected it, calling for complete and unconditional withdrawal as specified in UN resolutions. At first, France declined to join the air attack, arguing that it needed to husband its planes and bombs for the ground war. But more likely than not, France wanted to be in a position to resume its lucrative business as usual with Iraq after the war, which included significant arms sales and cheaper Iraqi oil.

Mitterrand, who served two terms (fourteen years) as president of France and who became only the second Socialist president in French history in 1981, was born October 26, 1916, in Jarnac at a time of great turmoil in world politics. Prior to World War II, Mitterrand obtained an undergraduate degree in literature and then a law degree.

Like George Bush and others of that generation, Mitterrand was greatly affected by World War II. Mitterrand was deported to Germany as a prisoner of war in 1940, only to escape back to France later that year. While it is not exactly clear what role he played upon returning to France, the official position is that he joined the resistance to the Nazis.

Mitterrand's career took off at a young age. By thirty, he was a government minister, and during his career held innumerable portfolios, including foreign relations, interior, and justice. Although he would face severe defeats in his run for president in 1965 against General Charles de Gaulle, and in 1974 against Valéry Giscard d'Estaing, Mitterand proved a resilient politician once he gained the presidency in 1981.

Mitterrand, who died in 1996, was rocked by a scandal in August 1994 that connected him with Nazi collaborators in the French government prior to the fall of France in 1940. But he will be most remembered for his strong commitment to European union and dogged efforts to promote close Franco-German relations. Indeed, no one could have imagined in 1940 that an imprisoned Mitterrand would half a century later witness German tanks parading down France's Champs-Elysées on Bastille Day as part of a Eurocorps battalion.

General Colin Powell (1937–   ), Chairman of the U.S. Joint Chiefs of Staff

During Desert Storm, Powell wanted to make sure that the U.S.-led attack would be massive and full-scale even into Iraqi territory itself, in an effort to "clean their clocks." In one of his more famous lines, he said that the U.S.-led coalition would isolate Iraq's army and then "kill it." Powell believed that the United States should not involve itself in a foreign war without the support of the American people. This explains why he urged the president to obtain the consent of Congress before launching the war. Powell also was concerned about Iraqi civilian casualties and wanted to avoid the impression that the United States eagerly sought to kill Iraqi soldiers. This may explain why he counseled against continuing the war on the "Highway of Death" and against Saddam's vaunted Republican Guard.

Colin Powell was the youngest chairman of the Joint Chiefs of Staff in American history when he accepted the appointment at age fifty-three in 1989, and the first African American to hold the position. In what could only be viewed as a Horatio Alger story, Powell, who was born to poor Jamaican immigrant parents in Harlem in 1937, and who attended the City University of New York, became one of the most powerful and visible blacks in America during the 1980s and 1990s, and a dominant voice for the U.S. military establishment.

In college, his main interest was the Reserve Officers Training Corps (ROTC), where he learned to love military strategy and various weapons, and where he was introduced to the "backbone of the military."[9] Powell would prove his mettle quickly in his college years. At summer ROTC training, he was named "Best Cadet, Company D." While Powell excelled in training, he was hardened in the jungle firefights of Vietnam. There he faced death and destruction, but more important for his own view of the war and the military, the emotionally draining picture of wasted lives as a result of bureaucratic and strategic incompetence. Armed with an M.B.A. and strengthened by his Vietnam experience, Powell was chosen as a White House fellow in the Office of Management and Budget (1972–1973). There he made his first major contacts with such future prominent political insiders and defense experts as Caspar Weinberger and especially Frank Carlucci, a mentor of sorts, both of whom later became secretaries of defense.

Under President Ronald Reagan, Powell served both Caspar Weinberger, the defense secretary, and Frank Carlucci, the national security adviser. Powell's tact and obvious intelligence, along with his knowledge of military strategy, won the confidence of his superiors. He became national security adviser in 1987, after the Iran-Contra scandal rocked the Reagan administration. Powell's impeccable integrity helped the Reagan administration survive the scandal. These roles during the 1980s familiarized him with the Persian Gulf, where U.S. forces were called on in 1987 to reflag Kuwaiti tankers that had been under attack by Iran.

As a four-star general, Powell also brought significant military experience and credibility to his official task. Unlike Cheney, Powell was a career military man and a product of the military environment. Indeed, he later admitted in his autobiography that he felt most comfortable in the military, with its chains of command and accountability. While he had his own views of foreign affairs, he believed that the military was an arm of American policy. He served at the president's behest, and did not try to push too hard his own views that economic sanctions against Iraq should be given a chance for a longer period of time. He argued within the administration and with military men such as General Norman Schwarzkopf about policy, but in the end the dutiful Powell deferred to the president.

Once Bush asserted that an offensive option was needed against Saddam, Powell argued that the American attack needed to be massive, quick, and decisive. Powell, who was wounded near the Laotian border in 1963 when he stepped into a pungi-stick trap, viewed the Gulf crisis with Vietnam in mind, although he would hasten to add that his strategy during the Gulf War had less to do with Vietnam per se than with three decades of experience.[10] In Vietnam, Powell thought Americans failed because they did not use their vast resources to hit the enemy hard with massive, quick, and decisive attacks, and because the policy goals of the war remained unclear. The loss in Vietnam hurt American prestige generally, and tarnished the military's reputation particularly. The Gulf War would be different.

Powell emerged from the war with popularity levels so high that he was widely touted as a serious contender for president in 1996, either as a Democrat or a Republican. His popularity increased even more after a successful national tour for his book, *My American Journey*, which chronicled his rise to power. While Powell finally cast his lot as a Republican, he decided to run neither for president nor as a vice presidential candidate on the ticket with Republican nominee Robert Dole. However, he continued to make speeches around the country, supported other Republicans politically, and held out the prospect for higher office in the future.

Sheikh Jaber al-Ahmad al-Sabah (1926–   ), Emir of Kuwait

After the invasion of Kuwait, Iraq installed a provisional government in Kuwait of nine hand-picked military officers whose origin is not altogether clear; this puppet regime replaced the ruling al-Sabah family. Sheikh Jaber al-Ahmad al-Sabah, emir of Kuwait, fled to Saudi Arabia to save his own life. From Saudi Arabia, the emir sought to generate support for his country behind the scenes and to protect his family's financial resources from Saddam. In addition, he obtained American support for the restoration of his position in Kuwait and made the necessary arrangements to support the American military deployment to the region.

The emir of Kuwait, born June 29, 1926, in Kuwait City, heads the al-Sabah royal family, which had established an autonomous sheikdom in Kuwait in 1756. The Emir is a shy man who prefers anonymity to notoriety. Indeed, during the Gulf War one scarcely heard a word from him, despite his leadership position. The emir, who has thirteen wives, assumed the throne on December 31, 1977, and has struggled to protect Kuwaiti security through the turbulent Iranian revolution, the Iran-Iraq war, and the Iraqi invasion of Kuwait.

Kuwait has had long-standing differences with Iraq over the latter's claims to Kuwaiti territory, and in the past the emir, who had a long track record of political appointments in Kuwait before assuming leadership in 1977, has negotiated on Kuwait's behalf in those disputes.

Lying at the heart of rivalry between Iran and Iraq and between Iraq and Saudi Arabia, Kuwait was not particularly secure prior to Iraq's invasion in 1990. Not only had Iraq threatened it for decades at various intervals, but the Iranian revolution also put the small oil sheikdom in a precarious position. Iran, which had little respect for the Kuwaiti monarchy and resented outright Kuwait's support of Iraq during the Iran-Iraq war, even bombed Kuwait in the mid-1980s. While facing serious external threats, the emir also had to deal with difficult domestic issues.

The emir flirted with aspects of democracy by reviving the national assembly (suspended since 1976) in 1980, but he dissolved the parliament again in 1986 because it was feared that it had become a tool of pan-Arab politics and internal subterfuge. The notion of democracy in Kuwait, in any event, was a limited one; women did not vote, and only certain men had that privilege.

Kuwait's lack of democratic tradition led some Americans, among them Patrick Buchanan, later a presidential candidate, to argue that saving the emir was not worth one American life. But clearly the issue of the Gulf War was much more complicated than that. The war was not about saving the emir. It was about stopping Iraq and protecting world oil supplies.

The allied success in Desert Storm restored the emir to power in Kuwait. In the postwar period, he oversaw the successful rebuilding of Kuwait and

sought to ensure that the West would remain vigilant against a still dangerous Iraq.

General H. Norman Schwarzkopf (1934–   ), Commander, U.S. Central Command

Schwarzkopf, the husky and sometimes exceedingly frank military hero
of the Gulf War, effectively commanded U.S.-led forces in the Gulf. The
military success of Desert Storm made Schwarzkopf an American hero,
despite his initial reluctance to use force against Iraq. With his witty
briefings to the press and clear sense of command, Schwarzkopf made the
war seem almost surgical and "clean." Smart bombs and light American
casualties were the mantra. The general emerged from the war as the
embodiment of what was good about the United States, the walking, talking
reminder that the U.S. armed forces were a competent and proud organization, and that Vietnam may have just been an aberration in history.

Schwarzkopf was born on August 22, 1934, in the small town of Pen-
nington, New Jersey. He came from a military family and entered the United
States Military Academy in 1952. Like Powell, Schwarzkopf served in
Vietnam, and this proved to be a defining experience in his career. In
Vietnam, he advised the South Vietnamese paratroopers in his first tour of
duty in 1965. By his second tour in 1969, the war had gone awry, and
Schwarzkopf, who commanded a battalion and at one point led a patrol from
the middle of a minefield, narrowly escaping death, began to doubt the
American leadership and became frustrated with the war effort. Perhaps as
the quintessential example of the confusion and poor planning in Vietnam
which so angered him, Schwarzkopf himself was bombed by U.S. Air Force
B-52s in an interservice fiasco.

After Vietnam, Schwarzkopf served in the mechanized infantry, attended
the Army War College, and served in the Pacific and on the Army staff at
the Pentagon. He also was the top Army officer during the 1983 invasion of
Grenada by U.S. forces. After serving as the Army's Deputy Chief of Staff
for Operations and Plans in Washington, D.C., Schwarzkopf became, on
November 23, 1988, the chief of U.S. Central Command (USCENTCOM),
based in Florida. USCENTCOM was responsible for protecting U.S. security interests in the Persian Gulf and for providing rapid deployment forces
for quick entry into crisis spots in the region.

Schwarzkopf had traveled widely in the Middle East and was somewhat
familiar with the region and its ways. Indeed, this education had started at
the age of twelve, when Schwarzkopf lived in Iran. Between 1942 and 1946,

his father was charged with creating and training an effective police force for the government of Iran, and the experience gave the younger Schwarzkopf important exposure to foreign cultures. Schwarzkopf's experience in the region likely helps explain why he encouraged a cautious approach in using force against Iraq in 1991. Like regional specialists, he saw the potential downside of such a war. His reservations and fears, however, would not be confirmed in actual warfare, where U.S. casualties were surprisingly low. Although he had endorsed a go-slow approach toward Iraq, Schwarzkopf accepted President Bush's orders for military preparations and backed the president fully once war came.

Schwarzkopf, an emotional and trusting commander, was known affectionately by his soldiers as "the Bear." He combined a certain sensitivity with a more volatile side. Powell, his military colleague, would even describe him as an "active volcano" with whom he would have occasional "transoceanic shouting matches . . . full of barracks profanity."[11] Interestingly, Powell gained respect for Schwarzkopf because he understood the "roots of his rages," which often had to do with feeling that his needs were not understood in Washington.[12] Again, such a concern may have had at its base lingering memories of Vietnam, where Schwarzkopf saw a serious disconnection between Washington and the reality on the ground.

Descended from German immigrants who came to the United States in the nineteenth century seeking a better life, Schwarzkopf believed in hard work and dedication as a recipe for success. He brought these solid values to the fore in his role during the Gulf War. After the war, Schwarzkopf retired to Florida, maintaining, however, an office in New York. While he generally kept out of the public eye, he did serve as a regular guest on NBC, and in September 1992 joined the Nature Conservancy's national board of governors.

NOTES

1. James A. Baker III, *The Politics of Diplomacy: Revolution, War and Peace, 1989–1992* (New York: G. P. Putnam's Sons, 1995), 360.

2. Ibid.

3. Colin Powell, *My American Journey* (New York: Random House, 1995), 465.

4. Bob Woodward, *The Commanders* (New York: Simon and Schuster, 1991), 35.

5. Ibid., 31.

6. "Javier Perez de Cuellar, United Nations Secretary-General," Biographical Note, Press Release, United Nations Department of Public Information, News Coverage Service, New York, January 17, 1990.

7. Baker, *Politics of Diplomacy*, 325.

8. Cited in Judith Miller and Laurie Mylroie, *Saddam Hussein and the Crisis in the Gulf* (New York: Random House, 1990), 12.

9. Powell, *My American Journey*, 32.

10. Author's interview with General Colin Powell, Chairman, Joint Chiefs of Staff, Alexandria, VA, May 30, 1996.

11. Powell, *My American Journey*, 492.

12. Ibid.

Primary Documents of the Crisis

ECONOMIC SANCTIONS

In the immediate aftermath of Iraq's invasion, the United Nations Security Council, led by the United States, passed a series of sanctions against Iraq. Resolution 660, which appears below, was the first, and with the exception of a Yemeni abstention, unanimously condemned the invasion and demanded that Iraq "withdraw immediately and unconditionally all its forces to the positions in which they were located on 1 August 1990." This set the tone for the resolutions that followed.

The next critical UN action imposed economic sanctions on Iraq (except for humanitarian or medical purposes) under Resolution 661, adopted on August 6, 1990. The vote was 13–0 with two abstentions (Cuba and Yemen). At first, it was unclear whether all countries would abide by the resolution, because it imposed severe economic hardships on some states, such as Brazil, Jordan, and Turkey, that depended on Iraqi oil and/or trade. Over time, however, almost all countries abided by the resolution. UN Resolutions 660 and 661 follow.

Document 1
UN SECURITY COUNCIL RESOLUTION 660

The Security Council,

Alarmed by the invasion of Kuwait on 2 August 1990 by the military forces of Iraq,

Determining that there exists a breach of international peace and security as regards the Iraqi invasion of Kuwait,

Acting under the Articles 39 and 40 of the Charter of the United Nations,

1. *Condemns* the Iraqi invasion of Kuwait;

2. *Demands* that Iraq withdraw immediately and unconditionally all its forces to the positions in which they were located on 1 August 1990;

3. *Calls upon* Iraq and Kuwait to begin immediately intensive negotiations for the resolution of their differences and supports all efforts in this regard, and especially those of the League of Arab States;

4. *Decides* to meet again as necessary to consider further steps to ensure compliance with the present resolution.

Source: The Middle East, 7th ed. (Washington, DC: Congressional Quarterly, Inc., 1991), 369.

Document 2
UN SECURITY COUNCIL RESOLUTION 661

The Security Council,

Reaffirming its resolution 660 (1990) of 2 August 1990,

Deeply concerned that the resolution has not been implemented and that the invasion of Iraq by Kuwait continues with further loss of human life and material destruction,

Determined to bring the invasion and occupation of Kuwait by Iraq to an end and to restore the sovereignty, independence and territorial integrity of Kuwait,

Noting that the legitimate Government of Kuwait has expressed its readiness to comply with resolution 660 (1990),

Mindful of its responsibilities under the Charter of the United Nations for the maintenance of international peace and security,

Affirming the inherent right of individual or collective self-defence, in response to the armed attack by Iraq against Kuwait, in accordance with Article 51 of the Charter,

Acting under Chapter VII of the Charter of the United Nations,

1. *Determines* that Iraq so far has failed to comply with paragraph 2 of resolution 660 (1990) and has usurped the authority of the legitimate Government of Kuwait;

2. *Decides*, as a consequence, to take the following measures to secure compliance of Iraq with paragraph 2 of resolution 660 (1990) and to restore the authority of the legitimate Government of Kuwait;

3. *Decides* that all States shall prevent:

(a) The import into their territories of all commodities and products originating in Iraq or Kuwait exported therefrom after the date of the present resolution;

(b) Any activities by their nationals or in their territories which would promote or are calculated to promote the export or trans-shipment of any commodities or products from Iraq or Kuwait; and any dealings by their nationals or their flag vessels or in their territories in any commodities or products originating in Iraq or Kuwait and exported therefrom after the date of the present resolution, including in particular any transfer of funds to Iraq or Kuwait for the purposes of such activities or dealings;

(c) The sale or supply by their nationals or from their territories or using their flag vessels of any commodities or products, including weapons or any other military equipment, whether or not originating in their territories but not including supplies intended strictly for medical purposes, and, in humanitarian circumstances, foodstuffs, to any person or body in Iraq or Kuwait or to any person or body for the purposes of any business carried on in or operated from Iraq or Kuwait, and any activities by their nationals or in their territories which promote or are calculated to promote such sale or supply of such commodities or products;

4. *Decides* that all States shall not make available to the Government of Iraq or to any commercial, industrial or public utility undertaking in Iraq or Kuwait, any funds or any other financial or economic resources and shall prevent their nationals and any persons within their territories from removing from their territories or otherwise making available to that Government or to any such undertaking any such funds or resources and from remitting any other funds to persons or bodies within Iraq or Kuwait, except payments exclusively for strictly medical or humanitarian purposes and, in humanitarian circumstances, foodstuffs;

5. *Calls upon* all States, including States non-members of the United Nations, to act strictly in accordance with the provisions of the present resolution notwithstanding any contract entered into or license granted before the date of the present resolution;

6. *Decides* to establish, in accordance with rule 28 of the provisional rules of procedure of the Security Council, a Committee of the Security Council consisting of all the members of the Council, to undertake the following tasks and to report on its work to the Council with its observations and recommendations:

(a) To examine the reports on the progress of the implementation of the present resolution which will be submitted by the Secretary-General;

(b) To seek from all states further information regarding the action taken by them concerning the effective implementation of the provisions laid down in the present resolution;

7. *Calls upon* all States to co-operate fully with the Committee in the fulfillment of its task, including supplying such information as may be sought by the Committee in pursuance of the present resolution;

8. *Requests* the Secretary-General to provide all necessary assistance to the Committee and to make the necessary arrangements in the Secretariat for the purpose;

9. *Decides* that, notwithstanding paragraph 4 through 8 above, nothing in the present resolution shall prohibit assistance to the legitimate Government of Kuwait, and *calls upon* all States:

(a) To take appropriate measures to protect assets of the legitimate Government of Kuwait and its agencies;

(b) Not to recognize any regime set up by the occupying Power;

10. *Requests* the Secretary-General to report to the Council on the progress of the implementation of the present resolution, the first report to be submitted within thirty days;

11. *Decides* to keep this item on its agenda and to continue its efforts to put an early end to the invasion by Iraq.

Source: The Middle East, 7th ed. (Washington, DC: Congressional Quarterly, Inc., 1991), 369–70.

PRESIDENT BUSH'S SPEECH OF AUGUST 8, 1990

On August 8, 1990, the day Iraq annexed Kuwait, President George Bush, speaking from the Oval Office, delivered a nationally televised address in which he explained U.S. policy and goals and sought to prepare the American people for a long-term crisis in the Middle East. This speech, which appears below, was critical because it clearly asserted the U.S. commitment to reverse Iraq's invasion of Kuwait and placed the U.S.-led coalition on the path to war with Iraq. Thereafter, Bush would not consider compromising the goals that he had established in this speech.

Document 3
ADDRESS TO THE NATION ANNOUNCING THE DEPLOYMENT OF UNITED STATES ARMED FORCES TO SAUDI ARABIA
George Bush

In the life of a nation, we're called upon to define who we are and what we believe. Sometimes, these choices are not easy. But today, as president, I ask for your support in a decision I've made to stand up for what's right and condemn what's wrong, all in the cause of peace.

At my direction, elements of the 82nd Airborne Division, as well as key units of the United States Air Force, are arriving today to take up defensive positions in Saudi Arabia. I took this action to assist the Saudi Arabian government in the defense of its homeland. No one commits American armed forces to a dangerous mission lightly, but after perhaps unparalleled international consultation and exhausting every alternative, it became necessary to take this action.

Let me tell you why. Less than a week ago in the early morning hours of August 2, Iraqi armed forces, without provocation or warning, invaded a peaceful Kuwait. Facing negligible resistance from its much smaller neighbor, Iraq's tanks stormed in blitzkrieg fashion through Kuwait in a few short hours. With more than 100,000 troops, along with tanks, artillery, and surface-to-surface missiles, Iraq now occupies Kuwait.

This aggression came just hours after [Iraqi President] Saddam Hussein specifically assured numerous countries in the area that there would be no invasion. There is no justification whatsoever for this outrageous and brutal act of aggression.

A puppet regime, imposed from the outside, is unacceptable. The acquisition of territory by force is unacceptable.

No one, friend or foe, should doubt our desire for peace, and no one should underestimate our determination to confront aggression.

Four simple principles guide our policy.

First, we seek the immediate, unconditional, and complete withdrawal of all Iraqi forces from Kuwait.

Second, Kuwait's legitimate government must be restored to replace the puppet regime.

And third, my administration, as has been the case with every president from President [Franklin D.] Roosevelt to President [Ronald] Reagan, is committed to the security and stability of the Persian Gulf.

And fourth, I am determined to protect the lives of American citizens abroad.

Immediately after the Iraqi invasion, I ordered an embargo of all trade with Iraq, and, together with many other nations, announced sanctions that both froze all Iraqi assets in this country and protected Kuwait's assets.

The stakes are high. Iraq is already a rich and powerful country that possesses the world's second-largest reserves of oil and over a million men under arms. It's the fourth largest military in the world.

Our country now imports nearly half the oil it consumes and could face a major threat to its economic independence. Much of the world is even more dependent on imported oil and is even more vulnerable to Iraqi threats.

We succeeded in the struggle for freedom in Europe because we and our allies remain stalwart. Keeping the peace in the Middle East will require no less.

We're beginning a new era. This new era can be full of promise, an age of freedom, a time of peace for all peoples. But if history teaches us anything, it is that we must resist aggression, or it will destroy our freedoms.

Appeasement does not work. As was the case in the 1930s, we see in Saddam Hussein an aggressive dictator threatening his neighbors. Only fourteen days ago, Saddam Hussein promised his friends he would not invade Kuwait. And four days ago, he promised the world he would withdraw. And twice we have seen what his promises mean. His promises mean nothing.

In the last few days I've spoken with political leaders from the Middle East, Europe, Asia, the Americas, and I've met with [British] Prime Minister [Margaret] Thatcher, [Canadian] Prime Minister [Brian] Mulroney, and NATO Secretary General [Manfred] Wöerner. And all agree that Iraq cannot be allowed to benefit from its invasion of Kuwait.

We agree that this is not an American problem or a European problem or a Middle East problem. It is the world's problem, and that's why soon after the Iraqi invasion, the United Nations Security Council, without dissent, condemned Iraq, calling for the immediate and unconditional withdrawal of its troops from Kuwait.

The Arab world, through both the Arab League and the Gulf Cooperation Council, courageously announced its opposition to Iraqi aggression. Japan, the United Kingdom, and France, and other governments around the world have imposed severe sanctions.

The Soviet Union and China ended all arms sales to Iraq, and this past Monday, the United Nations Security Council approved for the first time in twenty-three years mandatory sanctions under Chapter VII of the United Nations Charter.

These sanctions, now enshrined in international law, have the potential to deny Iraq the fruits of aggression, while sharply limiting its ability to either import or export anything of value, especially oil.

I pledge here today that the United States will do its part to see that these sanctions are effective and to induce Iraq to withdraw without delay from Kuwait. But we must recognize that Iraq may not stop using force to advance its ambitions.

Iraq has massed an enormous war machine on the Saudi border, capable of initiating hostilities with little or no additional preparation. Given the Iraqi government's history of aggression against its own citizens as well as its neighbors, to assume Iraq will not attack again would be unwise and unrealistic. And therefore, after consulting with [Saudi] King Fahd, I sent Secretary of Defense Dick Cheney to discuss cooperative measures we could take.

Following those meetings, the Saudi government requested our help and I responded to that request by ordering U.S. air and ground forces to deploy to the kingdom of Saudi Arabia.

Let me be clear: The sovereign independence of Saudi Arabia is of vital interest to the United States. This decision, which I shared with the congressional leadership, grows out of the longstanding friendship and security relationship between the United States and Saudi Arabia. U.S. forces will work together with those of Saudi Arabia and other nations to preserve the integrity of Saudi Arabia and to deter further Iraqi aggression.

Through their presence, as well as through their training and exercises, these multinational forces will enhance the overall capability of Saudi armed forces to defend the kingdom.

I want to be clear about what we are doing and why. America does not seek conflict, nor do we seek to chart the destiny of other nations. But America will stand by her friends. The mission of our troops is wholly defensive. Hopefully, they will not be needed long.

They will not initiate hostilities, but they will defend themselves, the Kingdom of Saudi Arabia, and other friends in the Persian Gulf.

. . . .

Standing up for our principles is an American tradition. As it has so many times before, it may take time and tremendous effort, but most of all, it will take unity of purpose. As I've witnessed throughout my life in both war and peace, America has never wavered when her purpose is driven by principle, and on this August day, at home and abroad, I know she will do no less.

Thank you, and God bless the United States of America.

Source: *Public Papers of the Presidents of the United States: George Bush, 1990*, Book II—July 1 to December 31, 1990 (Washington, DC: U.S. Government Printing Office, 1991), 1107–9.

KING FAHD'S SPEECH OF AUGUST 9, 1990

While Bush was informing the American people of the unfolding crisis in the Persian Gulf, King Fahd ibn Abdul Aziz of Saudi Arabia was doing the same with his domestic constituency. In a speech to his people, Fahd presents the crisis as one in which he had no choice but to allow Western intervention in the kingdom and to take measures to check Iraq. He also emphasizes how hard he tried to seek an Arab solution to the crisis, suggests that Iraq's invasion was a threat to the entire Arab world, and underscores that Western forces would remain in the kingdom only temporarily. The speech, as translated by the Saudi government from his broadcast August 9, 1990, appears below.

Document 4
FAHD SPEECH ON GULF CRISIS
King Fahd ibn Abdul Aziz

In the name of God, the Merciful, the Compassionate. Thanks be to God, Master of the Universe and Prayers of Peace be upon the last of Prophets Mohamad and all his kinfolk and companions.

Dear brother citizens, May God's peace and mercy be upon you.

You realize, no doubt, through following up the course of the regrettable events in the Arab Gulf region during the last few days the gravity of the situation the Arab nation faces in the current circumstances. You undoubtedly know that the government of the Kingdom of Saudi Arabia has exerted all possible efforts with the governments of the Iraqi Republic and the State of Kuwait to contain the dispute between the two countries.

In this context, I made numerous telephone calls and held fraternal talks with the brothers. As a result, a bilateral meeting was held between the Iraqi and Kuwaiti delegations in Saudi Arabia with the aim of bridging the gap and narrowing differences to avert any further escalation.

A number of brotherly Arab kings and presidents contributed, thankfully, in these efforts based on their belief in the unity of the Arab nation and the cohesion of its solidarity and cooperation to achieve success in serving its fateful causes.

However, regrettably enough, events took an adverse course, to our endeavors and the aspirations of the Peoples of the Islamic and Arab nation, as well as all peace-loving countries.

Nevertheless, these painful and regrettable events started in the pre-dawn hours of Thursday 11 Muharram 1411H., corresponding to 2nd August A.D. 1990. They took the whole world by surprise when the Iraqi forces stormed the brotherly state of Kuwait in the most sinister aggression witnessed by the Arab nation in modern history. Such an invasion inflicted painful suffering on the Kuwaitis and rendered them homeless.

While expressing its deep displeasure at this aggression on the brotherly neighbor Kuwait, the Kingdom of Saudi Arabia declares its categorical rejection of all ensuing measures and declarations that followed that aggression, which were rejected by all the statements issued by Arab leaderships, the Arab League, the Islamic Conference Organization, and the Gulf Cooperation Council, as well as all Arab and international bodies and organizations.

The Kingdom of Saudi Arabia reaffirms its demand to restore the situation in the brotherly state of Kuwait to its original status before the Iraqi storming as well as the return of the ruling family headed by H.H. [His Highness] Sheik Jaber al-Ahmed al-Sabah, the Emir of Kuwait and his government.

We hope that the emergency Arab summit called by H.E. [His Excellency] President Mohamad Hosni Mubarak of sisterly Egypt will lead to the achievement of the results that realize the aspirations of the Arab nation and bolster its march towards solidarity and unity of opinion.

In the aftermath of this regrettable event, Iraq massed huge forces on the borders of the Kingdom of Saudi Arabia. In view of these bitter realities and out of the eagerness of the Kingdom to safeguard its territory and protect its vital and economic potentials, and its wish to bolster its defensive capabilities and to raise the level of training of its armed forces—in addition to the keenness of the government of the Kingdom to resort to peace and nonrecourse to force to solve disputes—the Kingdom of Saudi Arabia expressed its wish for the participation of fraternal Arab forces and other friendly forces.

Thus, the governments of the United States, Britain and other nations took the initiative, based on the friendly relations that link the Kingdom of Saudi Arabia and these countries, to dispatch air and land forces to sustain the Saudi armed forces in performing their duty to defend the homeland and the citizens against any aggression with the full emphasis that this measure is not addressed to anybody. It is merely and purely for defensive purposes, imposed by the current circumstances faced by the Kingdom of Saudi Arabia.

It is worth mentioning in this context that the forces which will participate in the joint training exercises with the Saudi armed forces are of a temporary nature. They will leave the Saudi territory immediately at the request of the Kingdom.

We pray to Almighty God to culminate our steps towards everything in which lie the good of our religion and safety of our homeland, and to guide us on the right path.

May God's peace and blessing be upon you.

Source: The Middle East, 7th ed. (Washington, DC: Congressional Quarterly, 1991), 371–72.

PRESIDENT BUSH SPEAKS TO THE PEOPLE OF IRAQ (SEPTEMBER 16, 1990)

Forty-four days after Iraq invaded Kuwait, Bush decided to address the Iraqi people on the crisis. In an often repeated message, he emphasized that the Iraqi dictator, and not the Iraqi or Arab people, was the target. This speech aimed at undercutting Saddam's attempt to "Arabize," "Islamize," and "Zionize" the conflict. Indeed, in his speech, Bush used Saddam's own words about how wrong it is for one Arab state to occupy another, thus making him look aggressive and hypocritical. This address, which the president recorded in the Oval Office at the White House on September 12, and which was broadcast unedited on Iraqi television on September 16, 1990, appears below.

Document 5
ADDRESS TO THE PEOPLE OF IRAQ ON THE PERSIAN GULF CRISIS
George Bush

I'm here today to explain to the people of Iraq why the United States and the world community has responded the way it has to Iraq's occupation of

Kuwait. My purpose is not to trade accusations, not to escalate the war of words, but to speak with candor about what has caused this crisis that confronts us. Let there be no misunderstanding: We have no quarrel with the people of Iraq. I've said many times, and I will repeat right now, our only object is to oppose the invasion ordered by Saddam Hussein.

On August 2d, your leadership made its decision to invade, an unprovoked attack on a small nation that posed no threat to your own. Kuwait was the victim; Iraq, the aggressor.

And the world met Iraq's invasion with a chorus of condemnation: unanimous resolutions in the United Nations. Twenty-seven States—rich and poor, Arab, Moslem, Asian, and African—have answered the call of Saudi Arabia and free Kuwait and sent forces to the Gulf region to defend against Iraq. For the first time in history, 13 States of the Arab League, representing 80 percent of the Arab nation, have condemned a brother Arab State. Today, opposed by world opinion, Iraq stands isolated and alone.

I do not believe that you, the people of Iraq, want war. You've borne untold suffering and hardship during 8 long years of war with Iran—a war that touched the life of every single Iraqi citizen; a war that took the lives of hundreds of thousands of young men, the bright promise of an entire generation. No one knows better than you the incalculable costs of war, the ultimate cost when a nation's vast potential and vital energies are consumed by conflict. No one knows what Iraq might be today, what prosperity and peace you might now enjoy, had your leaders not plunged you into war. Now, once again, Iraq finds itself on the brink of war. Once again, the same Iraqi leadership has miscalculated. Once again, the Iraqi people face tragedy.

Saddam Hussein has told you that Iraqi troops were invited into Kuwait. That's not true. In fact, in the face of far superior force, the people of Kuwait are bravely resisting this occupation. Your own returning soldiers will tell you the Kuwaitis are fighting valiantly in any way they can.

Saddam Hussein tells you that this crisis is a struggle between Iraq and America. In fact, it is Iraq against the world. When President Gorbachev and I met at Helsinki [September 9], we agreed that no peaceful international order is possible if larger states can devour their neighbors. Never before has world opinion been so solidly united against aggression.

Nor, until the invasion of Kuwait, has the United States been opposed to Iraq. In the past, the United States has helped Iraq import billions of dollars worth of food and other commodities. And the war with Iran would not have ended 2 years ago without U.S. support and sponsorship in the United Nations.

Saddam Hussein tells you the occupation of Kuwait will benefit the poorer nations of the world. In fact, the occupation of Kuwait is helping no one and is now hurting you, the Iraqi people, and countless others of the world's poor. Instead of acquiring new oil wealth by annexing Kuwait, this misguided act of aggression will cost Iraq over $20 billion a year in lost oil revenues. Because of Iraq's aggression, hundreds of thousands of innocent foreign workers are fleeing Kuwait and Iraq. They are stranded on Iraq's borders, without shelter, without food, without medicine, with no way home. These refugees are suffering, and this is shameful.

But even worse, others are being held hostage in Iraq and Kuwait. Hostage-taking punishes the innocent and separates families. It is barbaric. It will not work, and it will not affect my ability to make tough decisions.

I do not want to add to the suffering of the people of Iraq. The United Nations has put binding sanctions in place not to punish the Iraqi people but as a peaceful means to convince your leadership to withdraw from Kuwait. That decision is in the hands of Saddam Hussein.

The pain you now experience is a direct result of the path your leadership has chosen. When Iraq returns to the path of peace, when Iraqi troops withdraw from Kuwait, when that country's rightful government is restored, when all foreigners held against their will are released, then, and then alone, will the world end the sanctions.

Perhaps your leaders do not appreciate the strength of the forces united against them. Let me say clearly: There is no way Iraq can win. Ultimately, Iraq must withdraw from Kuwait.

No one—not the American people, not this President—wants war. But there are times when a country—when all countries who value the principles of sovereignty and independence—must stand against aggression. As Americans, we're slow to raise our hand in anger and eager to explore every peaceful means of settling our disputes; but when we have exhausted every alternative, when conflict is thrust upon us, there is no nation on Earth with greater resolve or stronger steadiness of purpose.

The actions of your leadership have put Iraq at odds with the world community. But while those actions have brought us to the brink of conflict, war is not inevitable. It is still possible to bring this crisis to a peaceful end.

When we stand with Kuwait against aggression, we stand for a principle well understood in the Arab world. Let me quote the words of one Arab leader, Saddam Hussein himself: "An Arab country does not have the right to occupy another Arab country. God forbid, if Iraq should deviate from the right path, we would want Arabs to send their armies to put things right. If Iraq should become intoxicated by its power and move to overwhelm another Arab State, the Arabs would be right to deploy their armies to check it."

Those are the words of your leader, Saddam Hussein, spoken on November 28, 1988, in a speech to Arab lawyers. Today, 2 years later, Saddam has invaded and occupied a member of the United Nations and the Arab League. The world will not allow the aggression to stand. Iraq must get out of Kuwait for the sake of principle, for the sake of peace, and for the sake of the Iraqi people.

Source: *Public Papers of the Presidents of the United States: George Bush, 1990*, Book II—July 1 to December 31, 1990 (Washington, DC: U.S. Government Printing Office, 1991), 1239–40.

THE CONGRESSIONAL DEBATE ON AUTHORIZING THE USE OF FORCE

In January 1991 U.S. Representative Stephen Solarz (D-NY), one of two sponsors of the congressional resolution to support the president's initiative, offered a strong set of reasons to support the president's authority to wage war. This was among the most comprehensive statements by an American politician of why continuing economic sanctions ran too many risks and offered dubious benefits. Ultimately, Solarz's resolution carried the day, but opposition to it was strong.

Admiral William J. Crowe, Jr., chairman of the Joint Chiefs of Staff from 1985 to 1989, was perhaps the most stunning congressional witness. In testimony before the Senate Armed Services Committee on November 28, 1990, he argued that economic sanctions should be given a chance, because war in the Middle East would not solve the region's complex problems, would open a Pandora's box of uncertainties, including serious casualties, and was "nasty business." Many scholars also held Crowe's position. They believed a Middle East war would inflame the Arab world and damage the American position in the region.

Document 6 presents part of the debate from the *Congressional Record* in which Solarz defends his position and others challenge it. Document 7 consists of excerpts from the testimony by Crowe.

Document 6
THE CASE FOR INTERVENTION
A Debate from the House Floor, January 11, 1991

Mr. McCOLLUM. Mr. Speaker, I yield such time as he may consume to the gentleman from Pennsylvania [Mr. SANTORUM].

(Mr. SANTORUM asked and was given permission to revise and extend his remarks.)

Mr. SANTORUM. Mr. Speaker, I rise in support of the Michel-Solarz resolution and in opposition to the Gephardt-Hamilton resolution.

Mr. Speaker, I am honored to address this distinguished body as a newly elected Member from the 18th District of Pennsylvania, and to enter my statement as part of the public record.

We are facing perhaps this Nation's most difficult decision since the Gulf of Tonkin resolution of 1964. The Iraqi invasion of Kuwait was a grave injustice. Peace and international security have been threatened. Justice and freedom are being threatened. And now American lives are at stake as well.

Congress does have a role in offering leadership on this matter. I believe we have the right and responsibility to decide whether or not the President of the United States should have the authority to use force in this particular instance.

The President, however, believes that the United States Constitution gives him the authority to use force if necessary to get Iraq out of Kuwait. I believe that the President will authorize the use of force, pursuant to U.N. Resolution 678, with or without congressional approval if he feels it is necessary. Unfortunately, Saddam Hussein does not believe that President Bush will take offensive military action without Congress behind him. Therefore, to make Hussein realize that the threat of military action is real—and Mr. Hussein, make no mistake that it is real—I will stand behind the President and support the Solarz-Michel resolution.

As an editorial in the Pittsburgh Post-Gazette stated on Tuesday, "Prudence and the possibility of further diplomacy argue against an immediate attack on Iraqi positions. But favorable action by Congress would put Saddam on notice that the U.S. Government was behind the position of the United Nations—and this could influence him to obey the United Nations." In this scenario the threat of military action may be the best avenue to peace.

However, I believe it is important to send a message to the President as well. I do not support the sacrifice of thousands of Americans in this conflict. My constituents and the American people do not want to see their sons and daughters die in Kuwait. There are many ways in which powerful, decisive action can be taken militarily against Saddam Hussein without risking great numbers of American lives. President Bush, I will be writing you a letter to urge that you implement other avenues than the sending of thousands of American troops into battle. In casting this vote, I am not endorsing offensive action which would engage thousands of American soldiers. With the support of Congress and the American people, you have the most promising diplomatic tool yet to remove Saddam Hussein from Kuwait peacefully. Please use it.

I am not convinced that we are at the appropriate juncture to justify an all-out assault which may take thousands of American lives. We must, Mr. President, not resort to an all-out assault if military action is needed. And if military action is to be taken, we must not be engaged in it alone. The action must be taken together by all the nations participating in the multinational force present in the gulf.

This decision has not been made lightly. I have taken into account the hundreds of letters and calls directed to my office.

Fred Goehringer of Dormont, who has two sons in the gulf, asked me to support the President. Fred, I will support the President and your sons as you do. I will pray for your sons and for all the men and women deployed in the gulf.

Jim Bowden of Mount Lebanon, who has a brother in the gulf, called me to advocate peace. Jim, I appreciate your perspective as a Vietnam veteran, and I do not want another Vietnam. I believe that a vote in support of the President is our best chance to avoid another Vietnam and achieve peace.

Before I close I would like to address one more person. Mr. Hussein, I know that you are listening to these proceedings carefully. I want you to know that your occupation of Kuwait, your murder of innocent civilians, and your oppression of thousands more civilians is intolerable. The world is in agreement: You must withdraw your forces. We stand together on this and will do whatever is necessary to see freedom restored to a sovereign people. Do not think we will do otherwise.

Mr. McCOLLUM. Mr. Speaker, I yield 2 minutes to the gentleman from Michigan [Mr. CAMP].

(Mr. CAMP asked and was given permission to revise and extend his remarks.)

Mr. CAMP. Mr. Speaker, I rise in support of House Joint Resolution 62, to give our President full authority to resolve the Mideast crisis. It is only by giving the President our full support and this authority that we pursue our best course and our fervent hope for resolving this crisis peacefully.

This is a difficult time for all Americans, especially for the men and women and their families who have literally placed their lives on the line out of a sense of duty and respect to this country.

On Sunday, I was in Owosso, MI, wishing godspeed to 188 men and women headed for Saudi Arabia. They understand the importance of their mission, the importance of this time for our world. I think of them and their families at this moment and I thank them for their trust in our Nation, and their personal sacrifice, and their belief in our cause.

I make this decision in the hopes that the threat of war will avoid war.

We must send a strong and unified message to Saddam Hussein to get out of Kuwait. We must send a signal to the world community that we stand together, united against Saddam Hussein's acts of war, brutality and aggression. We hope and pray that war will not be necessary, that Saddam Hussein will at last listen to the message of a united international community. Our message is clear: We cannot and will not tolerate his acts of barbarism. We cannot and will not allow him to be rewarded for his acts of aggression. Saddam Hussein must leave Kuwait.

We should stand with our President today in the hopes that our men and women will soon be standing with us at home, secure in the knowledge that we did the right thing as a nation and they bravely served the cause of peace and justice.

Mr. McCOLLUM. Mr. Speaker, I yield 3 minutes to the gentleman from California [Mr. ANDERSON].

Mr. ANDERSON. Mr. Speaker, President Bush has formally asked Congress to endorse a resolution authorizing him to use "all necessary means" to force Iraq to withdraw from Kuwait. It has been my belief throughout this crisis that this was a step the President had to take if he were to use offensive force against Iraq. After a great deal of thought, and after listening to an exhaustive debate, my intention is to support the Solarz-Michel resolution.

This is not a step I take easily or without reservation. There is no graver matter than war and no man approaches the subject simply or easily. I have seen three great wars that America has fought in my lifetime and do not want to see another one. My colleagues know that I am not some young "hawk."

I vote for the Solarz-Michel resolution because I believe its passage is the best way to avoid war. With the Congress firmly behind him, President Bush can negotiate with Saddam Hussein from a position of strength. Saddam Hussein will not be allowed to hide behind any more false hopes that America does not have the resolve to do what is right. I firmly believe, ironic though it may be, that it is the threat of war that offers the best chance for peace. Should this resolution fail, we have effectively tied the hands of the President and told Saddam Hussein he has won. Should this resolution fail, we would only face further stalemate and intransigence on the part of Hussein. It is clear from Secretary of State Baker's meeting with Iraqi Foreign Minister Aziz in Geneva that Saddam Hussein will not back down. It is my deep and unabiding hope that the passage of this resolution will prove to Saddam Hussein that the President is not bluffing and then Hussein will withdraw peacefully. But should it not, I am prepared to face the consequences.

A congressional resolution authorizing the use of force against Iraq after January 15 is a step the United Nations has already taken. The President has made every effort to compel Iraq to leave Kuwait by peaceful means. I am satisfied he has exhausted diplomacy. I am not satisfied economic sanctions against Iraq will compel its withdrawal from Kuwait. Congress has insisted that the President come before it prior to the use of force. Now he has done so. This is a policy the nations of the world have resoundly endorsed. It is time for the U.S. Congress to stand up and be counted. The President deserves our support and will receive mine.

Mr. BERMAN. Mr. Speaker, I yield 5 minutes to one of the chief sponsors of the resolution, the gentleman from New York [Mr. SOLARZ].

Mr. SOLARZ. Mr. Speaker, if this debate has made any one thing abundantly clear, it is that virtually all of us, Democrats and Republicans, liberals and conservatives, agree on the proposition that it is a vital American interest to secure the withdrawal of Iraq from Kuwait. Where we disagree is over how best to achieve that objective. Should it be done through the protracted application of sanctions, or should it be done through the adoption of a resolution which would authorize the President to use force in order to achieve that objective—which would create the possibility of securing the withdrawal of Saddam Hussein without the use of force, but giving the President the right to use force if that should prove necessary.

Let me say, Mr. Speaker, that if I thought for a moment that there was any reasonable possibility whatsoever of securing the withdrawal of Iraq from Kuwait through the protracted application of sanctions, I would strongly favor that course of action. But neither Judge Webster, the Director of the CIA, nor any of our other coalition partners believe that the sanctions will be sufficient to induce Saddam Hussein to withdraw from Iraq. Nor do I.

Why do I think the sanctions will not succeed? If we consider the character of Saddam Hussein, and if we take into account the political dynamics of Iraq, it should become clear that the protracted application of sanctions is a formula for failure rather than a strategy for success.

Why is that? The sanctions, to be sure, are having an economic impact. Nobody can deny that. All of Iraq's oil exports have been cut off. Its industry is in a state of paralysis. Its gross national product has been cut almost in half.

Yet those who support the protracted application of sanctions as the best way of resolving this crisis have never demonstrated the connection between the undoubted economic impact of the sanctions and a political decision on the part of the Iraqi leadership to quit Kuwait.

There are, if you think about it, only two ways in which that can happen. Either Saddam himself has to make the decision to go, or Saddam has to be overthrown by a military junta which would then make the decision to go. The fact of the matter is that Saddam himself does not give a whit for the welfare of his own people. The fact that their per capita income will be reduced by 40 percent does not bother him. The fact that they will have less to eat does not bother him. He will hunker down and he will wait.

Anyway, his people will be able to feed themselves. It is a fertile country. Smuggling is going on across the Iranian, Jordanian, Syrian, and Turkish borders. He will wait. And while he waits there is a real chance this coalition against him will crumble, and the sanctions will erode.

He has totally tyrannized and terrorized his own military. There are five secret services. They are riddled with informers. His military officers know that he acts with utter ruthlessness against anyone whom he even suspects of wanting to overthrow him. If they did not get rid of him during an 8-year war with Iran in which they suffered 1 million casualties, they are not going to get rid of him now simply because the Iraqi people have a lower standard of living.

Believing that sanctions will work elevates wishful thinking to the level of hardheaded analysis.

Mr. PEASE. Will the gentleman yield?

Mr. SOLARZ. I only have 1 minute and then there is no time left.

Mr. PEASE. I suspect that the gentleman from California [Mr. BERMAN] would give you plenty of time if you wanted additional time.

Mr. SOLARZ. Let me finish and if I have any time left I will be happy to yield.

Mr. PEASE. The gentleman is making a brilliant point. I want to know how it applies to the possibility that the President's plan or course will work as well. What are the odds, in the gentleman's view, that Saddam will withdraw from Iraq as a result of our passage of this resolution?

Mr. SOLARZ. I think it is the last best chance for a peaceful resolution to this conflict.

But I want to conclude with one point in the limited amount of time that I have at this stage in the debate. To the extent that there is any possibility of getting Saddam out, it clearly requires a credible threat of force.

Some say that if the Hamilton resolution is adopted the credible threat of force will remain while we wait for the sanctions to work. But the truth of the matter is that if the Hamilton resolution is adopted there is nobody in the world, and certainly not in Iraq, who is going to believe that we will subsequently have the will to use force. They will break out the champagne bottles in Baghdad. Every one of our coalition partners, none of whom believe the sanctions alone can do the job, will conclude that if we are not willing to use force now we will not be willing to use it later. The option will disappear, and ultimately, therefore, we will be playing right into the hands of Saddam rather than delivering Saddam into the hands of the coalition.

Mr. SMITH of Florida. Mr. Speaker, I yield such time as he may consume to the gentleman from Maryland [Mr. MFUME].

(Mr. MFUME asked and was given permission to revise and extend his remarks.)

Mr. MFUME. Mr. Speaker, I rise in strong opposition to the Solarz-Michel resolution.

Mr. Speaker, I rise today to express my open and absolute opposition to war in the Persian Gulf. My fear against going to war in the gulf is not due to the fact that America and our allies cannot win in battle, but because our objectives and policies in this region have been inconsistent.

I am not comfortable with the stated objectives of why we are so ready to use force to dislodge Saddam Hussein from Kuwait. In August—when it appeared that Iraq was poised to attack Saudi Arabia's oil fields and hold foreign hostages at strategic locations—I concurred with the President's action to create an international force to defend the Saudi's oil fields and impose economic sanctions against Iraq.

Later, President Bush upped the ante with his steadfast promotion of the military option before we could determine whether sanctions and other international initiatives has a chance to take root. Additionally, President Bush began to talk about the need to stop Hussein's "naked aggression" and that he must leave Kuwait. For me, this is one of the most profound and bewildering turn of events of the entire crisis.

Why are we going to authorize the use of force and the death of thousands of American soldiers to dislodge Hussein from Kuwait and reinstall the Kuwaiti emir? Kuwait by no means represented Jeffersonian democracy. Many of the administration's past objectives and policy positions defended democracy and freedom. Where were these governing principles in Kuwait prior to August?

The Iraqis informed Ambassador April Glaspie that they intended to invade Kuwait in July and Ambassador Glaspie's response was that we don't get involved in such Arab affairs and that we do not have a defense treaty with Kuwait. Mr. Speaker, in part, we are responsible for creating the leviathan that challenges us now. Were we as concerned about Iraq's buildup when they were keeping Iran at bay? Of course not. Were we as concerned when Hussein and other Middle Eastern countries escalated their acquisition of arms? Of course not.

The international stance against Saddam Hussein is not truly as united as the President would like us to believe. The major league hitters in this conflict is plainly the United States versus Iraq. Unfortunately, the first and the last soldiers to die probably will be wearing American uniforms.

Now we are considering whether to give the President the authority to use force to dislodge Saddam Hussein from Kuwait. I do not favor this action and believe that we need to fully explore and exhaust our diplomatic options prior to playing the military hand.

I have heard many of our colleagues on the floor and in the media discuss the fact that we need to send a message to Saddam Hussein that his naked aggression will not be tolerated. Mr. Speaker, I want my message to be first sent to the parents and loved ones of those soldiers participating in Operation Desert Shield. My message would be that my conscience cannot rest knowing that your family members are being placed into a conflict that has yet to be clearly defined to anyone.

Mr. Speaker, let us not rush head first into chaos and uncertainty. Let us instead seek ways to leverage Iraq from Kuwait and further tighten the screws via international sanctions and continued isolation against Baghdad.

America has many pressing domestic economic problems. The cost of this war and its concomitant effects will only worsen our economic situation here with no visible relief in sight.

So, I urge those who want to go to war with Iraq to remember that although the Middle East is strategic for its oil, I do not wish to see the Saudi desert become the symbol of unclarified policy and the massive loss of brave American lives.

Source: Congressional Record, Proceedings and Debates of the 102nd Congress, 1st sess. (January 11, 1991), H305–H307 (Washington, DC: US GOP, 1991).

Document 7
GIVE SANCTIONS A CHANCE
Admiral William J. Crowe, Jr., U.S.N. (retired), Chairman of the Joint Chiefs of Staff, 1985–1989

War is always a grave decision and one which deserves both deep thought and wide public discussion. . . .

If Saddam Hussein initiates an attack on Saudi Arabia or U.S. forces, we have no choice but to react vigorously and to use force to bring Iraq to heel. It is imperative once we engage that we bring it to a successful conclusion no matter what it requires. It would be disastrous to do otherwise. I believe such a response would be defensible and acceptable to all constituencies, domestic and international.

For that reason alone, it is unlikely that Saddam Hussein will initiate further military action. Certainly everything we see to date suggests he is hunkering down for the long haul. If that predication proves correct, President Bush will be confronted with some very painful choices.

If deposing Saddam Hussein would sort out the Middle East and permit the United States to turn its attention elsewhere and to concentrate on our very pressing domestic problems, the case for initiating offensive action immediately would be considerably strengthened. The Middle East, however, is not that simple. I witnessed it firsthand. I lived in the Middle East for a year.

. . . .

I would submit that posturing ourselves to promote stability for the long term is our primary national interest in the Middle East. May I repeat it: that posturing ourselves to promote stability for the long term is our primary national interest in the Middle East. It is not obvious to me that we are currently looking at the crisis in this light. Our dislike for Hussein seems to have crowded out many other considerations.

In working through the problems myself, I am persuaded that the U.S. initiating hostilities could well exacerbate many of the tensions I have cited and perhaps further polarize the Arab world. Certainly, many Arabs would deeply resent a campaign which would necessarily kill large numbers of their Muslim brothers and force them to choose sides between Arab nations and the West.

From the Arab perspective, this fight is not simply a matter between bad and good. It is a great deal more complex than that and includes political and social perspectives deeply rooted in their history. The aftermath of such a contest will very likely multiply many-fold the anti-American resentment which we already see in the Middle East. In essence, we may be in a certain sense on the horns of a no-win dilemma. Even if we win, we lose ground in the Arab world and generally injure our ability to deal in the future with the labyrinth of the Middle East.

I firmly believe that Saddam Hussein must be pushed out of Kuwait. He must leave Kuwait. At the same time, given the larger context, I judge it highly desirable to achieve this goal in a peaceful fashion, if that is possible. In other words, I would argue that we should give sanctions a fair chance before we discard them. I personally believe they will bring him to his knees ultimately, but I would be the first to admit that is a speculative judgment.

If, in fact, the sanctions will work in twelve to eighteen months instead of six months, a tradeoff of avoiding war, with its attendant sacrifices and uncertainties, would in my estimation be more than worth it. . . .

In closing, I would make a few observations that perhaps we should keep in mind as we approach this process. Using economic pressure may prove protracted, but if it could avoid hostilities or casualties, those also are highly desirable ends. As a matter of fact, I consider them also national interests. I seldom hear them referred to in that fashion.

It is curious that just as our patience in Western Europe has paid off and furnished us the most graphic example in our history of how staunchness is sometimes the better course in dealing with thorny international problems, a few armchair strategists are counseling a near-term attack on Iraq. It is worth remembering that in the 1950s and 1960s, individuals were similarly advising an attack on the U.S.S.R. Would not that have been great? . . .

It would be a sad commentary if Saddam Hussein, a two-bit tyrant who sits on seventeen million people and possesses a gross national product of $40 billion, proved to be more patient than the United States, the world's most affluent and powerful nation.

Source: Testimony of Admiral William J. Crowe Jr., Senate Armed Services Committee (Washington, DC: US GPO, December 3, 1990).

UN RESOLUTION AUTHORIZING FORCE

On November 29, 1990, the UN Security Council passed Resolution 678, authorizing member nations to use "all necessary means" after January 15, 1991, to force Iraq to withdraw from Kuwait and comply with all UN Security Council resolutions related to its aggression. The vote was 12 to 2 with 1 abstention. The resolution was important because it signaled the resolve and unity of the U.S.-led coalition against Saddam.

Document 8
UN SECURITY COUNCIL RESOLUTION 678

The Security Council,

Recalling and reaffirming its resolutions 660 (1990), 661 (1990), 662 (1990), 664 (1990), 665 (1990), 666 (1990), 667 (1990), 669 (1990), 670 (1990) and 674 (1990),

Noting that, despite all efforts by the United Nations, Iraq refuses to comply with its obligation to implement resolution 660 (1990) and the above subsequent relevant resolutions, in flagrant contempt of the Council,

Mindful of its duties and responsibilities under the Charter of the United Nations for the maintenance and preservation of international peace and security,

Determined to secure full compliance with its decisions,

Acting under Chapter VII of the Charter of the United Nations,

1. *Demands* that Iraq comply fully with resolution 660 (1990) and all subsequent relevant resolutions and decides, while maintaining all its decisions, to allow Iraq one final opportunity, as a pause of goodwill, to do so;

2. *Authorizes* Member States cooperating with the Government of Kuwait, unless Iraq on or before 15 January 1991 fully implements, as set forth in paragraph 1 above, the foregoing resolutions, to use all necessary means to uphold and implement Security Council resolution 660 (1990) and all subsequent relevant resolutions and to restore international peace and security in the area;

3. *Requests* all States to provide appropriate support for the actions undertaken in pursuance of paragraph 2 of this resolution;

4. *Requests* the States concerned to keep the Council regularly informed on the progress of actions undertaken pursuant to paragraph 2 and 3 of this resolution;

5. *Decides* to remain seized of the matter.

SADDAM HUSSEIN PROMISES
"THE MOTHER OF ALL BATTLES"

In typical Saddam style, the Iraqi dictator addressed his nation on January 20, 1991, with the dual goal of communicating with the American public. By this time, Iraq had suffered severe air attacks on at least forty major political and strategic sites in Baghdad and at key locations outside Baghdad. In line with Saddam's basic strategy of preying on perceived American weakness, he asserted that Iraq could inflict heavy casualties on the treacherous U.S.-led coalition, and he portrayed the struggle as a holy war in which Iraq carried the Islamic banner for all the Islamic world against the satanic West. The following excerpts are from the transcript of a speech by President Saddam Hussein, as broadcast on Baghdad Radio and translated by Reuters.

Document 9
THE MOTHER OF ALL BATTLES
Saddam Hussein

O glorious Iraqis, O holy warrior Iraqis, O Arabs, O believers wherever you are, we and our steadfastness are holding. Here is the great Iraqi people, your brothers and sons of your Arab nation and the great faithful part of the human family. We are all well. They are fighting with unparalleled heroism, unmatched except by the heroism of the believers who fight similar adversaries. And here is the infidel tyrant whose planes and missiles are falling out of the skies at the blows of the brave men. He is wondering how the Iraqis can confront his fading dreams with such determination and firmness.

After a while, he will begin to feel frustrated, and his defeat will be certain, God willing. . . . We in Iraq will be the faithful and obedient servants of God, struggling for his sake to raise the banner of truth and justice, the banner of "God is Great." Accursed be the lowly.

At that time, the valiant Iraqi men and women will not allow the army of atheism, treachery, hypocrisy and [word indistinct] to realize their stupid hope that the war would only last a few days or weeks, as they imagined and declared. In the coming period, the response of Iraq will be on a larger scale, using all the means and potential that God has given us and which we have so far only used in part. Our ground forces have not entered the battle so far, and only a small part of our air force has been used.

The army's air force has not been used, nor has the navy. The weight and effect of our ready missile force has not yet been applied in full. The fact remains that the great divine reinforcement is our source of power and effectiveness. When the war is fought in a comprehensive manner, using all resources and weapons, the scale of death and the number of dead will, God willing, rise among the ranks of atheism, injustice, and tyranny.

When they begin to die and when the message of the Iraqi soldiers reaches the farthest corner of the world, the unjust will die and the "God is Great" banner will flutter with great victory in the mother of all battles. Then the skies in the Arab homeland will appear in a new color and a sun of new hope will shine over them and over our nation and on all the good men whose bright lights will not be overcome by the darkness in the hearts of the infidels, the Zionists, and the treacherous, shameful rulers, such as the traitor Fahd.

Then the door will be wide open for the liberation of beloved Palestine, Lebanon, and the Golan. Then Jerusalem and the Dome of the Rock will be released from bondage. The Kaaba and the Tomb of the Prophet Moham-med, God's peace and blessings be upon him, will be liberated from occupation and God will bestow upon the poor and needy the things that others owed them, others who withheld from them what they owed them as God had justly ordained, which is a great deal.

Then [words indistinct], the good men, the holy warriors, and the faithful will know the truth of our promise to them that when the forces of infidelity attack the Iraqis, they will fight as they wished them to fight and perhaps in a better way, and that their promise is of faith and holy war. It remains for us to tell all Arabs, all the faithful strugglers, and all good supporters wherever they are: you have a duty to carry out holy war and struggle in order to target the assembly of evil, treason, and corruption everywhere.

You must also target their interests everywhere. It is a duty that is incumbent upon you, and that must necessarily correspond to the struggle of your brothers in Iraq. You will be part of the struggle of armed forces in your holy war and struggle, and part of the multitude of faith and the faithful. If the opposing multitude captures you, you will be prisoners in their hands, even if they refuse to admit this in their communiques and statements.

You will inevitably be released when the war ends, in accordance with international laws and agreements which will govern the release of prison-ers of war. In this way you will have pleased God and honored, with your slogans and principles, the trust given to you.

God is great, God is great, God is great, and accursed be the lowly.

PRESIDENT BUSH'S LETTER TO SADDAM HUSSEIN OF JANUARY 9, 1991

In the famous Baker-Aziz meeting of January 9, 1991, in Geneva, Secretary James A. Baker gave Iraq's Tariq Aziz a letter from Bush informing Saddam that dire consequences would follow if he refused to withdraw from Kuwait. After assessing the letter's contents, Aziz told Baker that it was "full of threats" and worded in a manner unfit for official discourse. The letter, which appears below, was not particularly antagonistic and even hinted of possible better relations with Iraq once the crisis ended.

Document 10
BUSH LETTER TO SADDAM HUSSEIN
George Bush

Mr. President:

We stand today at the brink of war between Iraq and the world. This is a war that began with your invasion of Kuwait; this is a war that can be ended only by Iraq's full and unconditional compliance with UN Security Council Resolution 678.

I am writing you now, directly, because what is at stake demands that no opportunity be lost to avoid what would be a certain calamity for the people of Iraq. I am writing, as well, because it is said by some that you do not understand just how isolated Iraq is and what Iraq faces as a result.

I am not in a position to judge whether this impression is correct; what I can do, though, is try in the letter to reinforce what Secretary of State [James A.] Baker [III] told your Foreign Minister and eliminate any uncertainty or ambiguity that might exist in your mind about where we stand and what we are prepared to do.

The international community is united in its call for Iraq to leave all of Kuwait without condition and without further delay. This is not simply the policy of the United States; it is the position of the world community as expressed in no less than 12 Security Council resolutions.

We prefer a peaceful outcome. However, anything less than full compliance with UN Security Council Resolution 678 and its predecessors is unacceptable.

There can be no reward for aggression. Nor will there be any negotiation. Principle cannot be compromised. However, by its full compliance, Iraq will gain the opportunity to rejoin the international community.

More immediately, the Iraqi military establishment will escape destruction. But unless you withdraw from Kuwait completely and without condition, you will lose more than Kuwait.

What is at issue here is not the future of Kuwait—it will be free, its government will be restored—but rather the future of Iraq. This choice is yours to make.

The United States will not be separated from its coalition partners. Twelve Security Council resolutions, 28 countries providing military units to enforce them, more than 100 governments complying with sanctions—all highlight the fact that it is not Iraq against the United States, but Iraq against the world.

That most Arab and Muslim countries are arrayed against you as well should reinforce what I am saying. Iraq cannot and will not be able to hold on to Kuwait or exact a price for leaving.

You may be tempted to find solace in the diversity of opinion that is American democracy. You should resist any such temptation. Diversity ought not to be confused with division. Nor should you underestimate, as others have before you, America's will.

Iraq is already feeling the effects of the sanctions mandated by the United Nations. Should war come, it will be a far greater tragedy for you and your country.

Let me state, too, that the United States will not tolerate the use of chemical or biological weapons or the destruction of Kuwait's oil fields and installations. Further, you will be held directly responsible for terrorist actions against any member of the coalition.

The American people would demand the strongest possible response. You and your country will pay a terrible price if you order unconscionable acts of this sort.

I write this letter not to threaten, but to inform. I do so with no sense of satisfaction, for the people of the United States have no quarrel with the people of Iraq.

Mr. President, UN Security Council Resolution 678 establishes the period before Jan. 15 of this year as a "pause of good will" so that this crisis may end without further violence.

Whether this pause is used as intended, or merely becomes a prelude to further violence, is in your hands, and yours alone. I hope you weigh your choice carefully and choose wisely, for much will depend upon it.

George Bush

Source: *Public Papers of the Presidents of the United States: George Bush, 1991*, Book I—January 1 to June 30, 1991 (Washington, DC: U.S. Government Printing Office, 1992), 36–37.

SADDAM RALLIES HIS PEOPLE
(FEBRUARY 24, 1991)

Exalting the glories of the Iraqi nation and of God in a speech aired on Baghdad Radio on February 24, 1991, Saddam urged his soldiers to fight hard and with dignity and promised great victory in the ground war. Clearly, he aimed to lift the spirits of his people and, at the same time, to show resolve against the U.S.-led alliance. In painting Iraq as a victim of a U.S.-Saudi conspiracy to undermine the Iraqi nation, he also diverted attention from his own miscalculations by presenting one of the many conspiracy theories that often take root in the Middle East context. He suggested that the Gulf crisis was a setup by the United States. His summer 1990 meeting with April Glaspie, in which she suggested that the United States had no strong opinion on Arab-Arab border disputes, may have contributed to this belief. A partial text of Saddam Hussein's speech on Baghdad Radio appears below.

Document 11
SADDAM ON RADIO:
"ACTS OF TREACHERY" AGAINST IRAQ'S
"STRUGGLING FORCES"
Saddam Hussein

In the name of God, the compassionate, the merciful. It is possible that ye dislike a thing which is good for you and that ye love a thing which is bad for you. God knoweth and ye know not [Koranic verses].

O great Iraqi people. O valiant men of our heroic armed forces. O faithful and honorable people wherever you are. . . . At the time when it was decided that the [UN] Security Council would meet to look into the Soviet peace initiative, which we supported . . . the treacherous [U.S. President] Bush and his filthy agent [Saudi Arabian King] Fahd, and others who have consorted with them in committing crimes, shame and aggression, committed the treachery.

Those cowards who have perfected the acts of treachery, treason and vileness, committed treachery after they departed from every path of virtue, goodness and humanity. They have committed treachery and waged their large-scale ground assault against our struggling forces this morning. Their objective became known to all who have not known their objective so far.

They committed treachery according to their wont and qualities. They even betrayed those who along with them signed the infamous resolutions which were adopted at the Security Council before the military aggression against our country, deluding themselves that by those resolutions they were protecting international legitimacy.

They betrayed everyone but God is above all. . . . He will strike back their treachery on their necks and shame them until their ranks and their failing horde are repulsed. . . .

From the beginning, the evil ones worked on this path, the path of hostility and evil, in order to harm the Iraqi people and smother the shining candle in their hearts. Cursed be their intentions and cursed be their deeds.

However, they will realize after a while that God's unshakable desire will prevent them from inflicting evil on the people of faith and jihad. They will realize after a while that the great people of Iraq and the brave Iraqi armed forces are not like what they think or imagine.

Fight them, O Iraqis, with all the values that you imbibed from your great history and with all the values of faith in which you believed as a people who believe in God . . . fight them, O brave, splendid men. O men of the mother, of battles and al-Qadisiyah [a seventh-century battle that consolidated Islam in the region].

Fight them with your faith in God. Fight them in defense of every free and honorable woman and every innocent child, and in defense of the values of manhood, values and the military honor which you shoulder.

Fight them because with their defeat you will be at the last entrance of the conquest of all conquests. The war will end with all that the situation entails of dignity, glory and triumph for your people, army and nation.

If the opposite takes place, God forbid, there will only be the deep abyss to which the enemies are aspiring to push you . . . and a lengthy darkness will prevail over Iraq.

Fight them, O men. They do not carry the values that entitle them to be more manly, courageous and capable than you. When men collide with each other, the weapons of supremacy will disappear, and the only thing that remains to decide the final result will be the faith of the faithful and the courage of those who adhere to their noble, nationalistic and faithful stand of jihad.

Fight them and show no mercy toward them, for this is how God wishes the faithful to fight the infidel. Your sons, mothers, fathers and kin, and the entire population of Iraq and the world are beholding your performance today. Do what pleases God and bring dignity to the homeland and the people.

Fight them in the style of the faithful men. They are the camp of atheism, hypocrisy and treachery. You are the camp of faith, unshifting principles, loyalty and sincerity.

Fight them and victory will be yours, so will be dignity, honor and glory. God is greater. God is greater. God is greater and let the miserable meet their fate.

Victory is sweet with the help of God.

PRESIDENT BUSH SUSPENDS THE OFFENSIVE

In the following address, which was broadcast live on nationwide radio and television on February 27, 1991, President Bush accomplished several objectives. He announced the suspension of military operations against the demoralized and withdrawing Iraqi forces. In addition, he presented some requirements for a formal cease-fire, argued that the U.S.-led operation was not against the Iraqi people but against their unfortunate regime, and painted a picture of a future of potential peace in the region.

Document 12
ADDRESS TO THE NATION ON THE SUSPENSION OF ALLIED OFFENSIVE COMBAT OPERATIONS IN THE PERSIAN GULF
George Bush

Kuwait is liberated. Iraq's army is defeated. Our military objectives are met. Kuwait is once more in the hands of Kuwaitis in control of their own destiny. We share in their joy, a joy tempered only by our compassion for their ordeal.

Tonight, the Kuwaiti flag once again flies above the capital of a free and sovereign nation, and the American flag flies above our embassy.

Seven months ago, America and the world drew a line in the sand. We declared that the aggression against Kuwait would not stand. And tonight America and the world have kept their word.

This is not a time of euphoria, certainly not a time to gloat, but it is a time of pride, pride in our troops, pride in the friends who stood with us in the crisis, pride in our nation and the people whose strength and resolve made victory quick, decisive, and just. And soon we will open wide our arms to welcome back home to America our magnificent fighting forces.

No one country can claim this victory as its own. It was not only a victory for Kuwait, but a victory for all the coalition partners. This is a victory for the United Nations, for all mankind, for the rule of law, and for what is right.

After consulting with Secretary of Defense Cheney, the chairman of the Joint Chiefs of Staff, General Powell, and our coalition partners, I am pleased to announce that at midnight tonight, Eastern Standard Time, exactly 100 hours since ground operations commenced and six weeks since the start of Operation Desert Storm, all United States and coalition forces will suspend offensive combat operations. It is up to Iraq whether this suspension on the part of the coalition becomes a permanent cease-fire.

Coalition, political, and military terms for a formal cease-fire include the following requirements:

Iraq must release immediately all coalition prisoners of war, third country nationals, and the remains of all who have fallen. Iraq must release all Kuwaiti detainees. Iraq also must inform Kuwaiti authorities of the location and nature of all land and sea mines. Iraq must comply fully with all relevant

United Nations Security Council resolutions. This includes a rescinding of Iraq's August decision to annex Kuwait and acceptance in principle of Iraq's responsibility to pay compensation for the loss, damage, and injury its aggression has caused.

The coalition calls upon the Iraq government to designate military commanders to meet within forty-eight hours with their coalition counterparts at a place in the theater of operations to be specified to arrange for military aspects of the cease-fire. Further, I have asked Secretary of State Baker to request that the United Nations Security Council meet to formulate the necessary arrangement for this war to be ended.

This suspension of offensive combat operations is contingent upon Iraq's not firing upon any coalition forces and not launching Scud missiles against any other country. If Iraq violates these terms, coalition forces will be free to resume military operations.

At every opportunity I have said to the people of Iraq that our quarrel was not with them but instead with their leadership and above all with Saddam Hussein. This remains the case. You, the people of Iraq, are not our enemy. We do not seek your destruction. We have treated your POWs with kindness. Coalition forces fought this war only as a last resort and look forward to the day when Iraq is led by people prepared to live in peace with their neighbors.

We must now begin to look beyond victory in war. We must meet the challenge of securing the peace. In the future, as before, we will consult with our coalition partners. We've already done a good deal of thinking and planning for the postwar period and Secretary Baker has already begun to consult with our coalition partners on the region's challenges. There can be and will be no solely American answer to all these challenges, but we can assist and support the countries of the region and be a catalyst for peace. In this spirit Secretary Baker will go to the region next week to begin a new round of consultations.

This war is now behind us. Ahead of us is the difficult task of securing a potentially historic peace. Tonight though, let us be proud of what we have accomplished. Let us give thanks to those who risked their lives. Let us never forget those who gave their lives. May God bless our valiant military forces and their families and let us all remember them in our prayers.

Good night, and may God bless the United States of America.

Source: *Public Papers of the Presidents of the United States: George Bush, 1991*, Book I—January 1 to June 30, 1991 (Washington, DC: U.S. Government Printing Office, 1992), 187–88.

RESOLUTION 687 (APRIL 3, 1991)

The "Mother of All Battles" ended with the "Mother of All Resolutions." After Iraq's stunning defeat, the UN imposed Resolution 687 on Iraq on April 3, 1991. The main goal of the resolution, adopted in the Security Council by a vote of 12 to 1, with 2 abstentions, was threefold: to punish Iraq for the invasion, to keep Saddam's and Iraq's efforts to produce weapons of mass destruction in check, and to prevent any future challenges by Iraq against Kuwait. Iraq was prohibited from selling oil until it met the conditions of the cease-fire, which Iraq has since attempted to defy. Critical elements of the resolution appear below.

Document 13
UN SECURITY COUNCIL RESOLUTION 687

The Security Council,

. . . *Conscious* of the need to take the following measures acting under Chapter VII of the Charter, . . .

2. *Demands* that Iraq and Kuwait respect the inviolability of the international boundary and the allocation of islands set out in the "Agreed Minutes Between the State of Kuwait and the Republic of Iraq Regarding the Restoration of Friendly Relations, Recognition and Related Matters," signed by them in the exercise of their sovereignty at Baghdad on 4 October 1963 and registered with the United Nations and published by the United Nations in document 7063, United Nations Treaty Series, 1964; . . .

7. *Invites* Iraq to reaffirm unconditionally its obligations under the Geneva Protocol for the Prohibition of the Use in War of Asphyxiating, Poisonous or Other Gases, and of Bacteriological Methods of Warfare, signed at Geneva on 17 June 1925, and to ratify the Convention on the Prohibition of the Development, Production and Stockpiling of Bacteriological (Biological) and Toxin Weapons and on Their Destruction, of 10 April 1972;

8. *Decides* that Iraq shall unconditionally accept the destruction, removal, or rendering harmless, under international supervision, of:

(a) All chemical and biological weapons and all stocks of agents and all related subsystems and components and all research, development, support and manufacturing facilities;

(b) All ballistic missiles with a range greater than 150 kilometres and related major parts, and repair and production facilities;

9. *Decides*, for the implementation of paragraph 8 above, the following:

(a) Iraq shall submit to the Secretary-General, within fifteen days of the adoption of this resolution, a declaration of this locations, amounts and types of all items specified in paragraph 8 and agree to urgent, on-site inspection as specified below; . . .

12. *Decides* that Iraq shall unconditionally agree not to acquire or develop nuclear weapons or nuclear-weapons-usable material or any subsystems or components or any research, development, support or manufacturing facilities related to the above; to submit to the Secretary-General and the Director-General of the IAEA [International Atomic Energy Agency] within fifteen days of the adoption of this resolution a declaration of the locations, amounts, and types of all items specified above; to place all of its nuclear-weapons-usable materials under the exclusive control, for custody and removal, of the IAEA, with the assistance and cooperation of the Special Commission as provided for in the plan of the Secretary-General discussed in paragraph 9 (b) above; to accept, in accordance with the arrangements provided for in paragraph 13 below, urgent on-site inspection and the destruction, removal or rendering harmless as appropriate of all items specified above; and to accept the plan discussed in paragraph 13 below for the future ongoing monitoring and verification of its compliance with these undertakings; . . .

15. *Requests* the Secretary-General to report to the Security Council on the steps taken to facilitate the return of all Kuwaiti property seized by Iraq, including a list of any property which Kuwait claims has not been returned or which has not been returned intact;

16. *Reaffirms* that Iraq, without prejudice to the debts and obligations of Iraq arising prior to 2 August 1990, which will be addressed through the normal mechanisms, is liable under international law for any direct loss, damage, including environmental damage and the depletion of natural resources, or injury to foreign Governments, nationals and corporations, as a result of Iraq's unlawful invasion and occupation of Kuwait.

Glossary of Selected Terms

Arab League: Organization of twenty Arab states, officially formed on March 22, 1945; addresses, mediates, and improves cooperation on Arab social, political, economic, and military issues.

Baath "renaissance" party: Promotes pan-Arabism or Arab world unity, subscribes to socialist ideology, and seeks an independent, assertive Arab world position. Different Baath factions rule in Iraq and Syria, although Saddam and President Assad of Syria are enemies.

Deputies Committee: The crisis management group that reported to the "Gang of Eight" and provided it with information, analyses, options, and strategies for dealing with problems (see Chapter 4).

Desert Shield: The U.S.-led operation to defend Saudi Arabia following Iraq's invasion of Kuwait on August 2, 1990.

Desert Storm: The U.S.-led military operation, launched on January 16, 1991, and aimed at evicting Iraqi forces from Kuwait.

F-117A Stealth fighter: A fighter/bomber aircraft, specializing in precision bombing, and built to evade enemy radar. None were shot down during the Gulf War.

F-4G Wild Weasel: All-weather interceptor with electronic warfare capabilities that can hunt down surface-to-air missile batteries, thus preparing the way for U.S. bombing missions.

Gang of Eight: President Bush and his small group of seven principal advisers who made critical decisions during the Gulf crisis (see Chapter 4).

Global Positioning System (GPS): Guidance from these twenty-four satellites allowed U.S. troops to locate themselves, enemy positions, mines, and downed pilots, and to launch missiles, with pinpoint accuracy.

Gulf War Syndrome: Thousands of veterans of the Gulf War reported symptoms, including fatigue, memory loss, muscle pain, and insomnia, which are collectively known as Gulf War syndrome. Despite much research, no proof exists that there is a single cause for this syndrome such as war-time exposure to biological or chemical weapons.

Islamic fundamentalists: Refers to Muslims who are strict adherents to the Koran, the written word of Allah, as revealed through his prophet, Muhammad. Many of them believe that religion should significantly guide government.

Kurds: Twenty-five million ethnically related and distinct people, concentrated mainly on the border areas of Iraq, Syria, Turkey, and Iran, where they want an independent state. Bordering states oppose it, fearing it will destabilize them.

Ottoman Empire: Founded in the thirteenth century as an Islamic state by the Turkish leader Osman. It lasted until World War I when the empire was defeated. In 1923 the Islamic caliphate was abolished and a secular Turkey was established.

Shiites or Shia: In contrast to the "orthodox" majority of Sunni Muslims, Shiites follow Caliph Ali and his successors and hold different views on the nature and conduct of Islam. They are the majority in Iran, Iraq, and Bahrain, although in Iraq and Bahrain the political leadership is Sunni.

Sunnis: The majority of the elites and people in the Muslim world; the major "orthodox" division of Islam.

T-72 tank: Iraq's main, Soviet-built battle tank, known for its heavy protective armor and great accuracy within a one-mile radius. The U.S. M1 and M1A1 Abrams tanks, however, outmaneuvered and outperformed the T-72 during the Gulf War.

U.S. Central Command (USCENTCOM): One of ten U.S. commands in the world, USCENTCOM's mission covers nineteen Mideast region countries; founded in 1983 and led by General Norman Schwarzkopf during the Gulf War (see Chapter 3).

Annotated Bibliography

ABC News. *A Line in the Sand: What Did America Win?* 50 minutes, 1991. Distributed by ABC News. Examines the causes and consequences of the war and asks whether the war ended too soon.

————. *Schwarzkopf: How the War Was Won.* 70 minutes, 1991. Examines Schwarzkopf's role in the coalition victory in the Gulf. The video offers footage of his career, interaction with troops in the Gulf, and his final press conference in which he discusses how the war was prosecuted and won.

Atkinson, Rick. *Crusade: The Untold Story of the Persian Gulf War.* Boston: Houghton Mifflin, 1993. Argues that the Gulf War heralded a revolution in military weapons, doctrine, and tactics, and offers a useful account of how the temperamental Norman Schwarzkopf interacted with his senior American advisers.

Baker, James A., III. *The Politics of Diplomacy: Revolution, War and Peace, 1989–1992.* New York: G. P. Putnam's Sons, 1995. Illuminates pre-crisis diplomacy and postwar efforts to move the Middle East peace process forward.

El-Baz, Farouk, and R. M. Makharita. *The Gulf War and the Environment.* Lausanne, Switzerland: Gordon and Breach, 1994. Includes valuable scientific analysis on the use of satellites in understanding environmental damage, including satellite photos of the impact of the oil spill and oil fires; on the special Gulf marine environment and the impact on the desert ecosystem; and on the potential health effects of the oil spills and fires.

Bengio, Ofra, *Saddam Speaks on the Gulf Crisis: A Collection of Documents*. Tel Aviv: Moshe Dayan Center, 1991. Includes Saddam's speeches and interviews from the period February 1990 to February 1991, and allows the reader to see the entire period of the crisis through Saddam's eyes.

Blair, Arthur H. *At War in the Gulf: A Chronology*. College Station: Texas A&M Press, 1992. Includes an extensive chronology, with useful explanations of each important event in the crisis.

Bloom, Saul, John M. Miller, James Warner, and Philippa Winkler, eds. *Hidden Casualties: Environmental, Health and Political Consequences of the Persian Gulf War*. Berkeley, CA: North Atlantic Books, 1994. Examines the hidden environmental, health, and political consequences of the war, including the impact of the oil spill, oil fires, economic sanctions, Scud attacks, and the refugee crisis.

Blumberg, Herbert H., and Christopher C. French, eds., *The Persian Gulf War: Views from the Social and Behavioral Sciences*. New York: Lanham, 1994. Examines the crisis from the perspective of various actors, including Great Britain, Israel, the Soviet Union, France, and the Palestinians.

Cordesman, Anthony H. *After the Storm: The Changing Military Balance in the Middle East*. Boulder, CO: Westview Press, 1993. Offers an excellent discussion, including detailed tables and information, of trends in the proliferation of conventional weapons and weapons of mass destruction in the region.

Dunnigan, James F., and Austin Bay, *From Shield to Storm: High-Tech Weapons, Military Strategy, and Coalition Warfare in the Persian Gulf*. New York: William Morrow, 1992. Discusses the weapons and military tactics used during the war, and argues that the Gulf War was the first one in American history that U.S. armed forces were ready to fight.

Freedman, Lawrence, and Efraim Karsh. *The Gulf Conflict, 1990–1991: Diplomacy and War in the New World Order*. Princeton: Princeton University Press, 1993. Offers a detailed historical analysis of the Persian Gulf War, including maps and transcripts of key speeches and UN resolutions.

Gordon, Michael R., and Bernard E. Trainor. *The General's War: The Inside Story of the Conflict in the Gulf*. Boston: Little, Brown, 1995. Argues that Powell was critical in formulating the war plan against Iraq, including the military buildup, the left-hook ground war strategy, and, in the view of the authors, the grossly mistaken decision to end the war too soon.

Greenberg, Bradley S., and Walter Gantz, eds. *Desert Storm and the Mass Media*. Cresskill, NJ: Hampton Press, 1993. Perhaps the most comprehensive book on the media. Focuses on how leaders used the media to shape the war and their country's position in the conflict, the manner by which the media carried these rivalries, and the domestic and international public response to the crisis. Illuminates the role of the media as actual actors in the crisis.

Grossman, Mark. *Encyclopedia of the Persian Gulf War*. Santa Barbara: ABC-CLIO, 1995. Includes detailed information on weapon systems, individuals, concepts, and primary documents relevant to the Gulf War.

Hawley, T. M. *Against the Fires of Hell: The Environmental Disaster of the Gulf War*. New York: Harcourt Brace Jovanovich, 1992. Argues that air power singlehandedly won the Gulf War. Offers a wealth of interesting facts in reader-friendly form on the world's greatest oil spill, on the oil well fires, and on the possible Iraqi violations of international law, which Hawley believes may lead to a treaty explicitly prohibiting ecological terrorism during war.

Hazelton, Fran, ed. *Iraq Since the Gulf War: Prospects for Democracy*. London: Zed Books, 1994. Examines Iraq's prospects after Saddam, reveals the complexity of Iraqi politics, and underscores the difficulty attendant on uniting the diverse set of groups opposed to Saddam.

Hilsman, Roger. *George Bush vs. Saddam Hussein: Military Success! Political Failure?* Novato, CA: Lyford Books, 1992. Argues that Bush should have continued economic sanctions rather than launching Desert Storm, and that inasmuch as Saddam survived Desert Storm, he won out over President Bush.

Iraqgate: Saddam Hussein, U.S. Policy and the Prelude to the Persian Gulf War (1980–1994). Alexandria, VA: Chadwyck-Healey, August 1995. Reproduces on microfiche 1,900 rarely seen documents on how the United States helped build up Saddam prior to Desert Storm, on congressional investigations into the financing of Saddam by U.S. entities such as the Export-Import Bank, and on the Bush administration's response to the Iraqgate affair.

Johnstone, Ian. *Aftermath of the Gulf War: An Assessment of UN Action*. Boulder, CO: Lynne Rienner, 1994. Draws on extensive interviews with UN officials and analysis of UN documents to provide a useful record of how UN Resolution 687, the cease-fire resolution of the Gulf War, was drafted and implemented.

Lambakis, Steven. "Space Control in Desert Storm and Beyond." *Orbis* 39, no. 3 (Summer 1995): 417–33. Argues that the U.S. allies exploited unprecedented space-dependent military capability and satellites that provided near-total free communications and coordination, weather information, mid-course guidance for missiles, surveillance of Iraqi military movements, and guidance for smart bombs.

McCain, Thomas A., and Leonard Shyles, eds. *The 1,000 Hour War: Communications in the Gulf*. Westport, CT: Greenwood Press, 1994. Includes interesting pieces on the media and the military, on the use of technology in covering the war, and on the influence of CNN.

Miller, Judith, and Laurie Mylroie. *Saddam Hussein and the Crisis in the Gulf*. New York: Random House, 1990. Provides excellent details, in particular on Saddam's youth, background, and rise to power, and perceptions of Iraqi and Middle East politics.

Mueller, John. *Policy and Opinion in the Gulf War.* Chicago: University of Chicago Press, 1994. Evaluates U.S. public opinion on the Gulf War, drawing on an enormous body of polling research. Explains the impact of the crisis on Americans, their views of important developments during the crisis, their level of presidential support, and the impact of polls on policy.

NBC News. *The Shifting Sands of the Middle East.* 60 minutes, 1991. Distributed by Polygram. With Tom Brokaw as narrator, takes the viewer through stages in Middle Eastern history. Begins with a discussion of the Middle East as the birthplace of civilization, continues through colonial times, and concludes with an examination of the Gulf War.

Powell, Colin. *My American Journey.* New York: Random House, 1995. Offers an insider's account of key decisions during the Gulf crisis, and sheds light on Powell's own views of the war.

Sciolino, Elaine. *The Outlaw State: Saddam Hussein's Quest for Power and the Gulf Crisis.* New York: John Wiley and Sons, 1991. Effectively places the Persian Gulf War in historic context, offering interesting analysis of Saddam's desire to relive Iraq's glory days.

Sifry, Micah L., and Christopher Cerf. *The Gulf War Reader: History, Documents, and Opinions.* New York: Random House, 1991. Includes UN resolutions, political statements of leaders, background information on the crisis, and articles from leading analysts.

Simitar Productions. *The War in the Gulf: First Strike! Desert Storm, US Army.* 45 minutes, 1991. *US Air Force.* 45 minutes, 1991. *US Navy and Marine Corps.* 47 minutes, 1991. All distributed by Simitar Entertainment, Inc., Polymouth, MN 55447. Help the viewer understand the weapons systems of the war, such as the Patriot missile, AH-64 Apache helicopter, M1A1 Abrams tank, F-15 Eagle and F117 Stealth aircraft, and the Tomahawk missile. Each video focuses on a different branch of the armed forces.

Smith, Jean Edward. *George Bush's War.* New York: Henry Holt, 1992. Claims that Bush personalized the conflict too much, was obsessed with undermining Saddam, and thus lost perspective.

Khaled ibn Sultan. *Desert Warrior: A Personal View of the Gulf War by the Joint Forces Commander.* New York: HarperCollins, 1995. The commander of Saudi forces in the crisis, provides a useful insider account, from the Saudi perspective. Argues that, contrary to some views, the Saudis played a critical political role and an important military role in Desert Storm.

Timmerman, Kenneth R. *The Death Lobby: How the West Armed Iraq.* Boston: Houghton Mifflin, 1991. Provides an excellent chronology and information on how Saddam was armed by the West.

Watson, Bruce W., Bruce George, Peter Tsouras, and B. L. Cyr. *Military Lessons of the Gulf War*. London: Greenhill Books, 1993. Offers military lessons by individuals who observed the conflict in an official capacity, regarding such things as the importance of war preparation, electronic warfare, battleships, and the efficacy of high-technology equipment such as Stealth aircraft, Tomahawk missiles, and satellites.

Whicker, Marcia Lynn, James P. Pfiffner, and Raymond A. Moore, eds. *The Presidency and the Persian Gulf War*. Westport, CT: Praeger, 1993. Argues that Bush did not effectively consider alternatives to war, draw on the knowledge of advisers, or consult Congress.

Woodward, Bob. *The Commanders*. New York: Simon and Schuster, 1991. Provides useful insights, based on anonymous interviews, of key decisions, including the Saudi agreement to allow U.S. forces into the kingdom, Bush's decision in November 1990 to double the size of U.S. forces in the region, and the decision to launch Operation Desert Storm against Iraq's forces in Kuwait.

Yetiv, Steve. *America and the Persian Gulf: The Third Party Dimension in World Politics*. Westport, CT: Praeger, 1995. Argues that and shows how the 1979 Soviet invasion of Afghanistan and the Iran-Iraq war (1980–1988) reversed U.S. decline in the Gulf and prepared it for Operations Desert Shield and Storm. Develops a theoretical framework for studying how, under interdependence, conflicts between two actors often affect a third actor.

Index

About the Author

STEVE A. YETIV is Assistant Professor of Political Science at Old Dominion University in Norfolk, Virginia, and a research affiliate at Harvard University's Center for Middle Eastern Studies. He is the author of *America and the Persian Gulf: The Third Party Dimension in World Politics* (Praeger, 1995) and many scholarly articles on the Middle East and international relations. Yetiv has been featured on CNN, C-SPAN, National Public Radio, Voice of America, and numerous other media outlets. In October 1996, he was the recipient of the Secretary's Open Forum Distinguished Public Service Award from the State Department in recognition of his "contributions to national and international affairs."